NEGEV

Land, Water, and Life in a
Desert Environment

DANIEL HILLEL

PRAEGER

PRAEGER SPECIAL STUDIES • PRAEGER SCIENTIFIC

Library of Congress Cataloging in Publication Date

Hillel, Daniel.
  Negev, land, water, and life in a desert environment.

  Bibliography: p.
  Includes index.
  1. Negev region (Israel)   2. Desert ecology.
I. Title
DS110.N4H54   333.73   82-5218
ISBN 0-03-062067-8
ISBN 0-03-062068-6 (pbk.)

Published in 1982 by Praeger Publishers
CBS Educational and Professional Publishing
a Division of CBS Inc.
521 Fifth Avenue, New York, New York 10175 U.S.A.

© 1982 by Daniel Hillel

All rights reserved

23456789 052 987654321

Printed in the United States of America

Dedicated to Barbara, Bambi, and Eytan, founding members of Sdeh-Boker, who gave their young lives to the Negev, and gave the Negev a new life.

The wilderness and the parched land shall be gladdened;
And the desert shall rejoice, and blossom as the rose.
It shall blossom abundantly, and exult,
Even with joy and singing;
And the glory of Lebanon shall be granted it;
The splendor of Carmel and Sharon . . .
Strengthen ye the weak hands,
And make firm the tottering knees.
Say to them that are of a fearful heart:
"Be strong, fear not . . ."
Then the eyes of the blind shall be opened,
And the ears of the deaf shall be unstopped.
Then shall the lame leap as a hart,
And the tongue of the dumb shall sing;
For in the wilderness shall waters break forth,
And brooks in the desert.
And the parched land shall become a pool,
And the thirsty ground fountains of water;
In the habitation of jackals herds shall lie down,
Amidst lush grass and reeds and rushes.

Isaiah 35:1-7

Contents

Preface   xi

Acknowledgements   xv

Introduction   xvii

Part I: Deserts in General

1• The Desert Revealed   3

2• Arid Zones and Deserts   9

3• Features of the Desert   13

4• Water, the Universal Dilemma   31

5• Soil and Water in the Desert   35

6• The Desert Ecosystem   42

7• Plants and Water in the Desert   45

8• Animals and Water in the Desert   53

9• Man and Water in the Desert   62

Part II: The Negev in Particular

10• Journey to the Negev   69

11• Physiography, Climate, and Subregions   73

12• Water Regime and Habitats   87

13• Tides and Ebbs of Civilization   108

14• Catching and Storing Runoff   128

15• Harvesting Runoff from Hillsides   135

16• Farm Units and Small Watersheds   145

17• Harnessing the Floods   154

18• Tapping Groundwater   169

19• Crops and Cropping   179

- **20•** Grazing the Desert Range   185
- **21•** The Bedouin   202
- **22•** Irrigated Agriculture   217
- **23•** Sdeh-Boker and Ben-Gurion   224

    Epilogue: Modern Implications   237

    Bibliography   241

    Index   263

    About the Author   270

Preface

In antiquity the desert was regarded as a world unto itself, an extraterritorial realm separate from and additional to the other two known realms: the oceans and the habitable lands. Residents of the latter viewed the strange people of the desert with fear and hostility, perceiving them to be a threat to civilization—as indeed they often were. The desert itself was held in awe as a place of terror, a largely useless and dangerous land. One ventured into its mysterious vastness only at great risk.

Lately, however, perceptions of the desert have been changing, and interest in it has been increasing the world over. The explosive growth of population in our generation, and that anticipated in future generations, require us to seek new areas for settlement as land reserves in temperate regions continue to diminish. Our new technology makes possible the reclamation of what had so long been considered wasteland. The imminent need to develop and colonize the desert is nowhere more urgent and imperative than in Israel, a small and resource-poor country where more than half the land area is desert. For this reason Israel and its Negev can be regarded as a case study and pilot project for the development of similar desert regions elsewhere.

This book is partly about deserts in general, but mostly about one desert in particular: the Negev of Israel. It is the Wilderness of Zin and Paran and of Sin and Kadesh of biblical fame, the most storied and fabled of all deserts in Western civilization. Here Abraham and Isaac grazed their flocks, and the banished Hagar and Ishmael made their abode. Here Moses led the Children of Israel, twelve tribes of fervent, desperate desert nomads making their way to the Promised Land. Here the Judean kings—Solomon, Jehoshaphat, and Uzziah—dug cisterns, cleared highways, built guard towers, and mined copper. They also collected the runoff from slopes and built terrace walls across the creek beds in order to conserve water and soil, and to raise crops even in the desert. It was here in the Negev that the Nabateans founded some of their most astounding cities and further developed methods of land and water husbandry. The Romans and Byzantines built upon the Nabatean foundations with all their engineering and architectural skills. They fortified and maintained strategic outposts, towns, and villages in this frontier province of their far-flung empires. These achievements were followed by a long period of decline and isolation, as the once-thriving region became the abode only of aimless nomads barely able to eke out their subsistence in what had become a denuded wilderness. In all, since recorded history began, the Negev has seen at least five major civilizations come and go, each thriving and disappearing in turn, each leaving its indelible mark etched upon the ageless face of the land.

Western civilization is inextricably bound to the Negev and its environs, from which it has drawn, via its desert-born religions—Judaism, Christianity, and Islam—many of the mores and concepts, and much of the imagery and lore of the desert, including those pertaining to man's relation to nature and to God.

Any present-day description of the Negev Desert inevitably evokes memories and fantasies of its epic past, and of its spiritual as well as physical character. Fable, myth, and reality seem inextricably bound together. In some perceivable but inexplicable sense, a journey into the ancient Negev is a journey home, a return to the place and time, long abandoned yet unforgotten, from which our quest began before it went astray. It is a journey of fate and faith, impelled not merely by rational motives or scientific curiosity but also by a silent ancient call, an inner yearning for the Soul, once revealed in the desert, from which we have been separated but never completely severed. Can a return to the desert bring us any closer to our past, and make less obscure its enormous mystery? Can it help us recover from our flounderings and rediscover our original sense of direction? I am reminded of the ancient legend of the two Jerusalems, the Lower and the Upper. Lower Jerusalem is built of stone, and can be seen and touched. It is a city of great beauty, to be cherished, revered, and protected. But it is not perfect. Alas, it can be desecrated, abused, even destroyed. High above it hovers the Upper Jerusalem, and it is perfect: inviolable, indestructible, a city of complete peace, beauty, and justice. It is the ethereal Jerusalem, a city of the mind and of the spirit. To the faithful it is no less real, and certainly no less important, than Lower Jerusalem. In a somewhat similar sense there are two Negevs: the actual and the mythical, the physical and the spiritual. The aim of this book is to describe the one without dispelling the other.

Since the 1950s a rather large body of literature has accumulated regarding the Negev. Some of what has been written is strictly scientific, and highly specific and technical; some is popular to the point of being simplistic or even fanciful. My purpose here is not to provide an encyclopedic compendium on the Negev, but to paint a broad picture of the region from the standpoint of its land and water resources, and of their development and utilization, over the centuries. In attempting to compose an integral view of the Negev, I have drawn upon my personal experience there. Moreover, I have striven for the widest possible appeal, addressing myself to the educated layman rather than to the specialist. I hope that the personal view and the popular appeal will not detract from the soundness of the treatment. No book written by any author,

Preface

or even group of authors, can be completely objective; nor should it pretend to be. To the extent that this is a subjective book, let it at least be honestly so. In attempting to describe what is known about the Negev, one should also reveal that much is yet unknown. Indeed, our knowledge is tentative, and the desert retains many — perhaps most — of its mysteries.

Acknowledgements

The writing of any book is a lonely task, beset by many doubts. The writing of this book seemed at times to be particularly so, for it is a somewhat unusual book, at once professional and personal, largely objective, yet in some specific parts frankly subjective. More than once I wondered how, and even whether, I could balance these disparate elements while avoiding contradiction or blurring of distinction. With neither the benefit nor the constraint of external rules, the attempt turned out to be a tentative exercise. Perhaps I would not have perservered if it were anything less than a labor of love.

My daughters Adi and Sari took an interest in the writing and their enthusiasm sustained me at a crucial time. My esteemed colleagues Haim Gunner and Bernard Berger gave me their positive professional judgement at an early stage and deemed the effort worthy. So did other colleagues, by now too numerous to list, who have since examined the material. Linda Haight took meticulous care in typing the manuscript, which our editor Susan Goodman and editor-in-chief Ron Chambers made a special effort to transform into an attractively finished book.

I gratefully and cordially thank each of them.

Daniel Hillel

Introduction

Early in the fateful year 1914, on the eve of the cataclysmic event that we have come to call the First World War, two young British archaeologists named C. L. Woolley and T. E. Lawrence explored the Negev and northern Sinai, then frontier provinces of the Ottoman Empire. Ostensibly to study the antiquities of these deserts, the mission's real and clandestine aim was to gather intelligence for the British War Office in anticipation of the imminent conflict over the eastern approaches to the Suez Canal. However, archaeology was more than a mere guise or clever ruse by which to allay the suspicions of the Turkish authorities, for the study turned out to have authentic scholarly significance. It was published in 1915 by the Palestine Exploration Fund, under the title *The Wilderness of Zin*.

The younger of the two archaeologists, then only 25 years of age, soon went on to become the famed and fabled "Lawrence of Arabia," thereby transforming himself into a part of the region's history. *The Wilderness of Zin*, however, remained for many years the definitive work on the ancient civilization of the Negev. Sketchy and superficial though it may seem in the light of present-day knowledge, it was, for its time, a remarkable document, filled with fascinating data and intriguing insights.

Still, when the State of Israel came into being in 1948, the Negev seemed largely to be a tabula rasa, a vast and mysterious terra incognita of rugged mountains and barren valleys in which lay hidden (according to the evidence of Woolley and Lawrence) the ruins of no fewer than six ghostlike cities, remnants of long bygone civilizations. What a lure for inquisitive young adventurers!

An inquisitive young adventurer was I in 1951, when, at the age of 20, having just gained a master's degree in the earth sciences from an American university and regarding myself the "compleat" scientist, destined for great discoveries, I joined with a band of equally unrealistic dreamers of glory to embark upon the greatest adventure of our lives. Together, we founded the pioneering settlement of Sdeh-Boker in the very heart of the Negev highlands, where the depth of a year's total rainfall seldom exceeds the depth of a man's cupped hands, and where the loudest noise ever heard was the incongruous roar of the rare torrents tumbling down the wadis. In the beginning we were only ten men and two women, each hailing from a separate background and in search of individual purpose. With neither plan nor sponsor, we pitched our tents on the parched plateau near the chasm called the Valley of Zin. Through that valley ran the meandering course of the wadi named Nahal Zin, bone-dry save for the few spectacular hours in which it carried the torrential flash floods (unbelievable until actually seen) of the desert. Through the same valley ran the ancient trail the Bedouin call Darb el Sultan (perhaps an allusion to the biblical King's Highway), winding its tortuous way from or toward the distant rift valley of Arava and the mysterious Mount Seir rising beyond it.

Standing on the dizzying edge of that jagged precipice, gazing into the desolate, boulder-strewn ravine and across the cratered moonscape toward the mist-shrouded massif of Edom, in which nests the legendary temple city of Petra, we felt ourselves transposed in time, as if carried back into the dim past. In our mind's eye we could see Moses walking along the trail with staff in hand, leading the Israelites, a band of homeless and destitute fugitives, God-intoxicated and inspired by a vision of their own destiny and mission.

All too abruptly our fantasy and reverie were shattered by cruel reality. The Negev highlands were not peopled by benevolent ancestors but by belligerent Bedouin who regarded us as intruders, and they were abetted by saboteurs from across the hostile borders. Only four months after our arrival, Barbara, our first shepherdess, who had just turned 22, was ambushed and killed in broad daylight while tending sheep within sight of the settlement. Several months later and only three miles away, the young man whom we had fondly called Bambi and had elected to be our "farmstead manager" was ambushed while ferrying supplies in an open truck and shot fatally as he attempted to remove the saboteurs' roadblock. A year later my good friend Eytan and his four companions were killed on their adventure-driven hike across the border to visit the legendary ruins of Petra.

Our first year in the Negev was almost totally rainless. When the fervently anticipated wadi flood finally came, it cruelly washed away the dikes we had so laboriously built in crude imitation of the ancient dikes whose remnants we found all around us. It was then we realized that we ought to study the methods of past civilizations very thoroughly, in order that we might build more solidly upon, and extend, their experience. The Bible and *The Wilderness of Zin* were the only textbooks available to us at first.

In the years that followed, Sdeh-Boker became a major focal point in the exploration and development of the region, and its members took part in road construction, geological mapping, and mining, as well as in archeological, hydrological, and ecological investigations. Members of Sdeh-Boker also initiated the establishment of Mitzpe-Ramon, which eventually became a town; the opening of gypsum mines and marble quarries in the Ramon Crater; the location of scores of ancient settlement sites and cisterns; the excavation and partial restoration of the ancient city of Ovdat; and the founding of a regional research and educational center.

Much of the impetus and inspiration for these developments came from David Ben-Gurion, who during a chance visit to the then remote settlement in

1953 was so captivated by the region and the pioneering task of developing it that he soon resigned as prime minister of Israel and joined us as a working member. He lived out his life there, and is buried alongside his wife Paula at the very edge of the cliff overlooking the Valley of Zin.

Throughout the 1950s, I was personally involved in many of the activities mentioned, and carried out some of the earliest scientific investigations of the region's ecology, vegetation, soils, and water resources. For my studies of loessial crusts, I was awarded Israel's first doctorate in soil physics by the Hebrew University of Jerusalem. My first mentor there was the late Professor Avraham Reifenberg, who enlightened and inspired me with his own investigation of the age-old "struggle between the desert and the sown" (which, in slightly altered form, became the title of his excellent book, published in 1955). Being for some years the region's (practically only) resident scientist, I had the extraordinary opportunity to host, assist, and often collaborate in the work of several leading scholars who were drawn to the region during those early years. Among these were Nelson Glueck, whose book *Rivers in the Desert*, published in 1959, superseded *The Wilderness of Zin* as the major exposition of the Negev's archeology. Others who have contributed to our knowledge of the Negev's history, climate, geology, hydrology, soils, botany, and zoology are by now too numerous to list. But one who deserves very special tribute is the late Naphtali Tadmor, for a time my closest colleague and brother in spirit, who was surely the most dedicated, enthusiastic, and indefatigable of all the Negev explorers I have ever known.

Though I have maintained an active interest in the exploration of the Negev and other deserts, and have continuously pursued fundamental research into the hydrology and ecology of arid lands in general, my career as an environmental scientist and academician has gradually led me into spheres of activity far removed from the Negev. In 1979, however, I was asked to serve as consultant to a consortium of engineering firms preparing to construct air bases in the Negev highlands. By now the region was no longer remote and uninhabited, but had become a center of intensive settlement and development. This is what we had long yearned and worked for. And yet something seemed to have gone wrong. I came to realize that in our haste to "redeem" and "develop" the region, we are in fact, and perhaps thoughtlessly, endangering its very nature and age-old character. Modern roadways diminish the expanse and violate the primeval grandeur of the desert landscape, as do excavations, pipelines, and various protruding structures. Smoking vehicles and industries befoul the desert's crisp air, just as the shrill drone of aircraft and the clatter of trucks and tractors shatter its ageless silence. Earth-traversing and earth-moving machines scour and churn the soft soil, and torture the face of the land.

Altogether, the changes wrought and perpetrated by modern civilization rob the desert of its pristine purity and timeless majesty. More than irreversible physical change is involved: the soul and spirit of the desert are desecrated. Impatient travelers through the Negev who rush hither and thither while glimpsing the landscape only through the window of a speeding automobile cannot imagine the experience of wandering on foot, alone, over the trackless hills and valleys, hearing naught but the soft sound of the crumbling earth and the occasional plaintive cry of a lonely desert owl calling its mate from its sanctuary among the twisted, thorny branches of a stunted bush, or the sense of total serenity that comes to the weary wanderer as he rests the night in a hollow, submitting to the embrace of the warm earth while gazing heavenward at the incredibly clear star-studded canopy above. This, after all, is the same desert where, since time immemorial, seekers of the spirit have found solitude and inspiration, where Elijah heard the echo of the Almighty in the "still, small voice" of silence, and where the original and momentous revelation of the unity of God and the universe first occurred to mortal man.

Pondering all this, I find myself yearning, perhaps nostalgically, for some older concept of civilization and development that recognizes, respects, and harmonizes with the desert's own character, much as did the dwellers of the Negev in ancient times. Indeed, they were custodians of the desert's fragile environment, not its subjugators or destructive exploiters. This book is in part an exploration of their methods of land and water husbandry insofar as they might be pertinent to our civilization. For today, no less than in ancient times, human ingenuity and diligence can overcome scarcity even in the most difficult circumstances without destroying the very basis of all life: the sustainable harmony of land, water, and vegetation.

I

Deserts in General

1

The Desert Revealed

There is a fascination in the desert that seems to defy all logic. Like a vacuum that draws, so the desert's very emptiness, its impenetrable vastness, its enigmatic silence, its awesome grandeur and loneliness have captivated man's imagination.

There is mystery in the desert: the mystery of legendary treasures secreted among the uncharted cliffs, the gaping ravines, the badland labyrinths, the flowing sands, the immutable mountains.

There is the lure of romantic adventure in the desert: Marco Polo in the Gobi, Lawrence in Arabia, "Beau Geste" in the Sahara, the elusive Bedouin garbed in black flowing robes, suddenly descending like locusts upon their sedentary neighbors.

There is enchantment in the desert: the camel caravans silhouetted against the skyline; the crystal-clear nights and piercing sharp stars; the luring, deceiving mirage of shimmering water upon dry land; the unobstructed view of the luminescence of dawn, the sumptuous burst of splendor at sunrise; the infinite beauty and glory of sunset.

There is a spirit in the desert: the spirit sought by ascetic hermits who built lonely abodes there, away from the vain world of men and events, the spirit sought by the prophets of old who wandered into the vast stillness to escape the mindless conformity and humdrum trivial busy-ness of life in ordinary society, and to meditate and ponder the ultimate meaning of man's calling and God's purpose. Here in the desert spiritual man can be truly alone and one with nature's elements, free of conventions and unencumbered by imposed duties. Here he is reminded daily of the greatness of creation, and a realization of his own frailty gives him a sense of true humility.

And there is a challenge in the desert: a defiance of man's self-proclaimed mastery of the whole earth; a barrier to life, to progress, to economic development; a fortress holding out against colonization and civilization. It is a challenge compounded of the fascination, mystery, romance, enchantment, and the spirit of the desert. And of its promise.

Indeed, the desert is not without promise. To those who will wrestle with and decipher its secrets, the seemingly useless wasteland is in fact pregnant with hope and promise—the promise not merely of vast physical resources awaiting exploitation but, indeed, the hope of a new frontier, a new abode, a new opportunity, a new life.

The enigma and fascination of the desert were perhaps best expressed by Antoine de Saint Exupéry: "The love of the desert, like love itself, is born of a face perceived and never really seen."

The riddle of the desert is particularly intriguing to environmental scientists. Life in the desert is at once tenuous and tough, vulnerable and durable. The challenge is to decipher the dynamics of the desert's complex environment and the intricate adaptations of its plant and animal life forms. Here scientists trained in the conventionally separate disciplines of climatology, hydrology, botany, zoology, geography, geology, and soil science can each find fascinating problems in their own fields. More important, however, is the opportunity—ultimately, the imperative—to integrate sectarian or partial views in the development of a holistic, ecological approach to the desert environment and its living communities.

A space traveler from some faraway planet, coming toward our globe, observing its features while approaching ever closer, would first see its broad blue oceans and thin veil of swirling white clouds. Then, indistinctly at first, its island continents would appear. Coming still nearer, the visitor would begin to notice the roughly parallel bands of color spread upon the continents as if by an abstract painter. Soon the colors would become distinct: the white polar icecaps; the mist-shrouded pale green of the temperate latitudes; and the dark green, heavily clouded equatorial belt. In between the equatorial belt and the two pale green zones, north and south, our puzzled stranger would focus upon paired bands of a remarkably clear landscape, a sunbaked expanse of reddish-brown and buff-colored mountains and plains—the earth's desert belts.

Should our space traveler now slow his headlong rush toward the bulging earth and incline his ship into leisurely orbit around the globe, he would observe many more features of its continental surface. From his lofty vantage he would note the regularity of the planet's climatic pattern and its regional differences. Perhaps, as he continued to study the face of the earth, he would observe the circulation of the atmosphere resulting from the global radiation pattern. He would then realize that air heated along the equatorial belt evaporates water and it expands, rises, and flows poleward—north and south. As it thus rises, the warm and humid air cools, and precipitates its moisture;

Africa viewed from space. The tropical (equatorial) zone is marked by its cloud formation and dense vegetation; the subtropical arid zones are north and south of it. The Sahara Desert appears as a huge, barren, cloudless expanse of land, contiguous with the Arabian Desert of western Asia.

and as it moves away from the equatorial belt, now bereft of most of its original humidity, it sinks toward the ground, compressing and warming as it descends. If our space traveler were a scientist, he would take measurements and find that the subsidence of this warm and dry air occurs generally between the latitudes of 22° and 38°, thus forming a belt of clear skies. Elsewhere to the north and south, sweeping air masses collide, storms rage, and moisture-laden clouds spill their rains. Yet this subtropical belt remains relatively calm. At sea it is the zone that the ancient mariners called the "trade wind" zone.

Let our visitor approach still closer and concentrate upon these deserts. Let him soar over and inspect the deserts of the northern hemisphere: the Mojave, Sonora, and Chihuahua of North America; then the great Sahara of North Africa; then the Nafud and Rub al-Khali of Arabia, the Dasht e-Kavir of Iran, the Kara-Kum of Turkestan; the Thar and Sind in the northwest of the Indian subcontinent; the Takla-Makan and Gobi of Central Asia. Next, let him visit the deserts of the southern hemisphere: Atacama, Patagonia, and Gran Chaco of South America; Namib, Kalahari, and Karroo of southern Africa; and the great desert of Australia. Now he will begin to discern how local orographic and continental features can alter the broad picture: how some areas within the desert belt can be humid owing to maritime or topographic effects, and how some landlocked areas outside the desert belt can be dry and extensive enough to constitute separate deserts (for instance, the Gobi). Yet the major deserts of the world—the warm deserts—occur in consistent bands.

Supposing our extraterrestrial explorer were endowed with special scientific curiosity and wished to take an even closer look at the desert. He would then descend slowly and hover over some typical stretch of desert. Now he could see the actual physical appearance of the desert landscape: rugged, craggy mountains; bone-dry creek beds; sparse, stunted shrubs; salt-encrusted playas and shifting dunes. The landscape of the desert stands out in bold relief, unmitigated by the smoothing effect of a humid clime and unhidden by a mantle of soil or a veil of vegetation. It reveals some of the earth's boldest architecture, bare and parched. How can the waterless wasteland support any life at all?

But wait! A storm is brewing. Suddenly it is raining. Furiously, myriad tiny raindrops lash at the barren earth, slaking the loose, soft soil and turning its surface into a muddy ooze. Soon runoff begins. A part of the rain is no longer absorbed as fast as it hits the ground, but begins to trickle off the slopes, forming small gullies and rivulets. The latter converge into creeks, forming a gathering torrent, a flash flood, flowing seaward or toward some distant lake. Then, as suddenly as the storm began, it dissipates. The clouds blow away and the sky clears once again.

Our surprised visitor from outer space then wonders what will happen to all the moisture, and he decides to land on the ground and camp there long

An oblique eastward view from space of Egypt's Eastern Desert, the Gulf of Suez, the Sinai Peninsula, the Negev (a slightly darker wedge between Sinai and the trenchlike Arava Valley linking the Gulf of Aqaba and the Dead Sea), and beyond it the Idumean range and the desert of northern Arabia. Toward the north, Israel (and, beyond it, Lebanon and Syria) appear as an increasingly dark region of denser vegetation that is the result of greater rainfall.

enough to observe the happenings at close hand. Surely the drenching rain will have transformed the dry desert. Indeed, he sees an immediate awakening of plant and animal life. The sudden bloom of wild flowers on the momentarily satiated earth is a flamboyant spectacle. Alas, the bloom is only temporary. The water contained in the thin soil layer soon evaporates, or is drawn up and transpired by the ephemeral vegetation. Within days the sunbaked land dries out completely, with hardly a vestige of the brief rain remaining. The flash flood, having disappeared almost as fast as it had appeared, leaves practically no trace. Only in the depressions, where the soil had been wetted to greater depth, is the effect longer lasting. There, a lush vegetation grows for a few more weeks, only to shrivel and enter the long desert dormancy in expectation of another flood—next year, perhaps, or the year after . . .

Now the spaceman realizes that the desert is not entirely devoid of water. There is some rain, albeit infrequent, irregular, and scanty. And there is soil, and seepage, and life. The desert is in fact the home of an astonishing variety of plants and animals, which by elaborate adaptation of structure and behavior are able to thrive even where conditions of extreme heat and dryness would seem to preclude life. But can the desert's meager resources be managed to provide for human habitation as well?

At this point our visitor would be ready to begin reading the main part of this book.

2
Arid Zones and Deserts

What do we mean by the term "desert"? In what sense does it differ from what is commonly called an "arid zone"? Indeed, the two terms are sometimes used interchangeably, though the difference between them can be decisive. Aridity in general can be regarded as an imbalance between the demand for water and its supply, the latter being too scarce to meet the former. There obviously can be different degrees of aridity. Such are the vagaries of climate that even so-called humid regions can experience occasional drought and even prolonged dry spells, though in general a humid region, by definition, is one in which precipitation is practically always sufficient to sustain crop plants (and is at times excessive). A semiarid region is one in which precipitation is sufficient in most seasons but droughts occur frequently enough to make the practice of rainfed farming a somewhat hazardous venture. An arid zone is one in which rainfed farming is entirely marginal—successful in some years and hopelessly unsuccessful in others.

It is in the nature of arid regions that the unpredictable variations in precipitation tend to be greater, relative to the average, than in humid regions. Even if the seasonal average, per se, were adequate, rainfed farming would still be undependable in the long run. As a rule of thumb, the maximum annual precipitation in arid regions approximates 200 percent of the average, and the minimum is about 50 percent of the average. The variation of annual rainfall is therefore skewed; and since an unusually wet year raises the average more than an equally unusually dry year lowers it, it is apparent that more years are below average rainfall than are above it. Despite the hazards of drought in arid zones, sedentary agricultural populations can and do exist there, however marginal their agricultural economy. Extensive grazing, rather than continuous cultivation, becomes a major form of land use in such areas, which are often contested between nomadic or seminomadic herdsmen and sedentary farmers.

The situation is basically different in real desert areas, which can be thought of as "extremely arid." Here average annual precipitation is definitely insufficient to sustain agricultural crops, and hence ordinary rainfed farming is impossible. The biblical definition of the desert is "the unsown land" (Jeremiah 2:2), a land generally unsuited for agriculture because of its extreme aridity. Even extensive grazing is marginal, and may often be submarginal. For man to subsist in the desert without having to import most of his vital requirements, he must devise ingenious schemes to obtain supplementary supplies of water, either by wresting the precious fluid from underground aquifers, if available, or by collecting it off the slopes of barren ground during brief episodes of rainfall, or by conveying it from another region. With such means, spotty agriculture becomes possible (albeit risky); without them, even spotty agriculture is out of the question.

The qualitative distinction between arid regions and deserts can be formulated quantitatively, using rigorous criteria based on rainfall totals or probabilities and on rainfall-evaporation ratios. However, exact demarcations on what is a gradually varying continuum are necessarily arbitrary. In reality no clear-cut, fixed boundaries or distinct limits are recognizable universally, since factors other than those mentioned come into play. In marginal areas, for instance, soil characteristics—in particular the ability of the soil to retain moisture—influence the feasibility of rainfed agriculture. Moreover, agriculture tends to expand into marginal areas following a succession of more favorable years, only to contract with the inevitable recurrence of a succession of relatively dry seasons.

Thus, the transition belts separating the wilderness from the domain of civilization have experienced marked—and frequent—shifts. Such areas have been involved since time immemorial in the struggle between the desert and the sown. Any breakdown of central authority permitted incursion by nomads, the sons of the desert who would prey upon agricultural land and destroy the soil and water conservation works so laboriously and meticulously constructed by generations of diligent settlers. The drastic and wanton destruction of the climax vegetation for lumber and fuel; overgrazing by excessive numbers of livestock, particularly goats; erosion caused by this removal of protective vegetation and by injudicious cultivation—all these, and more—combined to alter the fragile ecological balance and to wreak practically irreversible damage. Such damage is particularly notable over parts of the Middle East, as is evidenced by the present, highly degraded landscape. This insidious process is not merely a thing of the past. Lately termed "desertification," it is in fact proceeding at an alarmingly accelerated pace on a global scale.

It was probably in the Fertile Crescent of the Middle East (stretching from the Persian Gulf northward through Mesopotamia, westward through Assyria and Aram—now Syria—to the Mediterranean, and southward along the coast through northern Israel) that Neolithic man first turned from gathering and hunting to agriculture (A. S. Leopold 1976). Rainfed crops were produced in the more humid areas, and irrigated crops in the river valleys. Whether earlier or later we do not know, but at some point an alternative or supplementary occupation to cropping came into prominence: the herding and pasturing of domesticated animals. The practice of agriculture caused denudation of the land and destruction of its native vegetation through clearing of fields, and even more through overgrazing. And it was here that man first began to play a role in the expansion of the deserts. This is not to say that deserts are basically man-made. In fact, they antedate humankind as we know it. However, man's activity has increasingly affected the nature and extent of the desert and of its fringe lands, and seldom for the better. Hence it has been said that the desert was made by God, but wasteland was made by man.

By some strange accident of history and geography, it happens that almost one-fourth of the world's population is struggling to eke out an existence in the earth's semiarid and arid zones, often at the very edge of the desert, where, by a cruel stroke of nature, the requirements of crop plants for water are the greatest, whereas the supplies by natural precipitation are the least. Agricultural plants, because of their physiology and interaction with the field environment, must transpire contantly if they are to be productive and, in fact, are required to transmit hundreds of times more water to the unquenchably thirsty air than they need only for growth.

Thus, in the arid zones the scales are weighted heavily, at the outset, against agriculture. The balance must be rectified by augmentation of water supply (that is, irrigation) whenever possible, and by strict water conservation at all times. In the desert, of course, the situation is even more extreme, and if water cannot be imported economically from some other region, then extraordinary means are needed to husband the exceedingly meager amount of water available locally. Throughout history, therefore, the settlement and civilization of the desert depended primarily on the acquisition and implementation of the special skills, techniques, and organizational systems required to meet the challenges posed by this difficult environment. Without these, the desert lies beyond the realm of civilization.

The very term "desert" is derived from the Latin word for "abandoned" or "deserted." Nothing could be further from the truth, however, than the popular notion of the desert as a totally forbidding and useless wasteland, sun-seared and wind-swept, waterless and endless, bereft of shelter and of life except for venomous snakes and malevolent scorpions lurking behind every rock. The desert is not so utterly hostile. It is, in fact, our civilization's major frontier and land reserve, offering perhaps 20 million square kilometers for possible future colonization. With so much space, mineral resources, and abundant sunshine, the desert is a wondrously rich frontier. But its potentialities are not simply there, to be had for the asking. Attempts to utilize and colonize it are destined to fail unless based on a thorough understanding of its specific and vulnerable ecology. Those who hasten to domesticate the desert may destroy it irreparably. Far from enhancing our civilization, they may diminish it for all time. Those who know the desert respect it as practiced mariners respect the sea, and proceed into it with caution and reverence.

3

Features of the Desert

Deserts are generally characterized by a total annual rainfall of less than 250 millimeters and a continental-type temperature regime of hot summers and often cool winters. They occupy about 14 percent of the earth's 143 million square kilometers of land area. Along the fringes of the deserts are the steppes, those equally vast semidesert, arid, or semiarid plains with an annual rainfall up to twice that of the desert but still largely insufficient or too variable for dependable, stable farming. The combined desert and steppe areas add up to over 40 million square kilometers—more than a quarter, and not much less than a third, of our globe's continental surface.

Though they tend to girdle the earth astride the tropics of Cancer and Capricorn, deserts occur in more or less distinct masses. The largest by far is the Sahara, which extends over an area of nearly 9 million square kilometers (practically as large as the United States, including all 50 states). The Sahara thus encompasses the greater part of northern Africa. About a tenth of it is covered with dunes, the sea of fluid, shifting sand made famous by films and lore. There are craggy mountains, too, some as lofty as 3,500 meters above sea level. But most of the Sahara consists of low, gravel-strewn plains with an average annual rainfall of no more than 25 millimeters. Dotted irregularly within this sere expanse are the oases at which dwell the Sahara's indigenous peoples: the Tuaregs, the Mozabites, the Reguibats, the Chamba, and others.

Continuous with the Sahara on the east is the Egyptian desert, divided into the Western Desert and Eastern Desert by the world's largest oasis, the thin emerald strip along the Nile. These deserts are connected by the Sinai and Negev to the Arabian Desert, including the great Nafud and the fearsome Rub al-Khali, altogether covering about 2.5 million square kilometers of the Arabian Peninsula. This is the sandiest of all deserts, with fully one-third of its area under dunes, and one of the very driest, with a total absence of any rivers or perennial springs of any size.

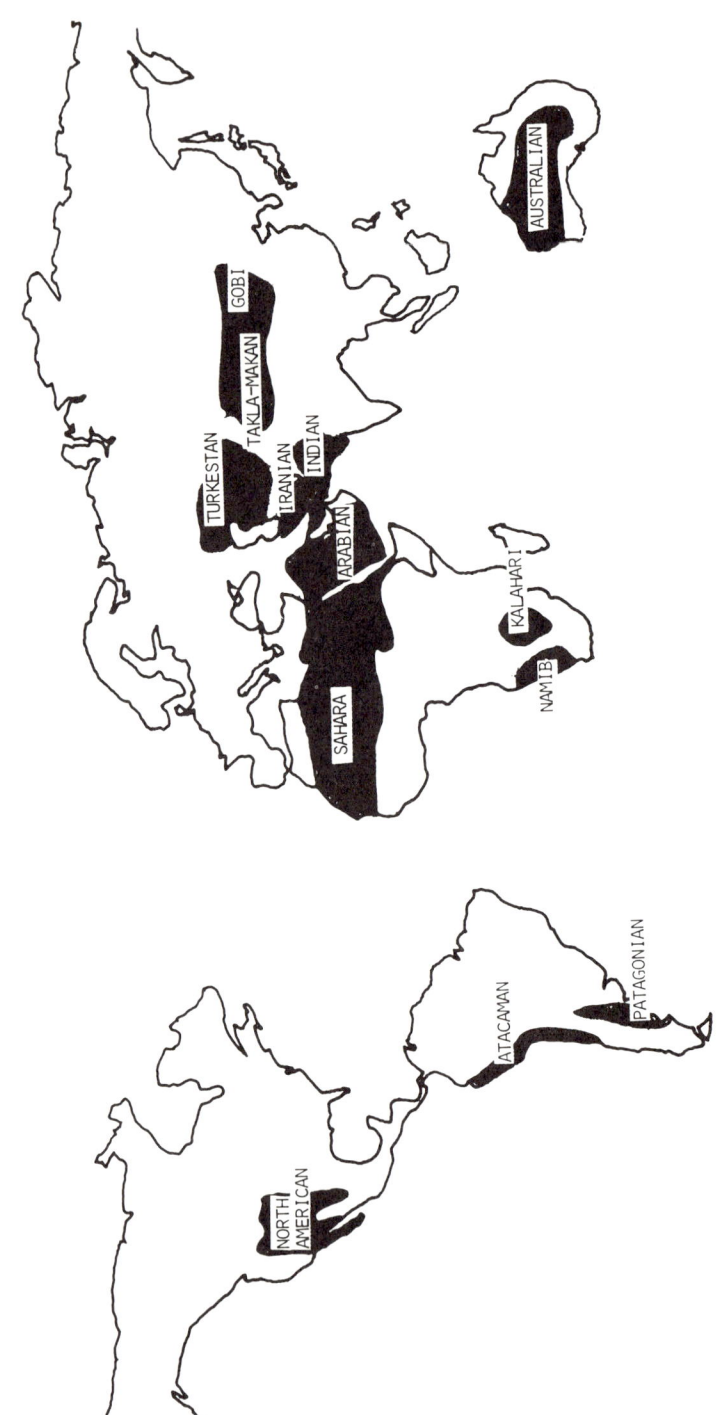

The major deserts of the world.

East and northeast of the Arabian Desert lies the Iranian Desert (including Dasht e-Lut, Dasht e-Kavir, and Dasht e-Margo), which occupies some 400,000 square kilometers. It is contiguous on the east with the 600,000-square-kilometer Thar Desert of Pakistan and northwestern India, and on the north with the 2 million-square-kilometer Turkestan deserts of Kara-Kum and Kyzyl-Kum lying east of the Caspian Sea. Still farther east is the Takla-Makan (500,000 square kilometers) of Sinkiang in western China, a landlocked region distant from any source of moisture. It extends eastward toward the great arid plains of northwestern China and Mongolia, and to the famed Gobi (1.25 million square kilometers), the high and rather cold and barren wasteland of east-central Asia.

Another desert mass, also in the northern hemisphere, is the North American Desert (1.25 million square kilometers), including the Great Basin, lying east of the Cascade and Sierra Nevada ranges; the Mojave Desert of southern California; the Sonoran Desert of Arizona and northwestern Mexico; and the Chihuahuan Desert of central Mexico. The most famous section in the North American Desert is Death Valley, grimly named for its harsh extremes of heat and aridity: it is the lowest and driest spot in North America, and one of the hottest places on earth (a temperature of 57°C was recorded there in 1913, the highest shade temperature recorded anywhere), with an average annual rainfall of only about 40 millimeters.

In the Southern Hemisphere the Australian Desert is the largest, covering 3.3 million square kilometers—nearly half the area of the Australian continent. With over 100 millimeters of average annual rainfall at its driest, this desert is not nearly so intensely arid as, say, the Sahara. The Kalahari in southern Africa covers about 550,000 square kilometers, and extends westward to the practically rainless but foggy coastal desert of Namib. The Patagonian Desert of Argentina (about 650,000 square kilometers), reminiscent of the Sonoran Desert of North America, extends northward to the Gran Chaco steppe of Bolivia and Paraguay. Farther to the north and west stretches the Peruvian Atacama Desert, a long and narrow band covering some 350,000 square kilometers of the west coast of South America. With no more than 15 millimeters of average rainfall per year, it is the least rainy of the major deserts of the world. Its coastal edge, however, is characterized by extremely frequent and dense fogs, condensation of which as dew may be of some biological importance.

Measured on the geological scale of time, so much longer than the historical scale to which we are accustomed, the particular deserts we have described are rather young features, just a few million years old. Throughout the 4 to 5 billion or more years of the earth's existence, the continents have been submerged and uplifted repeatedly, and have drifted together and apart in turn. It seems plausible that deserts have existed as long as the continents have been large enough to contain stretches of land isolated by distance or mountains from the sea or located in the latitudes of descending air. However, the deserts of the world, not unlike the continents, have shifted location, so that what was once a desert may now be a tropical rain forest, and vice versa. That is why we find marine or lacustrine fossils and deposits in the rocks of today's deserts, and arid-zone deposits underlying today's humid regions.

The occurrence and the location of deserts are not merely accidental. Rather, they result from consistent geophysical processes. To maintain dynamic equilibrium, the earth must dispose of the enormous amount of radiant energy (received in the equatorial region) by poleward convection (flow) through the earth's fluid cover—the gases of the atmosphere and the water of the oceans. Hence, a pattern of air-mass flow and ocean currents is set up. As the equatorial air is heated, it expands, rises, and blows away from the equator at high altitudes. The rising air creates a belt of generally low atmospheric pressure in the equatorial zone, and two belts of high pressure in the northern and southern subtropical zones where that air subsides. Still farther from the equator are two additional belts of ascending air with low pressure, located in the temperate latitudes. That air descends earthward and creates another pair of high-pressure areas at the polar regions. Wherever the air rises, it expands, cools, and precipitates its moisture. Wherever air descends, it compresses, warms up, and absorbs (rather than precipitates) moisture. Both the polar and the subtropical regions are zones of low precipitation and high atmospheric pressure. The polar regions, however, are too cold to be considered "desert" in the ordinary sense of the term. The subtropical zones, however, are generally warm and dry enough to have typical deserts.

The fact that the globe rotates about its axis (40,000 kilometers per 24 hours at the equator, zero speed at the poles) distorts the north-south pattern of air-mass flow. In effect, it deflects the flow rightward in the northern hemisphere and leftward in the southern hemisphere. The atmosphere therefore tends to circulate in a fairly well defined pattern of air swirls. As part of the descending air of the subtropical belts rushes equatorward, the ground-level winds tend to become easterly (the "trade winds") as they are deflected rightward. And, as part of that air flows poleward, it tends to form westerly winds (the "prevailing westerlies").

This idealized pattern of air circulation is modified by the irregular sizes, shapes, and positions of the continents, and is also altered by the tilting of the earth's axis in relation to the sun, a fact that causes the change of seasons as the northern and southern hemispheres tilt toward the sun alternately. Broadly speaking, however, the global movement of air dictates the zonation of aridity and deserts. Thus, for one example, the abundant rains that drench the southern coast of the African bulge (from Nigeria to Liberia) cannot penetrate the high-pressure belt to reach the Sahara. Simply being distant from the ocean can cause an inland area to be arid (for instance, the Gobi).

Even proximity to the oceanic moisture source is no assurance of humid-

Special Features

ity, however. A physiographic feature such as a coastal mountain range can create a "rain shadow" on its lee side and add greatly to the aridity of the region lying beyond it. In effect the mountain range intercepts the moisture-laden air blowing landward from the ocean, and as that air is impelled to rise up the slope, it cools, condenses its moisture, and drops its precipitation on the windward side and on the crest of the range. With much of its moisture thus extracted, the air descends on the leeward side, and as it descends, it compresses, heats up, and decreases its relative humidity. Indeed, it becomes hot and dry enough to desiccate the valley or plain lying beyond the range. An obvious example of this orographic effect is how the Cascade and Sierra Nevada ranges force the winds coming from the Pacific Ocean to discharge rain on their western slopes, and how the eastern side of the range, constituting the "rain shadow," remains dry. Indeed, the transition from the wet side to the dry side often occurs over a very short horizontal distance.

Nowhere is this transition more abrupt and dramatic than in Israel, when the Samarian and Judean mountain ranges run parallel to the Mediterranean coast. Their west-facing slopes receive from 500 to more than 700 millimeters of rainfall annually, and the climax vegetation is a forest of pine, oak, pistacia and carob trees. Just east of the watershed divide, however, begins the famed and spectacular Judean Desert, long the abode only of secluded hermits and monastic sects (like the ancient Essenes who left us the so-called Dead Sea Scrolls). Within a distance of little over 10 kilometers, rainfall decreases by two-thirds, atmospheric evaporativity increases, and all that grows on the barren slopes is a few scraggly desert shrubs. The city of Jerusalem is located on the knife's edge of that divide. Within the city's limits a casual tourist can readily walk across one of the sharpest and most startling of geographical boundaries: from rainfed, shaded groves to stark, rainless desert.*

The desert landscape is either monotonous or wondrously varied, depending on the present and past geological and climatic features of the location, as well as on the eye of the beholder. Viewed superficially, vast areas appear to consist of time-frozen oceans of sand or gravel-covered plains, stretching on and on to endless, flat horizons. This seeming uniformity is more illusory than real. Viewed closely, even the sand and the gravel plains reveal intricate patterns of variation in structure and water regime. Other parts of the desert, however, display dramatic landforms as dazzling as any in the world. In the desert the mountains and valleys, the geological faults and upthrusts, the sculpted works of relentless streams of water and gusts of wind

---

*Let the tourist beware, however. Venturing alone into the desert for even a day's outing can be dangerous. Some readers may recall the fate of the renowned Bishop James Pike of San Francisco, who ventured into the Judean Desert some years ago in a jeep, carrying a tourist map and a bottle of Coca Cola. His dehydrated body was found several days later. And this in a desert strip only 25 kilometers wide.

Naturally carved rock columns ("the pillars of Solomon") in the southern Negev Desert.

Special Features

are all on open display, unobscured by soil or vegetation. The landforms of the desert include jagged pillars and precipitous mountains thrust above the plain like an archipelago of volcanic islands rising out of the ocean, sharply etched rock ledges and pediments, deeply incised ravines, wrinkled ridges, rutted watercourses, mazelike badlands, and smooth playas. Desert cliffs and ravines often expose layer after layer of fossil-filled rocks from successively older geological periods, from recent to Precambrian. In a single short climb up a sequence of cliffs, shelves, and slopes, a trained observer can read the story of the land spanning hundreds of millions of years.

Desert sand is an ever-alive, restless, writhing body of golden, viscous fluid in constant, wind-whipped flow, a churning mass creeping along the valley floor in slow motion and lapping stealthily at the feet of the mountains. It moves in rippling, wavelike tides, steadily flowing hither, then shifting thither, as if by random caprice, only to turn again in its original direction. Sand consists primarily of fragments of quartz (a hard, glasslike material composed of silicon dioxide) along with lesser amounts of feldspar, mica, zicron, hornblende, and other minerals. It is derived from the disintegration of such primary (igneous) rocks as granite, or secondary (sedimentary) rocks such as sandstone. Originally irregularly shaped and angular, the particles are smoothed by repeated collision and mutual abrasion, and thus become nearly spherical. While a sandstorm may seem to hover or glide smoothly over the

A scraggly and practically leafless acacia tree grows in a gravelly wadi bed. Thrusting up behind it is a massive outcropping of water-carved, wind-polished, sun-scorched limestone.

surface of the land, the individual particles in fact advance by repeated skips and bounces, a jerking hopscotch motion called saltation. Sand deposits may occur in many locations, most commonly along seashores, in humid as well as in arid regions; yet nowhere outside the desert can sand and wind interplay so freely, unhindred by moisture (which tends to bind sand grains together) or by vegetation. When unchecked by vegetation, cementation, or windbreaks, moving sand can inundate whole valleys and devour agricultural land.

Dunes are mobile heaps of sand that can assume different forms, the most typical ones being the crescent-shaped barkhans and the elongated seifs. Barkhans, formed by winds of constant direction, are skewed hills: the side facing the wind rises gently to a sharp crest, beyond which the downwind side of the dune falls steeply. Grains of sand swept by the wind are carried up the long slope to the dune's crest, then tumble down the steep face, where they maintain the sand's angle of repose (approximately 31°). Though constant in shape and weighing perhaps a million tons or more, the barkhan in fact is an inexorably moving mass that can advance a score or more meters per year. In extreme cases wind-whipped dunes have been known to submerge an entire oasis within days. Where the winds are highly variable from season to season, barkhans, instead of advancing always in the same direction and at a uniform rate, may turn on themselves and coalesce to form grotesque, crazy-quilt patterns of twisted, star-shaped, or scorpion-shaped compound dunes that may

The wrinkled pattern of these shifting dunes results from the wind pattern — in this case the prevailing wind direction is evidently from right to left.

reach scores of meters in height and hundreds of meters in extent. From the air a region of sand dunes looks like a maze of wrinkles. Attempting to traverse such a region on foot can be treacherous. Winding through the dunes, an unguided traveler can quickly lose all sense of direction. The greatest area of continuous sand in the world is Rub al-Khali in Arabia, a vast sea of dunes first traversed and explored only a generation ago, scores of years after explorers had reached the North and South poles!

More diverse than the sands are the desert's mountains. Some are volcanic extrusions of black or gray basalt. Others are huge, blocklike massifs of granite. More prevalent are stratified sedimentary rocks such as limestone, dolomite, chalk, shale, or sandstone, originally laid down as horizontal deposits or beds, but later uplifted and deformed into wavelike ridges and troughs called anticlines and synclines. Occasionally the desert's mantle of rock formations is fractured and displaced along distinct fault lines. In places the mountains reveal intrusive plugs or dikes, the solidified remains of lavalike molten rock (magma) that once rose from the bowels of the earth and oozed its way into fissures. When softer than the bed-rock, such seams eventually erode to leave deep crevasses in the mountains; if harder, they become protruding walls. None of these geological processes is exclusive to the desert, but nowhere else are their effects so clearly in evidence. Indeed, the desert has been called a living school of geology and geomorphology (and, as we shall see, of hydrology and ecology as well).

Typical among the mountains of the desert are the relics of ancient plateaus known as mesas or buttes. When a stratum of hard, weathering-resistant rock is underlain by soft, erodible material, the process of geological erosion, once its cuts through the caprock, begins to undercut it, rapidly scouring away its vulnerable foundations. Over eons a continuous plateau is gradually dissected by deep canyons, which widen until all that is left of the ancient plateau are isolated, tablelike mountains, or mesas. As undermining and scouring continue, the mesas waste away, diminishing in width, until the vestigial mountains are reduced to isolated, islandlike relics, rising out of the flat desert like an archipelago out of the sea. They are often shaped like altars or truncated cones, called buttes. Often these are spectacular features, rising sheer out of the valley and capped by massive overhanging rocks. As those rocks crack, huge boulders tumble down.

Paradoxically, for a region whose distinguishing mark is the lack of water, the desert's base, once established by tectonic processes (large-scale shifts in the earth's crust), is primarily sculpted and etched by water. Working both mechanically and chemically, water not only wears away the surface but also continues to gnaw into the underlying flesh of the land as if it were a sharp-clawed monster. Trillions of raindrops pelt the surface, like so many explosive missiles. Water hydrates and dissolves minerals, seeps into pores, and cracks rocks as it freezes. Running water detaches and carries abrasive fragments.

This cone-shaped butte is of white chalk capped by a layer of black Campanian flint. Fragments of the black caprock are strewn on the slopes.

Borne by churning streams, such fragments scoop out channels. Entire mountain ranges, no matter how massive and hard, are gradually scoured and incised by the relentless attack of rain and runoff. The difference between hard rocks and soft rocks is merely a question of time. Eventually even the hardest rocks succumb.

All slopes reveal a regular pattern of gulleys converging into larger and larger rivulets and finally into streams. Where such streams emerge into broad valleys, they release their load of material raked from the mountains. This material, consisting mainly of gravel and sand and called alluvium, spreads out to form fan-shaped, sloping deposits that may coalesce into thick masses, smothering the valley with the fragmented debris of the mountains. The coarsest material in each alluvial fan is typically at the top of the fan while the finer material is carried farther into the valley. In closed basins having no outlet to

Special Features

Saline marshes in the northern Sinai.

the sea, the valley bottoms become temporary lakes — flooded intermittently during the rainy season, and dry the rest of the time. The mud shrinks and cakes as it dries, forming a web of deep cracks. Such desert lake beds are called playas (from the Spanish word for "beach") in the Americas, *sabkhas* in Arabic, and *kavir* in Persian. Playas are often saline, particularly in the presence of shallow groundwater that rises by capillary action and suffuses the surface with glistening crystals of salts. A saline swamp of this sort is called *mamlakha* in Arabia.

A rather rare occurrence in deserts is a permanent lake. The Dead Sea is one, and the Great Salt Lake in Utah is another. Both are landlocked, and both began as freshwater lakes that contracted as the region become arid. Other famous lakes are the huge Caspian Sea, which is not entirely in a desert, and Lake Chad, which expands and contracts intermittently, from 25,000 square kilometers to less than 10,000 square kilometers. The Dead Sea is the earth's lowest lake, located at the deepest pit of the Great Rift Valley, 394 meters below sea level. The lake is maintained and fed by a number of streams, the chief being the Jordan River. That river, its fame notwithstanding, is scarcely more than a small muddy stream, only about 25 meters wide and 1–3 meters deep along its lower reaches. Its headwaters are derived from the melt-

Saline marshes in the northern Sinai.

ing snows of Mount Hermon, from the foot of which it flows swiftly to the Sea of Galilee. Southward from the Sea of Galilee the river meanders lazily through the hot and arid lower Jordan Valley, finally dying a tired death in the saline waters of the Dead Sea. In recent decades the waters of the Jordan and its tributaries have been diverted for irrigation, and the river's flow has slowed to a trickle.

But whatever the amount of water entering the Dead Sea, none of it can leave except by way of evaporation—the lake evaporates an amount of water equivalent to a depth of about 2 meters per year. It has been doing this for many millennia—evaporating water while retaining all of the dissolved salts in the water—until it has become the world's most saline body of water (over 26 percent salt by mass, about seven times saltier than ocean water). Because of the density of its waters, the Dead Sea appears to be very calm, and bathers who brave the area's searing heat can float comfortably in its viscous brine, which is otherwise devoid of all life except for a few phenomenally adapted single-celled organisms.

There are, of course, numerous man-made lakes in various deserts, generally created by the damming of rivers. Among these are Lake Mead, formed in the Colorado River by the Hoover Dam. Larger and now even more fam-

A series of alluvial fans on the western shore of the Gulf of Aqaba, in Sinai.

ous is Lake Nasser, formed by the Aswan High Dam in the Nile River. Another lake made by man, albeit inadvertently, is the Salton Sea in the Imperial Valley of southern California. In the distant past this basin, called the Salton Sink, was an extension of the Gulf of California, but was gradually separated from the sea by accumulated alluvial deposits from the Colorado River's delta. For many centuries, perhaps millennia, it was a landlocked playa, about 90 meters below sea level at its lowest point, and would have remained so were it not for an accident that occurred in 1905. A man-made ditch called the All-America Canal, designed to divert water from the Colorado River to irrigate the Imperial Valley, was breached, and its water flowed unchecked to the valley bottom for about two years. The resulting lake, initially of fresh water, gradually became saline through dissolution of soil-borne salts, enhanced by drainage of brackish water from irrigated agricultural lands. The accumulation of these salts in the lake, and the progressive evaporation taking place from it, have already made the Salton Sea (750 square kilometers in size) saltier than the ocean.

A desert stream is called *wadi* in Arabic, *nahal* in Hebrew, *arroyo* in Mexican Spanish, and "wash" in the lingo of the American Southwest. By whatever name, such streams remain dry most of the time, then—suddenly and briefly—convey desert floods. Much of the water they convey seeps into the coarse gravel beds, where it may encounter an impervious layer and remain trapped as groundwater. Because of the fury of the floods and the coarse and abrasive debris that they carry, desert streams can be powerful erosive agents, clawing and gouging their way into and through even the hardest of rock formations. Nowhere is this power more manifest than in the unique *makhtesh* craters in the Negev, where ancient streams scooped out the very cores of several mountain ranges near their crests, forming enormous trenches or bowl-shaped chasms.

Less awesome than such craters but much more prevalent are badlands—erosion-rutted slopes resembling rugged mountains in miniature, with numerous deeply scoured labyrinthine channels, scratched into the land as if by a jagged, sharp-toothed comb, winding between knifelike ridges. The myriad irregularly directed channels and ridges create an endlessly complex maze in which a person attempting to cross the region can become utterly and hopelessly lost.

Thus far we have spoken only of the persistent erosive power of water. A less formidable erosive agent that nevertheless plays an important role in shaping the desert landscape is the ever-blowing wind. Gusting and whirling without obstruction over the bare face of the desert, it whips up, sorts, and transports everything loose, and sandblasts everything anchored. What it lifts up and deflates from one place, it deposits and piles up at another place—perhaps adjacent, perhaps a continent away. Because the soil of the desert is generally not cemented into stable clods by gluelike organic compounds, as are many soils of more humid climes, and because it is not covered by vegetation or bound by moisture, it is exceedingly vulnerable to wind action. Coarse, abra-

Desert badlands: relic beds of soft rock, incised and scoured by rain water to form a labyrinthine pattern of deep gullies and crumbly ridges.

sive particles swept up by the wind strike at plants, structures, and rock formations, and cause slow but cumulative damage. Particles carried aloft are deposited as the wind abates. Even small surface protrusions, such as boulders or shrubs, act as mini windbreaks, and result in the buildup of elongated hummocks on their downwind sides.

Windborne particles can travel very far, however, and end up hundreds or even thousands of kilometers from their source. The coarser sand particles are deposited nearer their origin, whereas the finer particles remain aloft much longer and are carried over greater distances to places where they are eventually laid down as loessial deposits. The thickest deposits of loess, hundreds of meters deep, are found in northern China, downwind of the great Central Asian deserts. Recent mineralogical evidence suggests that there is indeed a

A dust devil, a spiraling column of swirling dust whipped up by a sudden, transient whirlwind. Dust devils seem to be especially frequent about midday, when the ground-heated air tends to rise in sporadic convection currents.

global circulation of desert-originated dust, and that such material contributes appreciably as an admixture to soils in regions quite far from the desert.

Sandstorms and dust storms are whipped up by occasional violent winds that are capable of lifting clouds of dust dense enough to obscure the sun at midday. The usually marvelously clear desert air then becomes a thick, turbid, yellowish, eye-stinging, nostril-filling, gritty mass. Sandstorms often seem to glide low over the land, like a surging tide of thick fog. The tops of trees may protrude above the billowing mass while their trunks and limbs are stripped by the sharp little missiles of sand grains. The whistling sand grains grant no immunity to hard rocks, which they polish and sculpt into weird shapes. Desert winds damage plants not only by the stinging and pricking of sand but also by desiccation, wreaking special havoc upon young plants.

Removal by wind (deflation) of the finer particles is the cause of the typical "desert pavement," a ground surface covered with a residual layer of closely fitting gravel fragments swept clean of all dust or sand. The surface stones are polished by wind abrasion, and their sunscorched faces are often tinted by metallic oxides (of iron and manganese) called "desert varnish." The gravel-covered plains are variously called *hammada*, *reg*, or *serir* in different regions of North Africa and the Middle East.

Before leaving the topic of wind action in the desert, we ought at least to mention the frequent and sudden occurrence of dust devils. Out of a motionless plain there rises without warning a swirling pillar of white or yellowish dust, a whirlwind resembling either a frenzied dancing dervish or a vaporous genie popping out of a magic bottle. But then, a more serious vision comes to mind, the vision of the pillar of smoke that guided the Children of Israel through the trackless desert by day (and the pillar of fire by night). Alas, these particular "pillars of smoke," the dust devils, are too capricious for guidance, wandering as they do hither and thither, now seeming to collapse, now picking up again, abruptly changing direction, now disappearing, then reappearing in a different location. A dust devil, despite its bizarre appearance, is in fact caused by a gust of wind, curving perhaps around an obstruction and interacting with the rising convection of the desert's ground-heated air to form a mini tornado of upward-spiraling air that sweeps up dust from the ground as it travels over it.

An even more ethereal vision in the desert is the mirage, or fata morgana, an optical illusion appearing on clear, hot days. The phantom image is of a pond in the midst of the desert, and it can look tantalizingly real. To a thirst-racked traveler, ready to sell his soul for a drink of water, the sudden appearance of a brimming lake lying just ahead, but receding as one approaches, can become an unbearable taunt, a mockery, a cruel hoax. Yet even so unreal a phenomenon has a mundane physical explanation. The formation of a layer of buoyant hot air over the sunbaked ground surface causes the refraction (bending) of light so that the surface in effect reflects the blue sky, as if a mirror were placed on the desert floor. The rising waves of hot air play further tricks with that gleaming reflection, making it shimmer like laping water where in reality there is only dry dust. Often surface irregularities or protrusions appear as shade trees on the far shore. Ah, the desert is deceptive. Sometimes (as in the case of the mirage) there is less to it than meets the eye. But sometimes there is more. So much depends on the observer's eye.

4

Water, the Universal Dilemma

Water is literally the essence of life. In a symbolic sense it *is* life. The bubbling water of a rising spring seems indeed to be alive, and one can easily perceive why it has always inspired animistic and even divine associations. It was "living water" to the Hebrews, "running water" to the Mohammedans. As described in Genesis, God's first act after decreeing the appearance of light was to distinguish between the waters of the earth and those of the firmament (the atmosphere), and to separate the dry land and the sea. (Alas, in the case of deserts the separation was all too complete.) To represent water symbolically, the ancient Egyptians drew wavy lines reminiscent of wriggling snakes. This inspired the Hebrew and Phoenician letter *mem*, meaning *mayim* (water), which in turn became the Latin (and English) M.

Water rites were prevalent in many religions, and were associated with fertility in agriculture. The Sumerian term for water was *a*, which also signified sperm, generative power. Relict elements of an ancient cult of water, and rituals to induce rainfall, can be found in practically every religion and sect. The Greek god Poseidon (or the Roman equivalent Neptune) made the springs flow. Ancient rainfall rites still persist in North Africa, where rams and bulls are adorned and paraded in a manner reminiscent of the ancient Amon Ra representations in Egypt. In Scotland, Gaelic-speaking people still talk of the Bull of the Water, which dwells in their lakes (Furon 1967). Rivers and springs are held sacred in most arid and semiarid countries, most notably the Nile, the Mother Ganges in India, and the Jordan.

Water being at once the crux of the problem of life in the desert, and the key to its solution, it behooves us to digress for a moment and consider the availability and utilization of water in contemporary, global terms. Here our concern derives from a growing worldwide shortage in the midst of seeming plenty. For although water submerges nearly three-fourths of the earth's surface, it is not universally found where, when, and in the amount and quality needed.* Some 97 percent of the earth's water is in the oceans, too salty for drinking or irrigation. Another 2 percent is locked in glaciers and polar icecaps. The remaining 1 percent is anything but evenly distributed.

In the final two decades of this century, the world's demand for water is projected to double as cities grow and as industry and agriculture necessarily continue to expand. It still takes 20 tons of water to refine one ton of petroleum, as much as 250 tons of water to make one ton of steel, and 1,000 or more tons of water to produce one ton of grain! In the profligate United States, incidentally, an "average" person uses one-third ton of water at home every day, an amount that could suffice a desert Bedoui for over a month. To the water used directly at home we should add the huge amounts of water used indirectly to produce the food and other necessities (and amenities) of our extravagant civilization. Traced back through their production processes, the eggs we consume for breakfast require nearly half a ton of water each, and the steak we relish for dinner, 13 tons. With all the indirect uses, our daily consumption of water soars to some 8 tons for each American. This is perhaps 100 times more than needed for basic human subsistence.

A solution to the water shortage, it seemed not so long ago, would be desalinization. It is, incidentally, a rather old idea. Aristotle taught that "salt water, when it turns into vapor, becomes sweet, and the vapor does not form salt when it condenses." Julius Caesar used stills to convert seawater for his thirsty legions during the siege of Alexandria. However, only lately has desalinization been attempted on a large scale, and the attempt has been thwarted by the steeply increasing cost of energy, for desalinization (whether by vapor distillation, freezing, electrodialysis, or reverse osmosis) inevitably requires much energy. Even if desalinization of seawater does become feasible in terms of water cost, there will still be the problem of lifting and conveying the water inland to the places where it is most needed (that is, into arid regions, particularly deserts, that may be far from the coast). Desalinization is not the panacea the public had been led to expect.

The supply and distribution of water may someday be controlled by weather modification. Cloud seeding is a first step in that direction. But we still cannot predict seasonal weather or even specific weather events very effectively, let alone modify the weather pattern of a region. Nor can we yet tow icebergs from the Arctic or Antarctic without having them melt en route.

We are faced with the inexorable reality that, in the foreseeable future no less than in the past, the supply of fresh water, indispensable as it is, remains strictly limited. Hence water has repeatedly caused disputes. The very word

---

*An old frontier anecdote, popular in the American Southwest, illustrates the quandary of settlers in arid regions. "This would be a fine country if it just had water," observed an eager new settler. A disillusioned old-timer retreating from the area in his eastward-bound wagon responded, "yes, and so would hell!"

"rival" was used in Roman law as a term for those who shared the water of a *rivus*, or stream.

It is remarkable that certain earlier civilizations, technologically (it would seem) so much less advanced than ours, could thrive in arid regions and even in deserts. We ought to point out, however, that not all ancient civilizations managed equally well. Some, indeed, failed miserably. We need only fly over the land once called Mesopotamia ("the land between the rivers"), which, as every schoolchild knows, was a great "cradle of civilization," to observe wide stretches of barren, salt-encrusted terrain crisscrossed with remnants of ancient irrigation canals. Once these were thriving fields, created by enterprising irrigators whose very success brought about eventual failure as they inadvertently doomed their own land. Irrigation without adequate drainage of these river valley soils inevitably induces the insidious and inexorable process of soil salinization, which eventually poisons the once bountiful land and renders it sterile. This happens whenever the groundwater level, known as the "water table," moves toward the soil surface and the twin processes of capillary rise and evaporation of groundwater suffuse the soil with cumulative quantities of salt.

The universal tendency of farmers has always been to overirrigate ("if a little water is good, more must be better") and, once the soil begins to salinize, the temptation is to apply more and more water in an attempt to flush out the salt with fresh water. Alas, the salt reappears, it blossoms out in mockingly beautiful floral patterns after each irrigation, and more if it each time. Historians who fail to perceive the nature of such physical processes may ascribe the fall of an older kingdom and the rise of a newer one to the apparent failure of one king and the brilliant success of his rival on the battlefield, whereas the real — and invisible — battle had already been decided by soil degradation.

Not incidentally, the same processes that contributed to the decay of once-thriving agricultural centers along the Indus, Nile, Jordan, Tigris, and Euphrates still operate and can be observed in many countries, not excepting parts of the United States such as California, Arizona, and other southwestern states. Nowadays, however, we can monitor these processes and install drainage works to control what, in ancient times, was so much more difficult to control, if only because it was hardly understood.

Soil salinization was far from the only cause of environmental and agricultural failure in ancient times. Accelerated soil erosion was another cause, and an equally obvious one was the failure to plan for the inevitable periods of drought. The biblical story of Joseph the Provider, who had the foresight to store the excess grain of "fat" years for use in "lean" years is well known. Less famous, though no less poignant, is the sad fate of Fatehpur Sikri, the magnificent capital built in northern India in the late sixteenth century by the Mughal king Akbar the Great. He ordered a hilly eminence to be leveled. He then summoned the best architects and the best artisans to design and erect imposing and ornate palaces and mosques. No expense was spared. Blocks of red sandstone were shaped and fitted, and slabs of the finest white marble were carved into intricate patterns to serve as decorative facades. The nobles and officers of the kingdom built mansions. An impregnable city wall, with nine gates, was erected on three sides, and the fourth side, on the southwest, was protected by an extensive artificial lake many square kilometers in area.

King Akbar the Great was indeed a great leader, strategist, administrator, and philosopher. Alas, he was not a great hydrologist. The artificial lake, designed to serve as a reservoir and to provide a secure supply of water for Akbar's splendid capital, never filled to capacity. Following a succession of droughts, the lake went completely dry. Less than two decades after its completion, the splendor of its much-acclaimed architecture notwithstanding, Fatehpur Sikri was abandoned for want of water. It remained uninhabited by man, the abode only of wild beasts, for several hundred years, until redeemed in modern times to serve as a tourist attraction and a mute testament to the defeat of a great kingdom by the lack of that most ordinary yet most vital fluid, water.

Lest the reader derive the erroneous conclusion that the folly and fate of Fatehpur Sikri belong only to the distant past and are a mere historic curiosity, let us hasten to point out that many such cases have occurred in the recent past, and many are taking place in the present. A case in point is the Ogallala aquifer in the Great Plains region of the United States. In parts of this region, water is drawn from wells at a rate much exceeding the aquifer's natural recharge, and the water table has been falling progressively lower. Instead of cooperating to regulate pumping regionally and to replenish the aquifer insofar as possible, some of the landowners in the region have been competing in drawing water for their own immediate profit, without regard for the region's future. Since water is a fluid and recognizes no property boundaries, any individual who attempts to conserve water is in danger of having his water pumped out from under him by a less considerate neighbor. And so, in a case of private enterprise carried to its aberrant extreme, an entire thriving irrigation district is busily and rapidly putting itself out of business. It is now forecast that within the next few decades the water table will have fallen so far as to make the cost of further pumping (what with rising energy prices) prohibitive for irrigation. Akbar the Great could at least plead that he had acted out of ignorance.

5

Soil and Water in the Desert

We use the term "soil" to describe the fragmented outer layer of the earth's terrestrial surface. The intricate and fertile mix composing the soil, with its special and vital attributes, is the basic substrate of all terrestrial life. Soil is formed initially through disintegration and decomposition of rocks by physical and chemical weathering processes, and is subsequently influenced by the activity and accumulated residues of microscopic and macroscopic plants and animals. The physical processes causing disintegration of rocks into small fragments include expansion and contraction resulting from heating and cooling, stresses resulting from freezing and thawing of water and the penetration of roots, and scouring or grinding by abrasive particles carried by moving ice, water, and wind. The chemical processes tending to decompose the original minerals in the parent rocks include hydration, oxidation and reduction, solution and dissociation, immobilization by precipitation or removal of components through leaching or volatilization, and various physicochemical exchange reactions. The loose products of these various weathering processes are often transported by running water, glaciers, or wind, and deposited elsewhere.

Soil formation processes generally continue beyond the initial weathering of rocks and minerals. In the further course of soil development, the character of the minerals is modified by the genesis of secondary minerals (such as clay minerals) and the growth of organisms that contribute organic matter and bring about a complex series of physicochemical and biochemical reactions, including the clumping or flocculation of minute soil particles (colloids) and their more or less stable association with larger particles in composite aggregates that are often bound together by gluelike organic gels. The resulting soil is no longer a loose and haphazard assemblage of irregular particles, but a distinctly ordered and well-structured body with definite and consistent properties. The process of soil formation culminates in the appearance of a characteristic soil profile.

Typically, the soil profile consists of a succession of recognizable layers, or strata. Such layers may result from the pattern of deposition, or sedimentation, as can be observed in wind-deposited (eolian), and particularly in water-deposited (alluvial), soils. If, however, the layers form in place by internal soil-forming ("pedogenic") processes, they are called horizons. The top layer, called the A horizon, is the zone of major biological activity, and therefore is generally enriched with organic matter and often darker than the underlying soil. Next comes the B horizon, where some of the material migrating from the A horizon (such as clay or carbonates) tends to accumulate. Under the B horizon lies the C horizon, which is the soil's parent material. In the case of residual soil formed in place from bedrock, the C horizon consists of the weathered and fragmented rock material. In other cases the C horizon may consist of alluvial, eolian, or glacial sediments.

In arid regions soil formation processes and profile development are not nearly so pronounced as in humid regions. Chemical decomposition of minerals and the formation of secondary minerals are very slow, and little organic matter accumulates. Even so, a profile does develop in time. A typical feature of arid-zone soils is the dissolution of calcium sulfate, calcium carbonate, and other salts in the upper part of the soil profile, and their precipitation at some depth. Where advanced, such a process can result in an almost impervious, cemented B horizon, called caliche. The structure of arid-zone soils is generally unstable, and these soils are particularly vulnerable to erosion.

Water enters soil in a process called infiltration. During a rainstorm, water arriving at the soil surface permeates and penetrates it, then flows downward through the intricate network of soil pores. As the supply of water to the surface persists, the profile is wetted to greater and greater depth. Two forces cause the water to infiltrate: gravity and suction. The downward gravity force is constant, regardless of the condition of the soil. The suction force derives from the affinity of the dry soil for water. Dry soil is "thirsty" in the sense that it tends to "suck" water by capillary attraction, much the way an old-fashioned blotter could "suck up" ink. Thus, when the soil surface is wetted, the suction force by which the deeper layers draw water downward from the surface augments the force of gravity. Unlike gravity, however, the suction force is not constant. It is greatest initially, when the soil is driest, and diminishes gradually as the soil profile is wetted to progressively greater depth.

The rate at which a soil profile is able to absorb water supplied to its surface at atmospheric pressure has been called the soil's infiltrability (Hillel 1980b). It depends both on the forces (gravity and suction) drawing water into the profile and on a characteristic of the soil called the hydraulic conductivity. Different soils have a higher or a lower conductivity, depending on the sizes, number, and continuity of their conducting pores. While saturated, a coarse-grained soil such as a sand is more conductive than a fine-grained soil such as a clay, because the former has wider pores that offer less resistance to water flow.

As long as the rainfall rate does not exceed the soil's infiltrability, the rain penetrates as fast as it falls. However, when the soil's infiltrability drops below the rainfall rate (either because the suction force is reduced as the soil becomes increasingly satiated, or because the rain is particularly intense, or possibly because the soil surface is partially sealed by raindrop impact), the excess of rainfall over infiltration will accumulate at the soil surface. If that surface is level, ponding will occur; otherwise, the excess surface water will begin to trickle downslope as overland flow, also called surface runoff. At first, runoff will take place as sheet flow, but as the moving water gathers volume and momentum, it tends to concentrate in depressions and to furrow the surface, carving small flow paths called gullies. These gullies converge downslope in a dendritic pattern, creating larger and larger channels, which in turn collect in rivulets and streams.

When even a moderate rainstorm breaks on an entire catchment area, runoff flows from one tributary into another, and may gather suddenly in the

The lapping, churning water of a flash flood as it cascades over a paved roadway in the desert.

main stream, or wadi. As it gains power, its erosive effect multiplies and charges the water with silt and debris. If the rainstorm is localized, the flood stage will tend to diminish as the flowing water seeps into the gravelly channel of the main stream bed, and the flood may fail to reach the stream outlet and discharge into the sea. On the other hand, when a storm is heavy and widespread, all tributaries may flow simultaneously and a disastrous flood may occur in the lower reaches of the stream. Anyone who has not seen a desert flash flood cannot imagine its awesome power. The land may lie parched and placid for years, the stream bed dry as a bone, and as lifeless. Suddenly a wall of water, a torrent seemingly out of nowhere, will barrel down the channel, rolling boulders and uprooting trees and sweeping along any hapless creatures (grazing animals or careless humans) unfortunate enough to stand in the way of its raging fury.

The process of erosion, however, does not begin in the stream. Rather, it begins less spectacularly at the soil surface, under the seemingly gentle and benign raindrops that wet the ground and sustain all life. Those raindrops can wreak havoc. Not all soils are equally vulnerable, some being more stable than others. Indeed, lumps of soil stabilized by organic matter will withstand water and retain their shape through repeated cycles of wetting and drying. Not so, however, an unstable soil practically devoid of organic matter, such as a desert loess; a lump of it immersed in water will quickly collapse and lose its structure. When bombarded by myriad raindrops during a storm, each drop acting as an explosive missile, the bare surface of desert soil slakes down and becomes a thin layer of slick mud. Particles detached and splashed by the raindrops clog the soil's passages and reduce its infiltrability. Air trapped under the muddy surface seal cannot readily escape, and may in fact further retard water transmission downward into the profile. The soggy surface is now extremely vulnerable to erosion: the loosened fine particles are carried by running water as suspended sediment. To the onlooker it might seem that the soil is "melting away."

When the rainstorm ends and the sun comes out, the slaked surface begins to dry. As it dries, it shrinks to form a thin but quite dense and hard crust, which characteristically develops a polygonal cracking pattern. Crusting impedes not only water intake by the soil, but the germination and emergence of seedlings as well. It frequently happens in crust-prone soils that emergence and establishment of seedlings are confined entirely to surface cracks, while numerous seedlings lie smothered under the crust, unable to break through it and emerge into the light of day. As we shall see later, however, the soil crust is not always a bad thing, and in fact can be advantageous from our point of view whenever it becomes desirable to induce runoff from sloping ground in order to collect it as a source of water for human, livestock, or crop use.

The amount of water a soil stores for plant use depends not only on the amount of infiltration, but also on the amount subsequently lost from the root zone by evaporation and internal drainage. "Internal drainage" is the term ap-

Soil

The curled fragments of a clayey crust deposited by the muddy water of a flash flood. The sediment carried by the water is segregated as it settles, with the coarsest particles (sand) settling first and the finest particles (clay) settling on top. As the mud layer dries, the clay thus deposited at the surface shrinks and cracks, and sometimes separates and curls away from the coarser sandy material below.

plied to downward water movement that persists after cessation of the rain. In the course of this drainage, the soil layer wetted to near-saturation during infiltration does not retain its full water content. In fact, the water content of the initially wetted zone diminishes rapidly at first, then more and more slowly, until after some hours or days (depending on the soil), further drainage can be considered negligible.

The remaining water content and its distribution in the soil profile determine the effective reserve of moisture available to plants. Often in humid habitats, and sometimes even in arid-zone habitats if the soils are coarse-grained, much of the infiltrated water may escape to depths beyond root penetration, and continue to flow downward, eventually reaching the water table

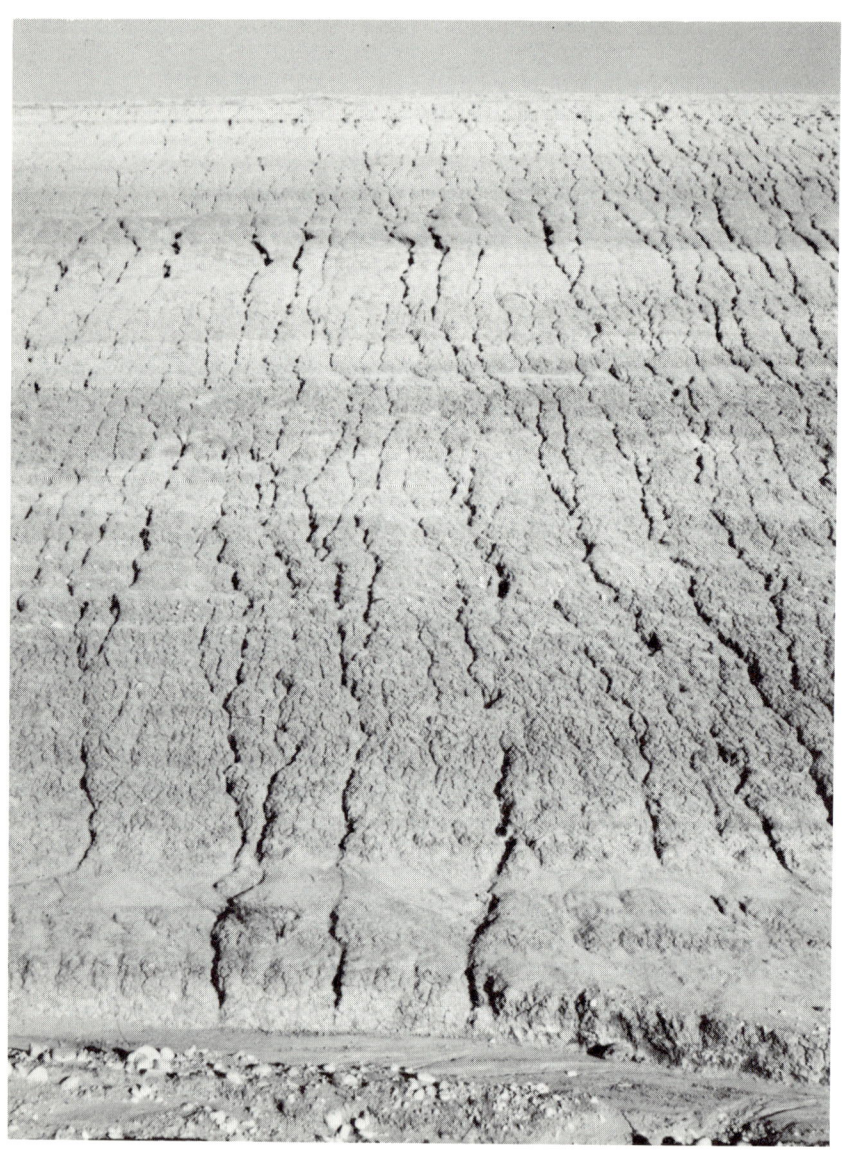
Rill erosion of bare, sloping ground in the desert.

and augmenting the groundwater reservoir. In the dry habitats of the desert, however, the paucity of rain prevents any appreciable amounts of direct groundwater recharge from occurring (except in extraordinarily wet seasons, as well as in stream beds). In these dry habitats water normally penetrates to shallow depth only, and that depth of penetration in effect determines the extent of the root zone.

In the desert, where the vegetative cover is sparse and the greater part of the ground surface remains bare, there is much direct evaporation from the unshaded soil. The evaporation of soil moisture deprives plants of a major portion of their potential water supply, which is meager in any case. This is especially critical during the most vulnerable stages in the life of plants, germination and seedling establishment. Should a seedling fail to win the race with evaporation (that is, fail to send its roots into deeper and moister layers quickly enough), it will desiccate and die. The ability of desert plants to perpetuate themselves even against such great odds depends on a number of interesting and clever stratagems that we shall consider in chapter 6.

For the moment, the important facts to bear in mind are that precisely because the supply of water is so sporadic in the desert while the demand for water is incessant, the soil's role as a moisture reservoir is crucial to sustaining life in this harsh environment. To be sure, the soil is an imperfect reservoir; it fails to absorb all the water delivered to it by rainfall, and even the water that it does absorb, it fails to safeguard against excessive downward seepage and evaporation. Moreover, the soil of the desert is often shallow, stony, steeply sloping, saline, and prone to crusting and to erosion by water and wind. With the scales weighted so heavily against them from the outset, plants and all other forms of life dependent on them would seem to stand little chance to survive here, much less to thrive. Such is the indomitable power and ingenuity of life, however, that it triumphs nevertheless, in myriad exquisitely intricate forms.

An interesting aspect of soil-water relations in the desert is that here coarse-grained soils (such as sandy or even gravelly soils) often offer more favorable moisture conditions for plant growth than do finer-textured soils (such as loams and clays). This is because a coarser soil is likely to have greater infiltrability, and therefore smaller runoff losses, deeper penetration of rainwater due to lesser retention per unit of depth, and lower evaporation losses (Hillel and Tadmor 1962; Hillel and van Bavel 1976; Hillel 1977a). In more humid areas, interestingly, the situation is often reversed, in that sand constitutes the driest habitat because of its excessively rapid drainage of the more abundant rainfall. This is only a single illustration of how notions and impressions derived from one context are inapplicable to another. In the desert the environment (or, rather, the set of micro-environments) is so highly specific that it must be studied meticulously within its own context in order to be understood.

6

The Desert Ecosystem

Ecology, as everyone now knows, has to do with the mutual relationships between living things and their environments. More specifically, the study of ecology has as its aim the elucidation of the principles by which the various species and groups of species composing an area's biological population are organized, and how they function individually and conjunctively within their common environment. Apart from its intrinsic interest, this study can guide us in assessing to what extent and in what way man can utilize a particular environment without changing it irrevocably for the worse. Unfortunately, however, ecology is anything but an exact science. There are too many variables of which we are unaware, or only vaguely aware, and hence are unable to measure. Lately, however, we have begun to acquire the ability to integrate disparate facts and processes that different scientists had hitherto perceived separately, as isolated phenomena. The classical analytical approach, attempting to disassemble every system into components that are to be studied one by one, has proved to be a hindrance in many cases. The task for ecologists is to reassemble and recompose the scattered pieces of the environmental jigsaw puzzle and view the picture as an integral entity.

Now enters the concept of ecosystem, the ecologist's designation for nature's comprehensive organization unit. It encompasses the host of plants, animals, and microorganisms that share a given domain and that might therefore influence one another through such modes as competition or symbiosis, predation, and parasitism. It also encompasses the complex of chemical and physical factors in the environment influencing those organisms and often influenced by them. The entire system is powered by energy, and the key to deciphering the way an ecosystem functions is to trace the flow of this energy into, within, and out of the system.*

In every ecosystem one can distinguish among four groups of species: primary producers—photosynthetic plants; herbivores—plant-eating animals; carnivores—animal-eating animals; decomposers—organisms subsisting on (and recycling) dead tissues of plants and animals.

The special task of desert ecology is to define how these various types of organisms adapt to, and cope with, the shortage of water, and how that shortage constrains and shapes biological activity. Since in the desert the availability of water is so highly variable, both spatially and temporally, we can expect life there to be characterized by relatively long periods of inactivity, or low-level activity, punctuated by short, sporadic bursts of intense activity.

In terms of their adaptation to a water-limiting environment, plants and animals can be classified into the following categories (Rita 1977):

1. Species that limit their activity entirely to moist periods, passing the dry periods in a dormant form—for instance, as spores in the case of microorganisms, as seeds in the case of annual plants, as bulbs in the case of geophytic perennials, as eggs in the case of some invertebrates, or as pupae in the case of insects.

2. Species that reduce but do not cease their activity during drought. Examples are desert shrubs that lose most of their foliage in the dry season. Some rodents, snails, and other animals spend the hot, dry season in a state of estivation, akin to the hibernation of cold-region animals.

3. Species that avoid drought by periodic migration to sources of water, or by developing mechanisms for absorbing water unavailable to most other species, or by storing quantities of water in internal organs.

4. Species able to continue activity for appreciable periods of time even in the absence of a water supply. This category includes some large mammals with specialized mechanisms for drought tolerance.

Because of the random nature of the water supply (rainfall in the desert being something of a fortuitous accident rather than a predictable, dependable event), reproduction of species in the desert ecosystem tends to assume an opportunistic nature instead of being a regular, seasonal, or otherwise prescheduled event. This means that the organisms take quick advantage of temporarily favorable cirumstances—that is, when the environment provides sufficient water. There is essentially no reproductive activity during the dry season even in species that remain active throughout the dry season.

---

*To be sure, we have given a rather idealized description of ecology, a science still in its infancy and still beset by many problems, not the least of which is the all-too-human reluctance of many scientists, consummate individualists that they are, to reach out and cooperate across interdisciplinary boundaries. In this, even the highly touted computer, so much in vogue nowadays as a comprehensive modeling tool, can only come to our aid, not to our rescue.

The availability of water is an essential condition for renewed activity in the form of germination of seeds or hatching of eggs. However, rainfall alone may not suffice to induce activity. The trigger in each case is likely to be a complex, optimal combination of water and other factors such as temperature, day length, and the presence or absence of stimulative or inhibitory substances. Even with all these precautionary preconditions, false starts are not avoided entirely, but for a species to survive in the long run, there must be a sufficiently varied set of responses to environmental stimuli to assure that, at least from time to time, a few individuals will achieve reproductive maturity and perpetuate the species in the particular environment.

The population density in the desert is highly unstable, depending strongly on the extremely variable environment. The population tends to dwindle through a succession of dry seasons, then to increase dramatically following a particularly favorable season. A self-destructive population explosion is avoided, however, by the fact that favorable sets of circumstances do not last very long, and are inevitably followed by unfavorable periods during which many of the new individuals die.

In any ecosystem green plants constitute the base of the biological pyramid. It is therefore fitting that we examine them more specifically, particularly with regard to their water relations under conditions of aridity.

7

Plants and Water in the Desert

Green plants are nature's only autotrophs, able to create living matter from purely inorganic raw materials. Terrestrial plants do this by combining atmospheric carbon dioxide with soil-derived water while converting solar radiation into chemical energy in the process called photosynthesis. This process not only produces food for all of the world's heterotrophs (that is, nonautotrophs, including humans and all other animals) but also releases into the atmosphere the elemental oxygen needed for respiration. In nature's cycle the process of respiration (by animals and plants alike) represents a reversal of photosynthesis, in the sense that photosynthetic products (carbohydrates, for example) are reoxidized to yield the original constituents (water, carbon dioxide, and energy) as separate entities.

Water plays a central role in the metabolism of plants, as a source of hydrogen atoms for the reduction of carbon dioxide in photosynthesis and as a product of respiration. Moreover, water is the solvent, and hence the conveyor, of transportable ions and compounds into, within, and out of all living plants. It is, in fact, a major structural component, often constituting more than 90 percent of the vegetative biomass.

Only a small fraction of the water absorbed by plants is used in photosynthesis, while most (at times as much as 99 percent) is lost as vapor in the process known as transpiration, which is analogous to the perspiration of animals. Transpiration is made inevitable by the exposure to the dry atmosphere of a large area of moist cell surfaces, necessary to facilitate absorption of carbon dioxide. Hence transpiration has been described, from the point of view of crop growers in arid regions, as a "necessary evil," since most crop plants are extremely sensitive, and vulnerable, to lack of sufficient water to replace the amount lost in transpiration. Water deficits impair plant growth and, if extended in duration, can be fatal. A plant not able to draw water from the soil at a rate commensurate with the evaporative demand of the atmosphere will soon begin to dehydrate. The problem is made particularly difficult by the fact that the evaporative demand of the unquenchably thirsty atmosphere in an arid region is practically continuous, whereas rainfall occurs only occasionally and irregularly. To survive during the long dry spells between rains, the plant must rely upon the diminishing reserves of water contained in the pores of the soil, which itself loses water by direct evaporation and by internal drainage.

Perhaps we can identify more readily with the plight of arid zone plants if we imagine ourselves to be living under a government that taxes away 99 percent of our income while requiring us to keep our reserves in a bank that is embezzled daily. The tax exacted from the plant is transpiration, and the plant's bank is the soil, embezzled by drainage and evaporation.

Plants live simultaneously in two very different realms, the atmosphere and the soil, in each of which conditions vary constantly, and not necessarily in conjunction. It is intriguing to ponder how the plant can sense the conditions prevailing in each of these realms, and then optimize its response to their separate or simultaneous changes. The aerial canopies of plants are designed to intercept and collect sunlight and carbon dioxide, both of which are diffuse rather than concentrated. To do so effectively, plant canopies tend to maximize their surface of exposure by branching and foliation. Indeed, the total leaf area of plants frequently exceeds the area of covered ground severalfold. Even more striking is the shape of roots, which proliferate and ramify throughout a large volume of soil while exposing an enormous surface area: a single annual plant can develop a root system with a total length of several hundred kilometers and a total surface area of hundreds of square meters.

The need for such exposure becomes obvious if we remember that the primary function of roots is to constantly extract water and nutrients from a medium that often contains only a meager supply of water per unit volume and only very dilute concentrations of nutrients. And while the atmosphere is a well-stirred and thoroughly mixed fluid, the soil solution is a sluggish and unstirred fluid that moves toward the roots at a grudgingly slow pace, so that the roots have little choice but to move toward it. Indeed, roots forage constantly through as large a soil volume as they can (so long as the soil is not excessively dry, dense, saline, toxic, or anaerobic), in quest of ever more water and nutrients.

The strategy by which any particular type of plant adapts to its environment may depend not only on the conditions prevailing at any moment, but also on an implicit set of expectations, so to speak, of what the future might bring. It is something of a mystery just how different plant species come to have different strategies of survival and how each can adjust its strategy in response to uncontrollable and often adverse conditions even though plants have no nervous system, no brain, and, alas, no access to a computer. The fact is, of course, that on the whole, plants manage very well, better in general than their presumably more sophisticated cousins the animals, and certainly better than human beings, whom the plants preceded and will undoubtedly outlast.

Ponder the dilemma of plants having to "decide" at any moment how to divide their limited growth potential between roots and shoots. Suppose that plants of two species are growing side by side in competition. Now let us employ a little teleology and characterize species A as the "optimist" and species B as the "pessimist." The optimist plants base their strategy on the assumption, so to speak, that the supply of soil moisture will remain plentiful, and hence only a small root system is needed to provide the plant's water requirements. Therefore, the optimists invest their resources in the growth of more branches and leaves. Thus they can develop a greater capacity for photosynthesis, produce more flowers, fruits, and seeds, and take over the habitat.

But what if these expectations prove to be wrong? Suppose the rains do not come, and soil moisture becomes limiting. Then the greater transpiration resulting from the greater foliage soon exceeds the supplying power of the restricted root system, and the plants are left, quite literally, high and dry. Now enter the pessimists. They are preprogrammed, as it were, to expect a long drought. Hence they tend to invest their energy (that is, their photosynthetic carbohydrates) in the development of more roots rather than more shoots.

If their anticipation of a drought is wrong, these overly prudent plants will be literally overshadowed by their more aggressive competitors, the optimists. If, on the other hand, the pessimists' expectations are borne out, their curtailed foliar transpiration, coupled with their enhanced root system's ability to provide (not for a "rainy day" but for the more dire eventuality of numerous dry days), will carry them through. The result will be that the meek shall indeed inherit the earth — at least for that particular season.

Our exercise in hypothetical teleology is not to be taken too literally, and was meant only to illustrate how plant species can differ in adaptation to environments with varying degrees of aridity. Plants that inhabit water-saturated domains are called aquatic plants, or hydrophytes. Plants adapted to drawing water from shallow water tables are called phreatophytes. Plants that grow in aerated soils, generally in semihumid to semiarid climates, are called mesophytes. Most crop plants belong in this category. Mesophytes control their water economy by developing extensive root systems and optimizing the ratio of roots to shoots (the former supply water and nutrients from the soil, the latter photosynthesize and transpire in the atmosphere) and by regulating the aperture of their stomates. These stomates are narrow openings in the leaves that serve as entry points for the carbon dioxide needed in photosynthesis while simultaneously permitting release of transpired water vapor.

Curtailment of transpiration, however, necessarily entails restriction of photosynthesis, and for this reason thirsty plants cannot be very productive. Plants that can nevertheless survive long periods of thirst and recover quickly when water is supplied, even briefly, are called xerophytes, or desert plants.

Such plants may exhibit special features, called xeromorphic, designed to store water and minimize its loss (for example, succulent tissues, thickened epidermis and a waxy surface cuticle, recessed stomates and reduced leaf area). Some plants are especially adapted to growing in a saline environment and are called halophytes. Finally, it takes an extreme degree of adaptability (or masochism?) for some plants (xero-halophytes) to grow in an environment that is both dry and saline at the same time.

The desert, although dry as a whole, contains pockets, or niches, where wet or moist conditions prevail, at least temporarily. Hence, all of the various types of plants mentioned are represented in it, sometimes in astonishingly close proximity to one another. Each viable species, availing itself of the diversity of the land, finds the particular locations and times at which circumstances are favorable for its growth and perpetuation.

The vegetation of the desert is remarkable for its diversity. To escape or withstand the pitiless drought and heat that continually threaten their extinction, desert plants have evolved highly specialized forms and functions. A desert habitat often displays, growing side by side, such diverse types of plants as puffy succulents covered by a thicket of thorns, shrubs with leafless twigs, bunch grasses, and long-leafed plants with subterranean bulbs, each type conditioned to cope with aridity in its own way. In typical habitats of a humid climate, where conditions are stable and uniform, plants generally compete for space and light until the best-adapted species, or narrow association of species, comes to predominate. In the desert, where the climate is unstable and the micro environment is spatially variable, plants compete for water rather than for light, and a wide spectrum of species exists in the same habitat to take advantage of varying circumstances. Some species gain prominence in wet seasons, others in dry; some concentrate in small depressions, others thrive on folds or ridges.

In principle, desert plants can adopt either of two alternative strategies for survival: drought evasion and drought resistance (Levitt, 1972). Drought evaders, generally annuals, survive the long dry period in a totally inactive state (for instance, as dormant seeds), ready to spring to life when conditions become favorable, and programmed, as it were, to complete the cycle of life in time to set seed again prior to the onset of the next dry season. Drought resistors are generally perennials able to remain active during the dry season by storing water in their fleshy leaves, stems, or underground organs; or by reaching and tapping subsoil sources of water; and/or by reducing their leaf area to curtail water requirements.

Drought evaders thus ignore the water supply problem, and need no special mechanism to resist drought. Consequently, they do not differ radically from annuals of more humid regions, except in their ability to complete their life cycle rapidly. Hence they are more ephemeral, and rather smaller, than their humid-region cousins, which may belong to the same genus. The seed crop that the desert-growing annuals produce must be enormous, since many —often most—of the seeds falling to the ground are consumed by desert animals living in the same ecosystem. There is obvious strength in numbers— that is, in spreading so many seeds that the probability of having at least a few survive to germinate seems assured.

How do the seeds that do survive the voracious animals sense when to germinate? Remember that germination is an essentially irreversible process —once begun, there is no turning back to dormancy; a seedling must either carry through to maturity or die. Unless the seedling can win the race against evaporation and advance its roots into the deeper and still-moist layers before it is overtaken and engulfed by dry soil, it is doomed. If all the seeds of a species were to respond too readily to the first wetting, the seedlings might then be caught by a dry spell at their most tender and vulnerable stage, and be annihilated without contributing to the perpetuation of their species, which is the ultimate aim of all forms of life.

How do the seeds of desert plants avoid being fooled into germinating after the false signal of a trivial shower that is insufficient to sustain subsequent seedling growth? As it happens, the seed coats of many desert plants are covered by water-repellent waxes or contain germination-inhibiting substances; hence they are unlikely to be affected by frivolous small rains. The longevity and tenacity of desert plant seeds is remarkable. Most seeds continue to lie in wait and remain viable, some even for many years, until a thorough soaking takes place, sufficient to wash away the germination-inhibiting factors and to ensure a deep wetting of the soil. An unusually moist season may bring out species that have seemed extinct for a decade or more.

The soil itself, because of its space-variable moisture regime (affected by stones, pits, or cracks), further enhances the nonuniformity of germination. Sometimes, incidentally, germinability is promoted by passage of the seeds through the digestive tracts of grazing animals, whose digestive juices evidently dissolve the waxy coating over the seeds, thus allowing water to penetrate and initiate germination. The germination of some seeds is further enhanced by abrasion. Seeds carried by flash floods are scoured by the jagged stream bed. This mechanism also helps to disseminate the seeds (as do the wind and animals), ensuring that they do not all cluster around their parent plant (A. S. Leopold 1976).

Drought-resisting plants are the true xerophytes. Most are perennials, and many belong to the chenopod family. They manage to live from one rainy season to the next by drawing water from a large volume of soil or from groundwater, by storing water in their spongy tissues during moist periods, to be doled out for use in subsequent dry periods, and by minimizing water use. Morphological and physiological devices to reduce transpiration include thickened and waxy cuticle (the plant's outer coating) to reduce cuticular water loss, recessed stomates or the presence of fine hairs over the stomates to reduce vapor diffusion, closure of stomates at midday and their opening to absorb carbon dioxide at night, and overall reduction of the plant's surface of exposure. Geophytes store water and food in roots and bulbs; their tops may die during the dry season, but life is preserved in underground organs. Species of perennial desert plants are not numerous, but they constitute the stable, permanent component of desert vegetation, less affected by seasonal variation. They are inherently slow-growing — the price they have to pay for curtailing water consumption.

Claims are often made that certain desert plants should be cultivated as crops because they require so little water. The unfortunate fact is that with little water, one gets little yield. Conversely, to obtain large yields, one must supply large quantities of water, commensurate with atmospheric evaporativity (which is generally higher in deserts than in humid regions). Many desert shrubs shed their leaves at the onset of the dry season, then rely on their green stems and twigs to perform photosynthesis. They therefore look gaunt and scraggly and hardly alive, when in fact they are tenaciously active. The long dry season is of course a very austere period, in which even water-storing succulents shrivel visibly.

The strikingly uniform spacing of desert shrubs on a plain is caused by the fierce competition by roots for the meager supply of soil moisture. Viewed from above, the shrubs seem sparse, spaced as they are several meters apart with much of the ground surface remaining bare. Under the surface, however, there is no room to spare. Every cubic decimeter of soil is tapped by lateral roots seeking to avail themselves of every bit of superficial moisture the sporadic rains might supply to the soil's top layer.

The trees of the desert grow mostly in creek beds (wadis), where, unlike in the plains, moisture penetration is deep and groundwater may be at a reachable depth. Such trees as mesquite, tamarisk, or acacia send taproots to depths of several meters. Young saplings of such species invest most of their growth potential in developing roots, and produce very little top growth until they reach an adequate water source.

In desert plants with shortened periods of stomatal opening, the efficient absorption of carbon dioxide must compensate for the loss caused by the prolonged closure of the stomates during the hot and dry period of the diurnal cycle. Plant physiologists now recognize three types of plants with respect to the biochemical pathways of their photosynthetic processes. One group is called C3, since the first stable synthetic product is phosphoglyceric acid, which contains three carbon atoms in its molecule. This pathway for photosynthetic carbon is known as the Calvin cycle. Another group, designated C4 plants, have as their first product of synthesis an organic acid with four carbons (oxaloacetic acid). The third group, designated CAM for crassulacean acid metabolism, open their stomates at night and absorb carbon dioxide in the dark, incorporating it into malic acid. During the day malic acid is decarboxylated and the available CO_2 is refixed by ribulose diphosphate in the Calvin cycle. Plants

An oasis at the shore of the Red Sea in Sinai. The palm trees are sustained by shallow groundwater replenished by occasional flash floods in the wadis descending from the mountains.

that have this twofold adaptation can also carry out photosynthesis in the normal way, and do so increasingly as the water supply improves and the difference in temperatures between day and night decreases. This means that the CAM pathway becomes increasingly important compared with the Calvin pathway as the climatically imposed transpirational demand increases and the drought intensifies.

The transpiration ratio (the amount of water transpired per unit amount of dry matter produced) of CAM plants is lower than those of the other two: 50–55, compared with 250–350 for C4 and 450–950 for C3 plants (Meidner and Sheriff 1976). However, the CAM pathway is the least efficient in terms of total dry-matter production. Of the three groups, therefore, the C4 plants appear to exhibit the greatest overall advantage in desert environments: high efficiency in absorption of carbon dioxide, water conservation, and an adaptation to high temperature and bright sunshine. Many desert plants are indeed C4 plants. CAM plants are also prevalent, and include a number of succulents.

In a special class are desert lichens, which are close symbiotic associations of certain fungi and green or blue-green algae, characteristically forming scaly colonies on rocks, tree trunks, or the soil itself. Studies carried out in the Negev by Lange and Bertsch (1965) on the lichen *Ramalina maciformis* showed that it is able to absorb appreciable amounts of dew during the night,* and to use this water to carry out photosynthesis during the early morning hours. As

---

*Higher plants apparently are unable to absorb dew to any significant degree.

the lichens dry out, however, they cease to photosynthesize, but continue to respire for a time. In midday and afternoon both photosynthesis and respiration cease, and the lichens become temporarily inactive.

As we have already mentioned, drought is the rule in the desert; rain, the rather infrequent exception. The appearance of much rain is so rare as to be a miracle. The resulting transformation is startling indeed. Seemingly overnight, the melancholy land that has lain brown and sere for so many months is gladdened and made a verdant Eden, with a magical display of bright color that pales the lushest of gardens. A carpet of flowers bursts out of the bare soil, and delicate leaves and blossoms enliven the thorny twigs. For a few glorious weeks the desert blossoms like the rose. Then, as the benevolent, nurturing golden sunlight of spring turns into the malicious white fire of summer, and as the meager residue of unreplenished moisture is boiled out of the soil, the leaves begin to wither, the exuberant blossom fades, fruits and seeds fall and are scattered by the wind, and somber dormancy returns to the desert.

8

Animals and Water in the Desert

The utter stillness of the desert on a summer day is deceptive. Although it may be invisible to the casual visitor, animal life in the desert is rich and vibrant. One need only know when and where to look in order to observe its teeming variety. Here, as elsewhere, whether they are herbivores (subsisting on plants and plant products directly), carnivores (consuming other animals), or omnivores (able to consume both plants and animals), animals depend ultimately on plants. Living animals usually contain from 60 to 80 percent of water by mass, water constituting over 95 percent of the body's molecules. Since a living creature is in constant interaction with the environment, continuously exchanging matter and energy with it, it is impossible to seal in the body's water hermetically. Animals are not in constant intimate contact with a potential source of water, the way plants are rooted in the soil. Hence the maintenance of their hydration in the desert, subject to the desiccating power of the hot and dry air constantly extracting water from every humid thing, is, it seems, in defiance of nature's basic laws. The evaporative power of the atmosphere is an ever-present threat to animal survival.

The problem for animals in the desert, therefore, is how to adapt themselves to cope with, or evade, drought. Desert animals do this more often by change of habit than by alteration of structure. There are, to be sure, some significant anatomical and physiological differences between many desert animals and their counterparts in moist climates, but these differences are minor compared with the striking structural differences exhibited by drought-resistant desert plants. A typical feature of desert animals is their pale coloration, so very similar to that of their environment. Blending into the background makes them practically imperceptible as long as they remain at rest. Walking in the desert, one is often surprised by the sudden start of a bird or some other animal where least expected.

To avoid the heat and aridity of the desert at its daytime worst, most desert animals are nocturnal and crepuscular—that is, they limit their activity to the cool hours of dusk, night, and dawn. A desert, seemingly devoid of animals during midday, literally "comes to life" as the sun descends and the heat of the day abates. One group of animals after another appears. Prominent among desert animals are the reptiles, lizards and snakes. Largely inactive during the heat of the day, the lizards begin hunting for the insects, and the snakes for the burrowing animals, that also become active at about the same time. Then the birds awaken and leave their nesting places to flutter about in search of feed, and bats emerge stealthily from their secret caves to hover overhead and sweep the sky for flying insects. Burrowing rodents climb out of their underground shelters and scamper around for seeds and other organic debris. The larger predators that feed on the rodents soon enter the scene.

Throughout the cool of the night and the early morning, the desert is astir with the intense activity of all its creatures, determinedly pursuing their separate yet interacting affairs. Finally, as the sun rises once again to flood the desert with its unblinking light and bake it with its searing heat, the animals retreat to their various shelters to while away the daytime hours in anticipation of another evening in which to resume their busy night life.

Nowhere is the crucial importance of water to life made more clearly and dramatically apparent than in and around a desert oasis. The abundance of sunshine, warmth, and mineral fertility of the soil, when combined with water, creates a veritable Garden of Eden where life flourishes in all its forms, in startling contrast with the sparseness of life in the surrounding open desert. The readiness with which barrenness responds to water and the generosity with which it gives forth life—whether temporarily, as following a rare drenching rain, or permanently, as in an oasis—is one of the desert's most outstanding characteristics.

Insects—including ants, beetles, flies, grasshoppers, wasps, moths, mosquitoes, and various other bugs too varied to mention—are undoubtedly the most numerous class of animals in the desert. One that demands special recognition is the migratory locust, which illustrates so dramatically the occasionally violent instability of life in the inherently unstable environment of the desert and its fringe zones. Locusts exhibit two distinct phases, differing greatly in form and behavior: the solitary phase and the swarming phase. Solitary locusts are in effect ordinary grasshoppers, each going about its business separately, in a more or less fixed domain, without any evident tendency to band together and migrate. These grasshoppers may exhibit a more or less stable pattern of life for generation after generation.

Then, unpredictably, a radical change takes place. Spontaneously the individualistic grasshoppers change into swarming locusts, with an uncontrollable instinctual impulse to gather together and begin to migrate en masse. The factor triggering this profound change seems to be excessive population density. As long as the grasshopper population remains thin, the solitary mode prevails. However, as soon as a critical population density is exceeded, perhaps following a succession of unusually favorable seasons, the swarming drive manifests itself. The young locusts assume a different appearance, with brightly colored, wide wings, and band together to feed and fly in huge swarms. As they fly, they drift randomly with the wind. At times they alight in the barren desert or even in the ocean, and die. Wherever they land on a vegetated area, however, they go to work. So voracious is their appetite that they can completely devour the foliage of a lush field or orchard within less than an hour. In biblical times they were considered a terrible scourge, and so they are today.

Insects of all kinds provide food for successively larger animals. The insectivores (insect eaters) include spiders, lizards, birds, and bats, which themselves serve as prey for still larger predators. In addition to the insects, the desert abounds with other arthropods, such as spiders, tarantulas, scorpions, and centipedes. Of these, scorpions seem to be among the most prevalent, and the most hazardous. Their sting can be very painful, though it is rarely fatal to adults. Their normal prey, as is that of the tarantulas, is insects.

Reptiles are common in the desert. Their platy or scaly skins help protect against drying; and their young, hatched from eggs deposited in the soil, emerge as small adults rather than as more vulnerable forms requiring metamorphosis (as is the case with frogs, for instance). Most numerous are the lizards, often seen scurrying over the dry, crusted earth in pursuit of ground insects, or basking in the morning sun atop a protruding rock. Like snakes, lizards are cold-blooded, requiring an external source of warmth to achieve the optimal body temperature needed for them to be active. Even lizards, however, cannot survive excessive heat, and seek shade at midday to keep their body heat within tolerable limits. Snakes, being legless and in direct contact with the sunbaked desert floor, are even more vulnerable to the midday heat (A. S. Leopold 1976). Most snakes are carnivorous, and feed on rodents, lizards, birds, and practically everything else that can be swallowed and digested. Our archetypal fear of snakes is, however, exaggerated, since only a few of the species living in any particular desert are venomous, and most of these are peaceful and anything but eager (unless provoked) to enter into conflict with so large and intimidating an animal as a man. They can be provoked inadvertently, however, because they hide, well camouflaged, in the sand and behind rocks.

Some of the birds found in the desert are merely migratory, spending only the most favorable season there and flying elsewhere to avoid the desert's harsher seasons. Those that remain must necessarily adapt themselves in order to avoid desiccation. Tending to be smaller and paler in color, and thus less conspicuous, than their counterparts in more humid regions, desert birds find shelter in thickets of desert shrubs, fissures in cliffs, or hollows beneath overhanging rock ledges. Having no sweat glands, birds cannot dissipate excess body heat by perspiration. Rather, they cool themselves by evaporating water from their lungs as they respire. To hasten this process of heat dissipation, birds tend to pant, much as dogs do in the midday heat.

Desert birds are either insect eaters, seed eaters, or flesh eaters. Some of the birds make do with the water contained in the food, whether it is plant matter or animal bodies. Other birds, however, require actual drinking water, and therefore must congregate near springs and water holes.

The most spectacular birds in the desert are the large carnivores: eagles, hawks, and vultures. Though they are not numerous, the clear desert air and unobstructed view of the landscape allow one to observe them more easily here than elsewhere. Soaring high on the currents of warm air rising from the hot desert floor, wheeling lazily as they soar, their expansive wings spread wide, their keen eyes sweeping the landscape in search of prey, they are magnificent birds to behold. Once they have spotted their prey, they swoop down upon it with a terrible swiftness, snatching it into the air or, failing that, landing upon it at full wingspan, feathers aflutter, haughty masters of the desert domain.

Desert rodents make their homes in chambers dug into the soft soil of the shrub-covered hummocks. Some live in mazelike colonies that riddle the soil with a honeycomb of tunnels practically invisible from above. How can such delicate creatures survive in the desert with nothing but dry seeds for food? The secret is literally buried in the ground. The soil is an excellent insulator against heat and aridity. A burrow only 20 centimeters below the ground surface can have a temperature $20°C$ cooler at midday, and similarly warmer at night, than the soil surface, and have a relative humidity of over 90 percent even when that of the external air falls to 20 percent or less. Moreover, the rodent's underground abode provides relative safety against predators and storage for seeds and other foods collected from the surface. This stored dry food absorbs moisture hygroscopically from the soil by vapor condensation, and the dampened food then helps supply the animal's water requirements. Some desert rodents are capable of estivating in their burrows during the drought's most severe period. They enter into a state of deep sleep akin to the hibernation of cold-region animals and to the dormancy of plants. Little energy or water is expended in this state, and the animal revives when its reserves approach depletion. Some birds are also capable of entering a torpid state and drowsing for days, awakening when weather conditions improve.

A most interesting group of rodents are the kangaroo rats of the American deserts and the strikingly similar (though not closely related) jerboas and gerbils of the African and Asian deserts. These charming little animals look and move like miniature kangaroos, hopping on their large, whiskered feet and powerful hind legs, using their tufted tails as rudder and counterbalance and their short forelegs as if they were arms and hands. Astonishingly quick, they can confuse and evade their pursuers by hopscotching and zigzagging unpredictably, even changing direction in midleap by whipping their tails. They are also amazingly efficient at water conservation.

Perhaps the most beautiful of all desert animals are the deerlike gazelles, oryxes, antelopes, and ibexes. These grazers move swiftly and gracefully, in huge gliding leaps, over the plains and slopes. They, too, are extraordinary water conservers.

In addition to its numerous herbivores, the desert serves as home for a variety of mammalian carnivores, including foxes, jackals, coyotes, hyenas, and wild cats (such as the lynx). They, too, are remarkably well adapted to desert life. Pondering the variety and ingenious adaptations of animals (as well as plants) to the desert, one cannot but marvel at the tenacity and hardiness of life on earth, even under the most difficult circumstances.

The manner in which desert animals control their water economy is the key to their survival. Most desert animals would die if subjected continuously to temperatures in excess of $45°C$, and cannot survive even short exposures to temperatures exceeding $50°C$ (A. S. Leopold 1976). Since the temperature of the sunbaked desert floor often exceeds $60°C$, and may at times be as high as $80°C$, it is obvious that desert animals must find ways to minimize exposure to high temperatures, or to avoid its consequences by physiological adaptation. Small animals such as rodents seek refuge by burrowing underground, and therefore can be called drought evaders. Large animals, however, cannot do so, and must find other means to control body heat without dehydration in order to survive and function under exposure to daytime desert conditions.

Most mammals, for instance, have a more or less constant temperature of $36-38°C$, only slightly below the threshold of excessive temperature ($42-45°C$). The heat load that the animal must release consists of the sum of radiant energy absorbed and the metabolic heat produced (proportional to the body's mass and the effort expended). The heat load being greater in the desert than elsewhere, the amount of water that an animal there must evaporate to prevent excessive heating is also greater. Thus, the obstacle to life in the desert is inherent in the fact that, since evaporation is the principal cooling mechanism for most animals, the physiological requirements for water are greatest just where water is scarcest. About 1.7 grams of water are needed to dissipate one kilocalorie of body heat. To avoid dehydration, the water thus evaporated must be replaced — if not by drinking, then by ingesting moist food.

There are several ways a body can cool itself by evaporation: from the skin, as in the case of perspiration by humans and horses; from the lungs through the nasal passages, as in respiratory cooling; and from the mouth by salivating. Often the mouth and nose are used together. Reptiles and birds rely on respiratory cooling, as do such mammals as foxes and coyotes. Other animals, such as the Australian koalas and wallabies, salivate profusely on hot days and lick their bodies to spread the cooling effect. Heat can also be released from exposed skin by radiation and by convection through the air. Some animals have large protruding skin surfaces (for example, the large ears of a rabbit) that may help in heat disposal. An amazing fact, recently discovered (Schmidt-Nielsen 1981), is that some desert animals can limit the loss of vapor in breathing by maintaining a nasal temperature considerably lower than that of the lungs. Cooler air holds less moisture at vapor saturation (for instance, at a body temperature of 38–40°C, a cubic meter of air at 100 percent relative humidity contains 44 grams of water; if the tempeature is lowered to 24°C, however, the same air at maximum humidity can hold only 22 grams). Thus, some of the water evaporated by the dry air entering the lungs is condensed in the intricate nasal passages and is thus retained by the body.

Animals with compound or rumen stomachs can subsist on the spartan diet provided by the dry and fibrous forage of the desert, but must also dissipate the heat produced by the bacteria in the rumen that help to digest the cellulose. In winter this extra heat can be advantageous, but in summer it is quite otherwise.

Apart from its function as a coolant, water serves to facilitate the excretion of waste products in feces and urine. Birds and reptiles do not excrete urine separately, but combine the highly concentrated uric acid produced in their kidneys with their feces. Most mammals, however, remove nitrogenous waste from the blood in the form of urea, normally excreted with excessive mineral solutes (salts) as a dilute solution (urine) separate from the intestinal waste. Desert animals are able to concentrate their waste to a greater degree than their humid-region counterparts, thus requiring less water for excretion. The ability to expel highly concentrated urine makes it possible for the animals so endowed to utilize saline water like that obtainable from the tissues of desert plants or from brackish springs. Furthermore, the feces of such drought-resistant animals as desert rats are exceedingly dry, containing less than 40 percent water by mass, rather than the 80 percent found in the feces of most mammals (Shkolnik 1977). Animals that consume highly proteinaceous food (such as carnivores) require that a greater amount of urea be eliminated in urine, and therefore need more water than do desert herbivores.

Of all the desert animals, the one most famous for its water economy is the camel, that great and magnificent beast known as the "ship of the desert" for its astonishing ability to carry men and heavy cargo across vast tracts of wilderness without water and without complaint. The camel has excited curiosity and amazement since ancient times. Early observers of this animal's behavior concluded that it has a hidden water reservoir inside its body, most probably in its prominent hump,* and this popular belief has persisted to our day. Indeed, camels can subsist for a long time on water drawn from their tis-

---

*I speak here mainly of *Camelus dromedarius*, the one-humped domesticated camel (also called dromedary) of northern Africa and western Asia. Its cousin, the Bactrian camel of Central Asia, carries two humps.

sues and water released as a metabolic breakdown product of fat. (As hydrogen is released from the decomposed fat, it is combined with respiratory oxygen to produce water.)

The camel's hump is filled largely with fat, and in a well-fed and well-watered adult camel may weigh about 10 kilograms. It has been estimated (A. S. Leopold 1976) that, as this fat is oxidized, about 1.1 kilograms of water are produced for every kilogram of fat used up. By combining this metabolic water with the water extracted from other tissues, a camel can continue to function for many days in the desert, even to the point of tolerating the loss of 30 percent of its normal body weight and—even more remarkable—a temperature rise of 5°C above normal, without sustaining permanent injury. One reason for this is the camel's ability to maintain the necessary consistency and viscosity of its blood despite the loss of body water. When finally allowed to slake its accumulated thirst, the camel can take in prodigious amounts of water, replenishing in one drinking practically all of the water (perhaps 80 or more liters) that it had lost during, say, a week of deprivation.

The camel was studied by Schmidt-Nielsen (1964a) and it appears, paradoxically, that its adaptation to the desert is based in part on the very characteristic that would seem to be its major disadvantage: its large size. Having a much larger body mass, and hence a much smaller surface-to-mass ratio than, say, desert rodents, the camel is able to use its body's thermal inertia to survive and function in the daytime desert while its temperature varies in a range of four to seven Celsius degrees. If a hypothetical animal weighing only 10 kilograms is exposed to daytime desert conditions, it may experience a temperature rise of over 5°C within half an hour. On the other hand, a 500-kilogram camel, although it will absorb more heat because of its larger surface area, will take over seven hours to experience the same temperature rise because of its much larger mass.

Indeed, the camel is endowed with an extraordinary ability to bear considerable changes in body temperature. In the course of a day, its body may warm up from perhaps 35°C at dawn to nearly 42°C in the afternoon. The heat thus accumulated is transferred to the cool air at night, as the camel increases the rate of blood flow to the skin, from which heat is dissipated outward. To dispose of the same amount of heat by evaporation without such changes of body temperature, the camel would have to lose about 5 liters of water (Shkolnik 1977). Thus, the camel's ability to accumulate heat by day and dissipate it by night saves it much water. Still, some evaporation does take place, for although the camel does not perspire appreciably, it does respire. In respiration, dry desert air is inhaled into the lungs, where it is humidified. Animals normally exhale vapor-saturated air at body temperature. The camel, however, not only cools the exhaled air but also reduces its relative humidity below saturation, so that much of the moisture that would otherwise be lost is recovered in the scroll-like nasal passages (Schmidt-Nielsen 1981).

Camels huddle at a shallow puddle of water to quench their voracious thirst after a long and arduous trek through the desert.

The amount of water excreted by the camel as urine is also remarkably small. In the camel, as in other regurgitating animals that subsist on a low-protein diet, the nitrogenous waste (urea or uric acid) is reabsorbed into the compound stomach, where part of it is reconverted by microbial action into amino acids. Hence, little water is required to expel the relatively small amount of nitrogenous waste products. Finally, as in the case of desert rodents, the camel's feces are quite dry.

Most of the medium-size animals (such as the deer, gazelle, ibex, sheep, goat, jackal, coyote, and dog, with a body weight in the range of, say, 10 to 20 kilograms) cool their bodies by evaporating water, and can increase their rate of heat dissipation by panting more frequently, as much as 200–400 times per minute (Shkolnik 1977). This mechanism seems to have an advantage over perspiration, since the latter requires that the temperature of the skin be maintained below that of the body's interior. In animals that dissipate heat by panting rather than by perspiring, the skin temperature can increase during the day so that no thermal gradient from air to skin can form.

A very interesting and important animal is the Bedouin's goat. Apart from the camel, this is surely the most desert-adapted of all domesticated animals. Often it is the only animal that accompanies man into the farthest reaches of the desert, not only surviving there but sustaining its master even in the most barren environment. The Bedouin's goat, weighing 15–25 kilograms, is smaller than the similar black Arab goat (weighing 30–50 kilograms) raised by villagers in the semiarid to subhumid eastern Mediterranean region. The desert goat has smaller, sideways-pointing ears, and brown rather than blue eyes. In the far reaches of the Negev and Sinai deserts, flocks of these goats have been observed to thrive on the sparsest vegetation and under exposure to the merciless summer sun, even when allowed to drink only about every four days. In the laboratory they were found to subsist for two weeks without drinking water and without loss of appetite, even when given only dry feed (Shkolnik 1977). Detailed studies showed that this goat's metabolic rate is lower than could be expected from its body weight. A priori, therefore, it requires less food and water than most other animals of similar size.

Like the camel, the desert goat is able to conserve body water by minimizing its various losses, to continue functioning even in the face of prolonged exposure to drought, and to replenish its lost fluids by drinking prodigiously when water is finally made available. According to Shkolnik (1977), some goats are able to imbibe up to 40 percent of their body weight within a few minutes. After such a heroic feat, those goats were found to contain as much as 85 percent water by weight (a state of hydration greater than that of nondesert goats) as if they were "stocking up" for an anticipated period of drought. The ability of the desert goats to function for several days without water in effect extends the area of usable range from the immediate vicinity of a water source (such as a spring or a cistern). Merely doubling the radial distance from the water source quadruples the grazing area.

9

Man and Water in the Desert

True to their common aquatic origins, human beings depend on water no less vitally than do all other animals. As newborn infants we are 90 percent water, and although we tend to dry up a little as we grow older, we still remain more water (about 70 percent) than anything else. Our all-important gray matter is, incidentally, one of the more watery (85 percent) of our tissues.

It is a truism that people can live for weeks without food, but generally cannot survive more than a few days without water. In the desert they require drinking water daily. Without dependable access to a spring, stream, well, cistern, pipeline, or some other source or storage of water, human activity in the desert is impossible, and life itself is in danger. A man stranded in the open desert on a summer day without water or shelter will feel no discomfort at all in the early morning, the temperature being a comfortable 20°C. By mid to late morning, having lost perhaps 2 liters without knowing it, and with the air temperature having risen to 35°C, he will feel rather warm and thirsty. By midday, with the air temperature at 40°C and our man having lost 4 or 5 liters, he will feel very thirsty indeed, and drowsy with heat. By midafternoon, with the temperature of the air approaching 45°C and his loss of body water by perspiration exceeding 7 liters, the man will be fatigued and perhaps delirious. After sundown he will experience relief from heat, but then shiver through the cold of the night. When dawn arrives, he may at first welcome the warmth of the rising sun, only to die the painful death of dehydration and heat prostration sometime during his second day in the desert. This is undoubtedly an upsetting description, but unfortunately a realistic one.

I shudder as I recall with what misconceptions regarding our own water needs we went into the desert in the early 1950s. We believed, for instance, that to drink water on a hot day only induces sweating; hence, one should refrain from drinking in daytime, so as to "condition" the body to make do with less water. Contemptuously, we held the Bedouin to be slothful for not working throughout the day, as we did, and to be foolish for wearing all that clothing when it felt so much better to expose oneself to the sun and the breeze — as much, at least, as minimal modesty allowed. Finally, we believed that an increased intake of salt is needed for the body to compensate for the loss of salt in perspiration, which one experiences in a hot climate.

We were wrong on practically every count. As subsequent research has shown, the rate of perspiration depends primarily not on drinking, but on the climatically and physiologically imposed heat load. Avoidance of drinking can quickly cause heatstroke. Even mild water deficits can eventually impair one's health, and the habit of working outdoors at full pace through the midday hours exacerbates the situation. Moreover, excessive exposure of skin to direct sunshine incurs the risk of skin cancer. An "attractive" suntan is not necessarily a healthy thing. I might point out, in our defense, that we were not alone in our misconceptions. We received our notions from what was then "good authority." Medical science, after all, was developed primarily in the temperate-humid zones, and relevant research into the physiology of man in the desert began in earnest only during the Second World War.

In the mid-1950s experiments were conducted in Israel in which two physically similar groups of soldiers were marched through the desert in summertime. The members of one group were allowed to drink water at any time, without limitation, while the others were made to adhere strictly to a scheduled water ration then considered adequate. From time to time the physical state and performance of the two groups were tested similarly. The results were startling. The well-watered soldiers maintained normal body weight and temperature, remained alert, and were able to function well both physically and mentally throughout the arduous exercise. The soldiers whose water supply was limited gradually became lethargic, suffered measurable weight loss and even elevated temperature (early signs of dehydration that could lead to heatstroke), and performed their tasks sluggishly.

Humans are versatile and adaptable creatures, but they cannot escape the laws of physics. They can live well in the arctic and in the desert, but only if they maintain the heat balance and water balance of their bodies. To function properly, the human body must maintain its temperature within very narrow limits, say 35° to 40°C. The survival limits are 32° and 43°C. Exceeding this narrow range for any length of time causes death. Humans are much more sensitive in this respect than some of the other mammals described in the preceding chapter. Since it is impossible for humans to adapt physically to aridity in the manner of camels or goats, they must adapt culturally by developing appropriate living and working habits.

The physiology of man in hot and dry climates was reviewed by Sohar (1979). To maintain the required temperature, the human body must release heat at a rate commensurate with its production and absorption. Heat is produced in the body by the "internal combustion," as it were, of carbohydrates in a process associated with respiration. The rate of heat production depends on the level of a person's physical activity. At rest, the basal metabolism generates about 1 kilocalorie per hour per kilogram of body mass. Thus, an "average" person weighing, say, 75 kilograms would generate about 75 kilocalories per hour just lying still. The same hypothetical person would generate about 180 kilocalories per hour sitting, 200 walking slowly, 550 carrying a load up a hill, and over 1,000 running a marathon.

In addition to generating heat, the body may absorb heat from its surroundings, particularly in a warm climate under intense radiation. Assume that a person can be represented by a rectangle about 170 centimeters tall and 40 centimeters wide, thus presenting an area of nearly 7,000 square centimeters. In the desert at midday, the incoming flux of solar radiation may exceed 1 calorie per minute per square centimeter. A naked person exposed perpendicularly to the sun's rays may experience a total flux of well over 400 kilocalories per hour. Allowing for the fraction of radiation that is reflected and for the generally nonperpendicular position, we can estimate that a naked (or scantily clad) sunbather in the desert may absorb 300 kilocalories of heat per hour. If fully clothed, the person would absorb 150 kilocalories per hour (more or less, depending on the color of the clothing), an amount that is still greater than the basal metabolism generates at rest.

The total heat load of a body—the sum of the heat generated metabolically and that absorbed from the environment—is the amount of heat the body must dissipate in order to prevent a progressive rise in temperature leading to a dangerous condition known as heatstroke. A body can dispose of its excess heat by several mechanisms. Radiation is the principal mode of heat disposal by a warm body in a cool environment. Heat can also be transferred from a warm body to a contacting cooler object by conduction, and heat can be carried away by convection currents if the body is surrounded by either air or water. In a warm environment, however, the objects around the body are likely to be at about the same temperature as the body, or even warmer. The temperature gradient between the body and its surroundings may be either nonexistent or negative, and the body is then incapable of disposing of all its excess heat by radiation, conduction, or convection.

Enter another mode of heat dissipation: evaporation, a form of latent heat transfer. If the body can release water over its surface, and if the surrounding atmosphere is warm and dry enough to evaporate the water, then the amount of heat involved in transforming a unit mass of water from the liquid state to the gaseous (vapor) state, known as the latent heat of evaporation, is absorbed, mainly from the body. Considering the fact that almost 0.6 kilocalorie is required to evaporate just 1 gram of water in the range of temperatures ordinarily encountered in the desert, we can see that the process of "evaporative cooling" can be a very efficient one indeed. Thus, in a warm, dry climate the human body's principal mode of heat dissipation is by evaporation of perspired water. Perspiration itself does not cool the body; only its evaporation does. In a warm, humid climate, for instance, a person may perspire profusely, but to no avail if the perspiration merely accumulates or trickles off without evaporating. In a warm dry climate, on the other hand, no perspiration may be visible, because it all evaporates from the skin just as soon as it appears.

Thus, the role of perspiration in heat dissipation depends both on the body's ability to release water and on the atmosphere's ability to evaporate it. The latter, called the evaporative power of the atmosphere, depends, in turn, on temperature, relative humidity, and wind. A dry atmosphere is obviously more strongly evaporative than a humid one, and a light wind that sweeps away the vapor from the evaporating surface further enhances the process.

As long as the body is not severely dehydrated, drinking seems to have little influence upon the rate of perspiration, which is largely dictated by the total heat load to which the body is subjected. According to Sohar (1979), the process is regulated by the part of the brain known as the hypothalamus, which senses the temperature of the blood. As that temperature rises, so does the rate of perspiration. But whether perspiration can dissipate the body's excess heat ultimately depends, of course, on the evaporation rate. Our hypothetical person, sitting idly—fully clothed—in the desert sun, absorbing 150 kilocalories per hour and generating 100 kilocalories metabolically, will generally have no difficulty disposing of his 250 kilocalories/hour heat load by perspiring at a rate of just under half a liter per hour.

Should he then decide to walk briskly rather than just sit, his metabolism might generate three or four times as much heat as before, which, added to the amount of radiant energy absorbed, would constitute a total heat load of about 500 kilocalories per hour. To dispose of this much heat, our man in the desert would have to perspire nearly a liter of water per hour. In about two hours he would lose close to 3 percent of his body's weight, or 4 percent of his body's total water content (normally about 70 percent). Since most of the water in the body is bound within the cells and only 15 liters or so are readily mobile ("fluid") water, hiking in the desert for two hours at midday would cost our man more than 10 percent of his extracellular water. Obviously, he would quickly become quite thirsty.

Now let us suppose that our man becomes even more ambitious and begins to work strenuously, and—in the interest of "comfort"—also removes his hat and shirt. Under these conditions his body produces 500 kilocalories and absorbs perhaps 200, for a total heat load of 700 kilocalories per hour. And now our man may have gotten himself into serious trouble: his heat load could exceed the atmosphere's evaporative power. If the climatically limited evaporativity is equivalent to only 600 kilocalories per hour (a little over a liter of evaporation per hour), then the excess heat of 100 kilocalories will accumulate in the man's body, raise his temperature gradually (at a rate of 1°C or more per hour), and eventually cause heat prostration. Should he persist in his strenuous activity and fail to replenish his body fluids by drinking adequately, our hapless man could reach the point of dehydration causing loss of consciousness and even death. Even if he were supplied with unlimited water, he simply could not perspire enough to dispose of the high heat load, and could not possibly sustain his physical activity.

And now we understand why the Bedouin are so heavily clad and like to sit in the shade during the heat of the day. They may not know the physical theory, but they are well versed in the practice of desert survival.

People living and working in a desert climate might well perspire in excess of 10 liters of water per day. A curious fact is that the mere sensation of thirst may be an inadequate warning system. A person's actual water requirements may be greater than what his thirst alone dictates. People who live and work continuously in a desert environment and drink only to satisfy thirst may in time develop such conditions as kidney stones, simply because, with insufficient replenishment of body liquid lost by evaporated perspiration, the concentration of urine in the bladder may be great enough to cause the precipitation of calcium salts. In this connection it is now clear that few people living in an arid climate ever lack for salt, which is generally present in more than adequate quantities in normal food. The practice of swallowing salt tablets can do more harm than good, because it taxes the kidneys unnecessarily and increases the difficulty of disposing of the excess salt in the absence of sufficient water to flush it out.

According to Sohar (1979), people can to some degree become acclimated to living in the desert because they develop a greater ability to perspire earlier and to exude less salt, and to have a lower pulse rate and temperature. The danger of heatstroke is greatest for those unacclimated to the desert. If lost in the desert, such a person (perhaps a pilot who is required to make a forced landing in the desert, as in the case described so beautifully by Saint-Exupéry?) would do well to rest in a shaded and windless shelter (preferably in a cool cave) during the hot daytime hours, to remain fully clothed (uncomfortable as that may seem), and to walk only at dusk, night, and dawn. Staying with a failed vehicle until discovered by a search party is generally preferable to striking out on one's own to search for help. Cautious inactivity may be better under these circumstances than courageous (or foolhardy) action. If the stranded person fails to find cisterns, water holes, or seep wells, he may be able to distill his own water from the moist subsoil, or from succulent desert shrubs (Jackson and van Bavel, 1965). All he needs in order to construct a solar still are a thin sheet of clear plastic (foldable), a digging implement (a sharp fragment of flint might do in a pinch), and a container (a gourd shell, a helmet, or a plastic bag).

II

The Negev in Particular

10

Journey to the Negev

> I remember thee the affection of thy youth
> The love of thine espousals
> How thou wentest after me in the wilderness
> In the land unsown.
> Jeremiah 2:2

The Negev is a rugged land of great beauty and stark contrasts; of dark, gravel-strewn plains and wind-whipped golden sands; of thrusting buttes and altar-shaped hills; of glistening white chalk interbedded with massive black flint; of huge, gaping craters scooped into high plateaus; of awesome, jagged cliffs plunging into shadowy ravines; of winding dry riverbeds and variegated badlands scoured and carved into the land by the relentless erosion of countless eons; of wavelike anticlines fissured and rifted by the fury of pent-up forces rising out of the bowels of the earth; and of mountains and valleys lying still under the steady gaze of a merciless, unblinking sun. The Negev is a land of vivid, bright days and luminous skies, of clear nights and piercingly sharp stars. It is an ancient land in whose stillness the past echoes even as the future already looms, and before whose eternity ephemeral man can only stand in awe and humility.

I first visited the Negev Desert in 1945, and the memory is etched in my consciousness. Over the years the recollection has loomed larger than the reality could have been, and has assumed the dimension of myth. It is a memory not merely of an event, but of a discovery suffused with a mystic and numinous sense of wonder, reverence, and endless fascination. Being scarcely 15 years of age and seeking adventure, I managed somehow to attach myself to a small convoy of trucks ferrying supplies from Tel-Aviv to the pioneering outpost of Revivim, located on the sandy plains of the northwestern Negev. On a present-day map Revivim is seen only at the edge, rather than at the heart, of the Negev. But back then it seemed to lie beyond reality.

In my childhood, available maps of the Holy Land generally included only the area between Dan in the north and Beersheba in the south, whereas practically the entire Negev—an area fully as large as the remainder of the country—was either totally ignored or, at most, inserted as a small-scale addendum at a lower corner of the map, showing no noteworthy geographical features or historical landmarks anywhere south of Beersheba. And so it was that I knew nothing factual about the Negev, and my decidedly unfactual impressions were composed only of biblical passages and postbiblical fables greatly embellished by my own fantasy.

We set out from Tel-Aviv in the pale light of dawn. It was springtime, and the morning air was fresh with the moisture of the sea breezes and perfumed with the fragrance of orange blossoms. Riding in the back of the truck, sitting precariously on top of the quivering crates, clutching the swaying wooden frames of the speeding vehicle, facing into the cool wind, I floated high above verdant fields and luxuriant orchards. But soon I began to notice a change in the scenery, subtle at first, then increasingly obvious. The lush plantations of the Valley of Sharon gave way to the open grain fields of the Shefela plain, then to the uncultivated grasslands of the transition zone, whose pale green cover in turn faded into the drab color of bare earth and sparse shrubs growing amid protruding gray boulders. In the short distance of some 140 kilometers, the face of the land had metamorphosed from fertile farmland to bleak and barren desert.

Gazing at the sunbaked, shimmering expanse, I then caught sight of the ancient city of Beersheba. In its desolate setting it seemed, from afar, as ethereal and dreamlike as a mirage, a haze-veiled ghost town out of the biblical past. The ethereal vision dimmed, however, as soon as we entered the town. The scene was one of abject squalor. On either side of the single paved road stood clusters of crumbling houses jerry-built of rough-hewn stones plastered with flaking mud. Black-robed, barefooted Bedouin roamed the alleyways and clustered in the teeming *souk* at the south end of the town. The milling mass of people and goats and camels seemed oblivious to the road's existence, and mindless of our right-of-way. We were unwelcome intruders, to be treated with contempt and ignored by all except the children, who jeered and spat and pelted us with fistfuls of gravel. It was some time before we emerged from the *souk* and from its hovering cloud of dust and living odors. We then descended to and crossed the wide wadi, and continued our way southward.

The road was narrow and winding. It led through a desolate terrain with rounded low hills of stratified chalk interbedded with black chert, and across an area of crescent-shaped, windswept dunes of glistening sand. Occasionally we saw a lonely tamarisk or flat-topped acacia. But there were no settlements in sight, no signs of life save for a few curious clusters of stunted almond or fig trees growing in a shallow depression, a wandering camel appearing out of nowhere only to fade away and blend again into the landscape, a small flock of grazing goats, or a rare huddle of Bedouin tents. Revivim itself was not even a settlement, just an experiment, with a handful of brave but inexpert and isolated pioneers striving with great devotion and little visible success to make crops grow in the desert sand without a dependable source of water.

Though I did not realize it at the time, that first journey to the Negev turned out to be a fateful event in my life, the sort of definitive and formative experience that is infused into one's very being and becomes a lifelong theme. As I ponder that journey and its aftermath, I fancy that in some mysterious nonphysical way it may not have been my first journey at all, but a spiritual revisit to a place filled with ancestral memories and yearnings that, once reawakened, could never again be put to rest.

Five years and one war later, I returned to the Negev, which had in the meanwhile become the frontier province of the newborn State of Israel. This time I was able to go beyond the northwestern plains into the central highlands and the Arava, and all the way to the Red Sea. To get there, I had to attach myself to an Israeli Army reconnaissance unit and spend several bone-jarring

A natural sphinx in the Negev Desert.

days traveling cross-country along trackless, boulder-strewn, tortuous wadis, crossing deep gullies and protruding hummocks, scaling steep and slippery slopes of loosened rocks, traversing plateaus covered with a natural pavement of knife-sharp fragments of flint, and wading through soft loessial plains. The last seemed at times to be the most treacherous. Once pulverized and churned by prior traffic, the soft, parched earth turned into fluff that provided hardly any traction. A vehicle would sink into the chalky powder and come to rest on its axles, its wheels spinning crazily and spewing up puffs of dense yellow dust into the hot windless air.

Something strange and wonderful happened to me on that trip, too. All the physical discomfort notwithstanding, I simply and wholeheartedly and unreservedly fell in love with the Negev. I was bewitched and intrigued and captivated by the land and all its hidden secrets. And so it was that I resolved to return and devote myself to its exploration.

Perhaps only those who have willingly submitted to the searing heat of the desert by day and shivered unsheltered in the chill of its nights; suffered the caking dust in their eyes and tasted the saline grit in thirsty mouths; stumbled over the jagged rocks and sought rest in the soft, warm sand; climbed the lofty peaks and gazed over the vast primeval vistas; descended into the shadowy ravines and searched through ancient caves; witnessed the desert gush forth with waters in a sudden flash flood of winter and sprout a carpet of flowers in the brief blossom of springtime; or listened for—and heard—the eloquence of total silence, as in the all-engulfing silence one senses while floating all alone in weightless suspension over the dense blue brine of the Dead Sea, as if hovering between two utterly still skies, can ever truly understand the haunting fascination of the desert, and of this among all deserts, the Negev.

11

Physiography, Climate, and Subregions

> Every valley shall be uplifted
> And every mountain and hill made low
> The crooked shall be made straight
> And the rough places plain.
> Isaiah 4:40

The word *negev* means "dryness" in the original Hebrew, and later came to connote "south" as well. The Negev region is Israel's southern desert. In comparison with other deserts, the Negev is rather small. It is, in fact, only a minuscule part of the great desert belt of North Africa and Southwest Asia, and, being on its fringe, it is not, for the most part, an extremely arid desert. It is, however, geographically and historically distinct. The very compactness and distinctness of the Negev make it an ideal laboratory for studying the experience of the past and the potentialities of the present with regard to the development and utilization of land and water resources in a desert environment.

The Negev is shaped like an isosceles triangle, with its northern base running from the Mediterranean coast south of Gaza to the southern basin of the Dead Sea. From these extremities the sides of the triangle stretch well over 160 kilometers south to the apex at Eilat on the tip of the Gulf of Aqaba. The Negev thus appears to be thrust, like a giant dagger or wedge, into the great Eastern Desert, separating Sinai from Arabia. The boundaries of the Negev coincide roughly with the present-day borders of Israel with Egypt (on the west) and the Kingdom of Jordan (on the east).

The northern boundary of the Negev is rather indistinct. Toward the northwest the loess-covered Negev plains change gradually into the grassy Shefela plain (the abode of the ancient Philistines) and the thinly wooded Judean foothills. Toward the northeast the Negev blends into the Judean Desert, overlooking the Dead Sea, without any clear line of demarcation. The eastern boundary of the Negev is the most distinct. It is the narrow, fault-lined Arava Rift Valley, a spectacular gash in the earth's crust, a sunken valley (or graben, in the jargon of the geologists) sharply marked on both sides by high cliffs. The natural western boundary of the Negev is the broad creek bed of Wadi El-Arish, probably the biblical Nahal Mitzrayim, which runs some kilometers beyond the present-day frontier between Egypt and Israel. It marks the transition between the rugged highlands of the Negev and the generally flat gravel plains (called *hammadas* or *regs*) of the northern Sinai.

The climate of the Negev is rather typically continental and desertic. Mean annual rainfall decreases from 200–300 millimeters in the northwest to about 25 millimeters in the extreme south, and is confined to the winter months, November to April. The distribution of rainfall within the rainy season is highly irregular, and the total seasonal rainfall fluctuates widely from year to year. A single freak rainstorm, a chance cloudburst, can spell the difference between a "wet" season and a "dry" one. The winters are relatively cool in the highlands and warm in the Arava; the summers are hot and dry everywhere, and exceedingly so in the Arava. The skies are generally clear, and insolation (radiation intensity) is high. This, coupled with the dry winds that sweep over the land, causes high rates of potential evaporation.

The geological history of the Negev spans about a billion years, from Precambrian formations to recent sedimentary deposits of Tertiary age. The igneous (granite) and metamorphic (gneiss and schist) Precambrian massif outcrops only at the southern tip of the Negev and occupies only 54 square kilometers here, but this formation continues into Sinai and is very extensive there. A deposit of Nubian sandstone, hundreds of meters thick, normally rests on the Precambrian formation. This sandstone is typically colorful (often wine-red), quite porous, and only weakly cemented. It is mostly of continental (eolian, fluviatile, or lacustrine) origin, rather than of marine origin (as are nearly all subsequent sedimentary rocks, resulting from periods of submersion by the sea). A typical outcropping of Nubian sandstone occurs at Solomon's Pillars, about 30 kilometers north of Eilat.

Most of the Negev—over 90 percent of the land area—consists of marine sedimentary rocks, primarily limestones and chalks of varying degrees of hardness, ranging in age from Triassic through Jurassic and Cretaceous to Tertiary and Quaternary. There is some evidence of minor volcanic activity in the geological history of the Negev, including magmatic plugs and dikes, and a few extrusive features. Thus, the landscape is of rocky hills and mountains, gravel-paved plateaus, coarse sediments, and sands. Outside the northwestern subregion there are only a few extensive tracts of potentially arable soil. The typical soil of the Negev is loess—a buff-colored, fine-grained, wind-borne deposit of desert dust. In the northwestern Negev, where it is most extensive,

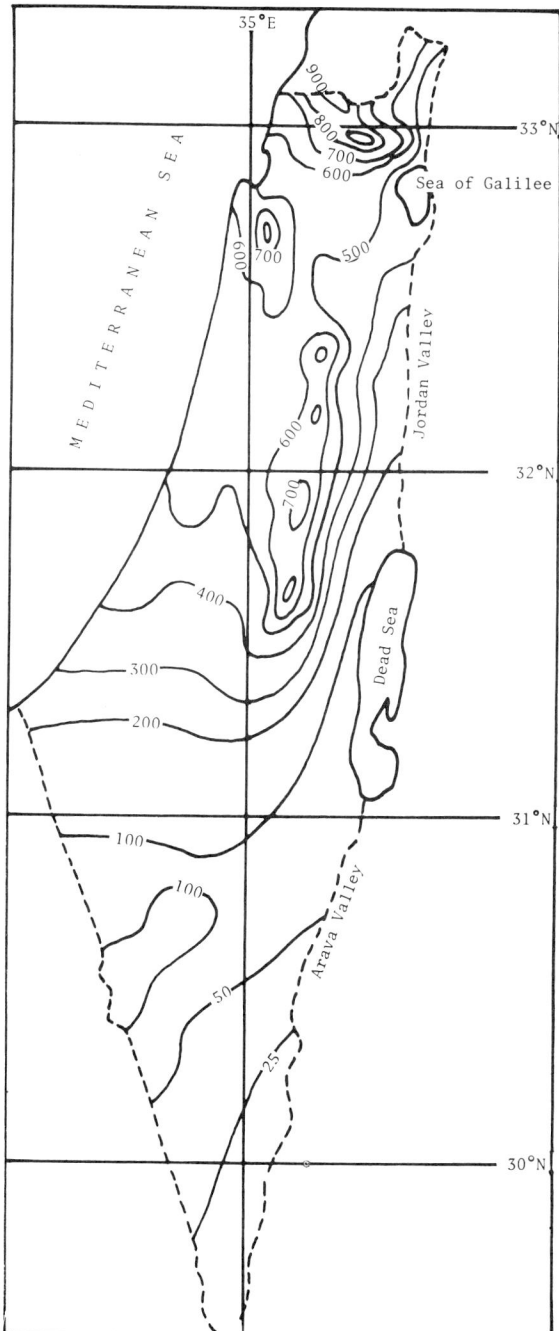

Rainfall map of Israel, with isohyets (lines of equal rainfall) marked in millimeters of mean annual rainfall. Rainfall is concentrated in the mountains of northern Galilee and along the central mountain ridge of Samaria and Judea. The eastern slopes of these mountains, being in their "rain shadows," are relatively arid.

and in some valleys in the central Negev, the mantle of loess can attain a thickness of many meters, but in most places it is shallow. Though an unstable soil, highly erodible by both wind and water, loess has favorable water-retaining characteristics that make it highly productive in places where water is available.

Within the large triangle of the Negev, which occupies some 12,500 square kilometers (well over half the State of Israel), differences in topography, elevation, aspect, geology, hydrology, climate, and vegetation enable us to recognize four fairly distinct subregions: the northwestern plains, the northern highlands, the southern highlands, and the Arava Valley.

The northwestern plains are an area of flat to gently undulating terrain, some 30 to 60 kilometers wide. The underlying bedrock is Eocene chalk and limestone. Rock outcrops frequently reveal interbedded layers of soft white lime and nearly horizontal thin bands of flint concretions. The soils are eolian (wind-deposited). The areas nearest the coast and Sinai tend to be more coarse-grained (sandy), and those farther north and farther inland tend to become gradually finer-grained (silty and clayey). This reflects the tendency of the winds to deposit the larger and heavier particles closer to the origin of the material and to carry the lighter particles farther before depositing them. As we are now aware, the circulation of dust is global, and high-altitude winds can convey volcanic ash as well as Saharan dust even to the farthest islands in the Pacific Ocean.

Hence, it is difficult in general to pinpoint the exact source of eolian material. That of the Negev, however, appears to be largely from adjacent desert areas, which frequently experience deflation by gusty winds. (A full-blown desert dust storm that can darken the sky and choke living things is a truly memorable event; fortunately, it is not very frequent.) Inland enclaves of sand dunes occur in the southern part of the subregion. The natural vegetation consists of desert shrubs and short-season annuals, including grasses and legumes. In a good year the plains are lush with pasture, enough to fatten and multiply the Bedouin's flocks of goats and sheep. In a drought year the same hapless animals, now emaciated and lethargic, may search in vain for a single blade of grass and be forced to subsist on scraggly shrubs.

The northern plains subregion of the Negev constitutes Israel's main agricultural land reserve, its most extensive area of arable soil. Rainfed agriculture ("dryland farming") is submarginal, too risky because of the frequency of drought. Irrigated farming is very successful here, but it depends almost entirely on the increasingly expensive importation of water from the north, since local groundwater resources and their natural replenishment are exceedingly meager.

The greater part of the Negev is mountainous, with several prominent ranges. The highest of these is the Ramon, which attains an altitude of 1,000 meters and separates the Negev highlands into northern and southern subregions.

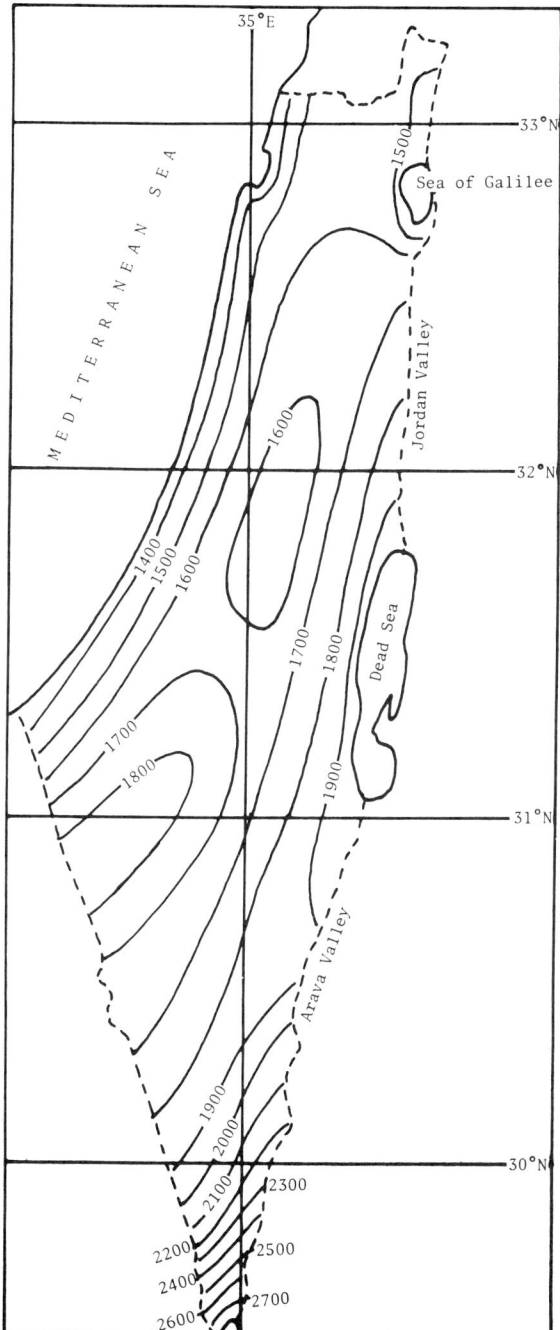

Evaporativity map of Israel, showing lines of equal mean annual evaporation (millimeters), as measured with a pan evaporimeter. A comparison with the rainfall map reveals that the areas with the least rainfall suffer the greatest evaporative demand, and thus are even more arid than the rainfall alone would suggest.

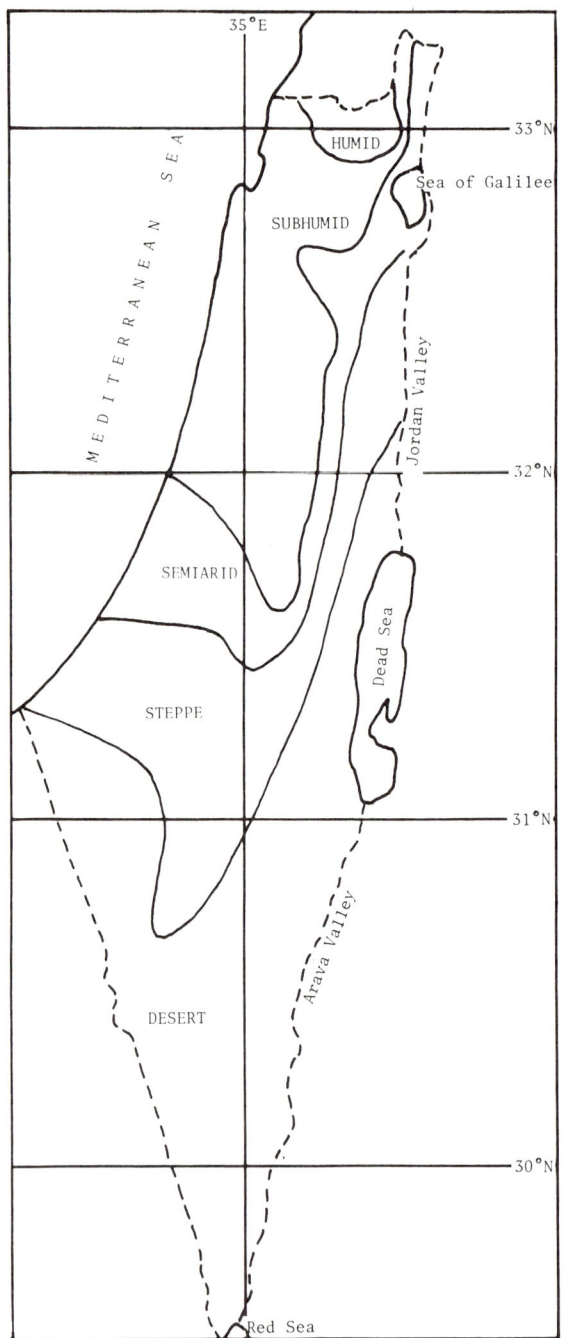

Ecological regions of Israel, which gradually change from relatively humid conditions in the north to increasingly arid conditions in the south. The northern Negev is transitional between arid steppe and extremely arid desert. Such demarcation lines, drawn on what is in reality a continuum, are necessarily somewhat arbitrary.

Physiography & Climate

The northern highlands consist of parallel anticlinal ridges and synclinal valleys running from northeast to southwest. These ridges are characterized by fairly gentle northwest-facing slopes and relatively steep southeast-facing slopes. The exposed strata are of upper Cretaceous limestone and dolomite (Cenomanian-Turonian), overlain in places by Senonian marls and chalk capped by beds of erosion-resistant flint. A unique and spectacular feature of the Negev highlands is the occurrence of several large craters in the anticlinal ranges. These craters, or cirques (now recognized internationally by the Hebrew name *makhtesh*), are several kilometers across and several hundred meters deep. They did not result from tectonic or volcanic activity, but were gouged into the anticlinal landscape by geologic erosion. This gigantic scooping out of the bedrock exposes a variegated succession of strata down to Jurassic and even Triassic formations. Also typical and striking are the altar-shaped hills (mesas) and truncated cones (buttes) of soft rock, generally chalk, topped by a layer of hard, erosion-resistant rock, flint or dolomitic limestone. Particularly spectacular are the eastern fringes of the Negev highlands, where the lofty land descends through a series of cliffs, cascading ledges, and narrow gorges down to the Arava Valley.

Because of the higher elevation, the northern highlands intercept rain-bearing clouds and are wetter than the adjacent subregions at the same latitude. The mean annual rainfall is on the order of 100 to 120 millimeters. This subregion is also cooler than other parts of the Negev, with occasional frost in winter. The prevalent soils here are residual, stony serozem on the hills, eolian loess in the plains, and a mixture of eolian and alluvial (water-deposited) material in the valleys. The natural vegetation is transitional between desert and steppe associations. Owing to its transitional character, the composition and intraregional distribution of the vegetation are determined by secondary, microclimatic factors (such as localized differences in relief, exposure, and moisture regime) rather than by primary macroclimatic factors.

The southern highlands lie south of Ramon, the Negev's highest mountain range. Crossing that range southward from its northwest-facing side to its lee side, one notices an abrupt change in hydrological and ecological conditions. Annual rainfall drops from more than 120 millimeters at the range's crest to less than 75 millimeters, then continues to diminish, as one goes further south, to little over 25 millimeters at the southern tip of the Negev triangle. Completely desertic conditions prevail in this subregion, the landscape consisting almost entirely of rugged rocky hills and of *hammadas*. The latter are wide expanses or plateaus with a natural surface cover of stones and pebbles (called desert pavement) resulting from the deflation of the finer soil material by winds. Some soil material is found underneath the desert pavement, but the soil, such as it is, is quite shallow, gravelly, and fairly saline. The vegetation is very sparse, consisting of dwarf desert shrubs. Numerous acacia trees, however, grow in the local depressions and watercourses.

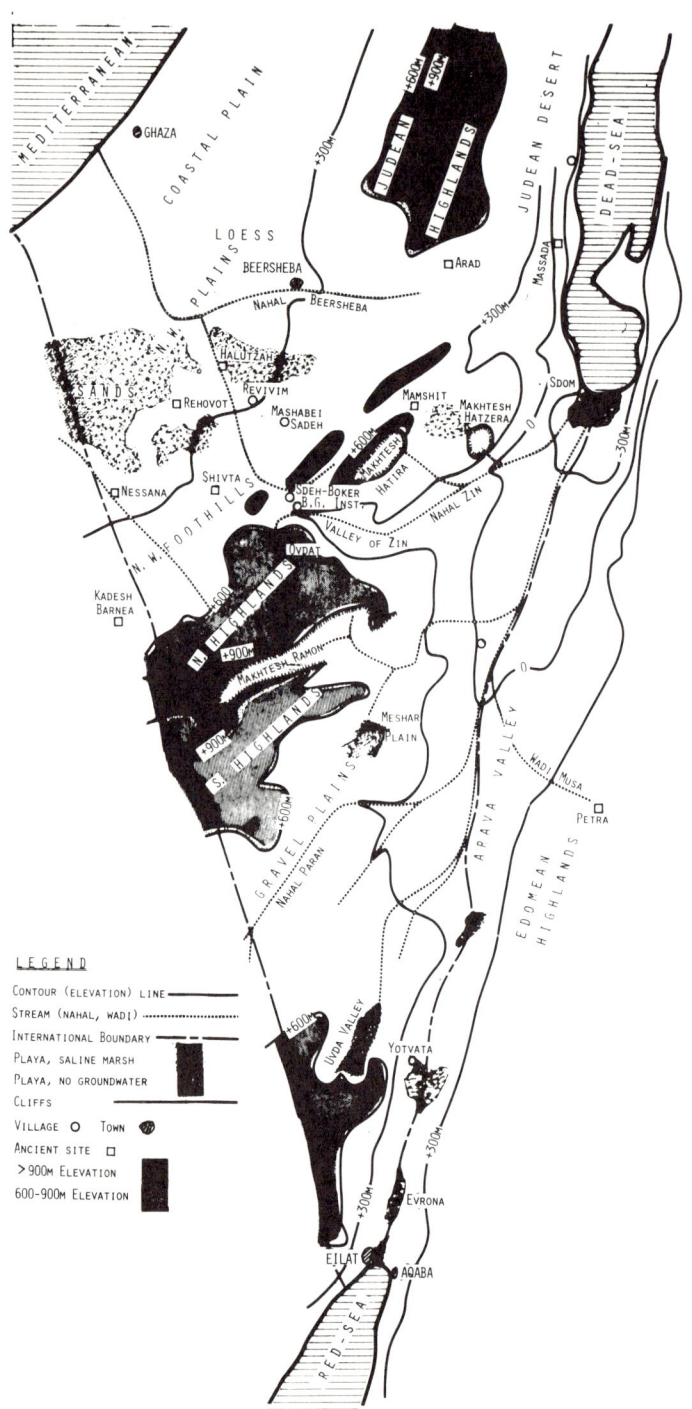

General map of the Negev, showing topography, drainage pattern, major subregions, and settlements.

Physiography & Climate

Variegated sedimentary rock formation at the Hatira Crater, in the northern Negev highlands.

The Arava is a narrow, cliff-lined valley running the length of the Negev triangle on its east side. It is the segment of the Great African-Syrian Rift extending between the Dead Sea and the Gulf of Aqaba. The Great Rift is a series of massive trenches some 6,000 kilometers (3,700 miles) long, extending from Mozambique up through eastern Africa, along part of the Red Sea and the Gulf of Aqaba, through the Arava, the Dead Sea, the Jordan Valley, and northward between the mountain ranges of Lebanon and Anti-Lebanon in Syria to southern Turkey. Along its course it contains a number of deep valleys with flat floors and clearly marked sides—in effect, depressions between raised plateaus. Other great gashes or depressions in the earth's surface, such as the Grand Canyon or the great fjords, were carved out by rivers or glaciers, but the origin of the Great Rift is tectonic—that is, attributable to movements of the earth's crust. According to the theory of plate tectonics, the Great Rift is a line along which continental plates are separating and drifting apart. Indeed, the mighty fault-lined cliffs rising sheer to hundreds of meters from the sunken floor of the Arava make this dramatic theory entirely believable. Corresponding geological formations on either side of the Arava are not merely separated laterally, but also shifted longitudinally, so it appears that the tectonic crustal movement is one in which adjacent plates are both tearing apart and sliding alongside each other with the eastern (Edumean) block having shifted several score kilometers northward relative to the western

The southern Negev highlands.

(Negev) block. The collapse of the Arava and Jordan Valleys is part of a very extensive tactonic movement that may eventually open up a new ocean floor. (This is not likely to happen any time soon, however.)

Geologically, the Arava Valley is a graben, derived from the German word for trench. In the context of geomorphology it describes an elongated depression resulting from the sinkage of the earth's crust between two fault lines. According to Bentor (1979), the line of faults that separated and lifted the Edumean Plateau above the Negev probably began as early as the latter part of the Precambrian period. The Arava graben, however, formed mainly during the relatively recent Miocene and Pleistocene periods. An oblique stretching and shifting occurred that caused a second line of faults to form on the Negev side. The crust between the two fault lines, about 15 kilometers wide, sank correspondingly. The Pleistocene deposits at the bottom of the valley are at least 3500 meters thick in the Dead Sea area. Consequently, the large mass of semiliquid salt buried underneath oozed out to form a plug rising

Physiography & Climate

Sedimentary badlands and igneous (granitic) domes in the southern Negev highlands. The Gulf of Aqaba lies below, and the hills of northwestern Arabia are in the far background.

220 meters or more above the valley floor, thus forming Mount Sodom. This legendary mountain consists of pure crystalline salt, into which the rainwaters have dissolved spectacular chimneys and grottoes.

The Arava Valley is 180 kilometers long and only 8 to 20 kilometers wide. On the east the Edumean mountains rise to between 1,000 and 1,500 meters above sea level, and on the west lie the less prominent mountains and high plains of the Negev highlands. The valley floor rises slowly from sea level at Eilat (on the Red Sea) to a watershed divide not far from the center of the valley, then descends rather more steeply (from a maximum elevation just over 200 meters above sea level) to the Dead Sea, which is the lowest point on the earth's continental surface at -394 meters. Thus, practically the entire northern part of the valley is below sea level.

The Dead Sea has a most intriguing geological history (Bentor, 1979). During transition from Pliocene to Pleistocene, there were large floods which scoured the Negev highlands and deposited conglomerate material in the Arava. At the same time, the sea penetrated the land from the north, through the Jezreel valley, and inundated the Jordan Valley. In this lagoon, a tremendous deposition of salt took place during the early Pleistocene. Some of this salt, later uplifted, is seen in Mount Sodom. When the lagoon was sev-

An oasis in the Arava Valley. In the foreground are low circular mounds, relics of an ancient chain-well system. Beyond these is an expanse of cultivated fields, irrigated with pumped groundwater. In the distant background is the massive mountain range of Edom.

ered from the sea in the middle Pleistocene, the long and narrow basin became a giant playa, in which clays, sands and marls settled and salts precipitated. About 100,000 years ago, a new lake formed in this basin, called the Lisan Lake (after the eastern peninsula of the Dead Sea, named "Lisan," or "Tongue," in Arabic). The deposits of this lake are friable white rocks with thin layers of a calcitic clay known as Lisan marl. Lisan Lake apparently dried up about 16,000 years ago, and about 2,000 years later the present lake formed, with its characteristic sediments of clay, chalk, and gypsum. The water of the Dead Sea is rich in valuable potassium and bromide salts, which are extracted in a large industrial complex at the southern end of the lake.

The climate of the Arava Valley is extremely hot and dry. Rainfall, being highly chancy, varies between 20 and 50 millimeters per season. Northerly chimney winds sweep along the valley, and counter the moderating effect one might otherwise expect from the proximity of the Red Sea. The potential evaporation approaches 2 meters per annum.

Igneous rock formations at the southern apex of the Negev triangle.

A gravel-strewn plain, variously called "hamada" or "reg." The finer material having been deflated by wind, the surface is covered with a continuous layer of gravel, called "desert pavement." Note that the sparse vegetation is practically confined to the few gullies which drain the surface of the plain. In the background is a mesa (table-mountain) of limestone.

The valley floor is lined with coarse erosional deposits of stones, gravel, and sand. The vegetation is extremely sparse. In a few locations, however, where the drainage from mountain wadis (which emerge into the valley as alluvial fans) gives rise to perched water tables, there are oases that abound with vegetation. Often the shallow groundwater is brackish.

Because of the diversity of the Negev's subregions, it is difficult to describe each of them in equal detail. I propose, therefore, as a case study, to focus primary attention upon the northern highlands, a subregion that abounds with evidence of ancient settlement and of land and water development schemes, both past and present.

12

Water Regime and Habitats

> . . . As a hiding place from the wind
> And a covert from the tempest;
> As rivers of water in a dry place
> As the shadows of a great rock in a weary land.
> Isaiah 32:2

As seen by an ecologist interested in the relationship between the varied forms of life and their environments, the northern Negev highlands is anything but a homogeneous place in which the same conditions prevail everywhere. For while the region as a whole is a desert, and its overall climate is fairly uniform, there exist within it ecologically specific realms in which conditions are either drier or wetter than average, and the contrasts can be astonishing indeed. This is not merely a matter of random variation, but a consistent pattern governed by definable physical factors or combinations of factors involving the nature of the bedrock, the soil, and the topography. When viewing the Negev from the air, one cannot but notice the striking difference between the barrenness of the plains and the luxuriance of the depressions and wadis. On the ground one also notices the change in plant species and density between the plains and the slopes, and among slopes of different steepness, direction (whether north-facing or south-facing), and geological formations. Close examination of the reasons for these outstanding differences reveals that they relate to the variable water regime. Let us therefore describe the three principal plant habitats of the region — rocky slopes, loessial plains, and wadi beds — in terms of their water regimes.

Rocky slopes occupy about 80 percent of the total area. The soil cover is shallow and discontinuous: where the bedrock outcrops in the form of ledges

Rocky slopes in the Negev highlands. The land in the foreground, which slopes northward, exhibits a relatively dense growth of sagebrush, whereas the south-facing slope across the valley has much sparser vegetation.

or boulders, soil may be completely absent; yet in pockets between boulders the soil may reach a depth of 60–80 centimeters. The soil is stony to the extent of at least half its volume, and is generally rich in lime, somewhat alkaline, and, beyond the depth of rain penetration (30–50 centimeters), highly saline. The vegetation is characterized at the higher altitudes by a species of sagebrush, *Artemisia herba alba* (an aromatic plant from which the Bedouin brew a zesty, if somewhat bitter, tea), and at lower altitudes by the more desertic bean caper, *Zygophyllum dumosum.* The north-facing hillsides and the talus of thicker soil at the base of many slopes often have denser vegetation and, because of their moister conditions, also harbor plants of a more humid clime. The total plant cover, however, is not greater than 10 percent of the surface, and is often much less. The vegetation has doubtless been affected by centuries of overgrazing by the Bedouin's goats. The original vegetation was certainly denser, but probably not basically different. Control of overgrazing since the 1950s has resulted in a noticeably thicker vegetative cover, as can be seen in satellite photos (in which the Negev appears darker than the immediately neighboring

Clumps of plants growing in pockets of soil among outcroppings of bedrock. In addition to direct rainfall, these pockets receive some of the water that trickles off the adjacent rocks. The wide-leafed herb in the foreground is *Urginea undulata* of the lily family.

area of Sinai), though regeneration of depleted vegetation in desert areas generally is not very rapid.

Loessial plains occur mainly near watershed divides and in the wider synclinal valleys. The soils are eolian loess of a fine-sand or a silt-loam texture, or they may be alluvial (water-laid) deposits of somewhat coarser texture along the main watercourses. The eolian soils are deep and texturally uniform, but tend to be saline below the depth of rainfall penetration (about 30 centimeters), whereas the alluvial soils often contain interbedded layers of silty, sandy, and gravelly deposits, generally salt-free. The vegetation is characterized by an association of low desert shrubs of the chenopod family, in which the jointed saltwood *Haloxylon articulatum* and *Anabasis hausknechti* or *A. aticulata* predominate. Above-ground distances between shrubs may be several meters, but just below the surface the shallow roots (not generally deeper than 30 centimeters) extend laterally so that the entire volume of soil that is wetted annually by rains is effectively tapped. The density of the stand of shrubs is largely in equilibrium with, and a function of, the mean annual rainfall. In relatively wet seasons smaller grassy plants, such as sedge (*Carex* spp.) and feather grass (*Stipa tortilis*) may grow profusely, albeit ephemerally, in the open ground between the shrubs.

Wadi beds occur in narrow and winding bands that altogether constitute somewhat less than 5 percent of the total area. Three main wadi types can be discerned: large regional wadis, generally with gravel-bedded channels; synclinal valley wadis, often loessial; and small tributary mountain wadis, generally with stony loess beds. The gravelly wadi beds are from 50 percent to 100 percent fine to coarse gravel, often interlayered with sand. Considerable quantities of water seep into the gravel during flash floods, and in certain locations, where the gravel is underlain by clay or by unfractured bedrock, perched water tables are formed and their groundwater can be tapped by shallow wells. Water yields, however, are generally meager and subject to the vagaries of fluctuating rainfall.

The vegetation of the gravelly wadi beds consists of deep-rooted bushes typified by the sparrow wort, *Thymalaea hirsuta*, and the leguminous white broom, *Retama roetam*. More palatable species of bushes, such as saltbush, *Atriplex halimus*, and *Colutea istria* (a legume), have been decimated by longterm overgrazing, but are now making a comeback. Occasional tamarisk, acacia, and even pistacia trees grow in the wadi beds, and are a dramatic phenomenon in the middle of the otherwise treeless desert. These trees were very probably more numerous in ages past, but were cut down for construction and fuel, and prevented by seedling-devouring goats from regenerating themselves.

Loessial wadis generally occur in the synclinal valleys as broad and gently grading courses. The fine-grained soil is often interlayered with gravelly horizons. Where natural water spreading takes place during winter flash floods, a rich vegetation abounds. In addition to shrubs and trees, many annual and perennial plants typical of the more humid Mediterranean associations grow here, including numerous species of pasture grasses and legumes of the *Hordeum, Phalaris, Oryzopis, Lolium, Cynodon, Poa, Avena, Medicago, Trifolium, Trigonella. Astragalus*, and other genera. The pattern of water spreading is greatly influenced by past and present practices of land management and flood-water irrigation.

As already stated, the mean annual rainfall of the region is on the order of 100–120 millimeters. Rainfall generally occurs in 15 to 25 rainy days, mainly between November and April. Mean annual rainfall, however, is an inadequate indicator of growing conditions, since great fluctuations occur from year to year both in the total amount and in the temporal and spatial distribution of the rains. Moreover, even knowledge of the amount and distribution of annual rainfall, were it available, would not of itself tell us much about its ecological effectiveness. An "effective" rain is one that adds available moisture to the root zone of plants, generally below the depth that is subject to immediate evaporation. As a rough rule of thumb, only a rain that penetrates to at least 10 centimeter of the soil can be considered effective for vegetation on slopes and plains, and only rains causing runoff from the slopes to collect in the channels are effective for the deep-rooted vegetation of the wadi beds. In most instances, rains large enough to be effective on the slopes and plains also cause some runoff, and are therefore effective in the wadis as well.

Effective rains seldom occur more than four or five times during a typical season, and generally include no more than half the total seasonal rainfall. In some seasons there may be only one or two effective rains, perhaps early in the season without any follow-up, or perhaps too late in the season to allow normal growth. In other seasons several effective rains may be clustered at an unfavorable time in, say, midseason, when the temperatures are low and the soil is likely to be at its wettest, so that all the rain coming at once is neither necessary nor desirable. In any case, the number and timing of the effective rains bear no consistent relation to the total quantity of seasonal rainfall. However, these effective rains, and their temporal distribution, determine the commencement, length, and quality of the growing season. Desert plants must therefore have the ability to lie dormant for long periods until conditions are suitable for their particular needs.

I resided in the Negev highlands for almost a year before I witnessed a single truly effective rain. We had devoted the entire summer of 1952 to preparation for the rainy season. We built dikes with stone spillways and planted trees (laboriously irrigated with water we had to haul by tanker from a shallow well some 20 kilometers away). The task of building those dikes lasted beyond the summer and into the autumn. Day after day, while rushing to complete our plan, we would gaze worriedly at the skies, praying that the rain would be delayed. Alas, our prayers were answered only too well. For when the work was completed and the rains could come—the sooner the better, as far as we were now concerned—the rains still did not come. October passed, and then November. December was clear and cold. The sun was bright, but gave little warmth. Cold winds swept over the dry plain and raised swirling columns of dust. Sometimes the skies were overcast and flashes of lightning would be seen over the mountains, but no rain came. The dreary weather of expectancy lasted on and on; and as more and more weeks passed, the dreaded word was sounded: drought.

One night when I was on guard duty and the black sky rested heavy above and the air was still and strangely warm, it began to rain, gently at first, and pleasantly. I felt the drops stroking my face and dripping into my collar, and I prayed for more, much more. The rain continued for a while, then stopped. It started again, in greater earnest. There was lightning and thunder; the rain beat down on the thirsty earth and on our tents and makeshift huts; and the air was full of the sound of singing raindrops. I stood in the drenching goodness of the rain, tasting and drinking its sweet moisture, shivering in its delightful chill. But then the rain stopped, the puddles quickly disappeared into the soft earth, the winds came up, and the clouds were dispersed. The stars reappeared, and the rain did not return.

In the morning the world seemed different somehow. The air smelled of moisture and the earth was still soggy. But there had been no runoff. The rain was insufficient. One could kick through the moist layer and find dry dust just a few centimeters below the surface. And in the days that followed, the surface layer desiccated once more, as if there had been no rain at all. Again the days were bright and the skies a steely, stubborn, stingy blue. The desert did not change.

The weather tormented and toyed with us a few more times in January and February, but the showers were largely ineffective and our hopes were dashed time and again. There we were, a forlorn band of foolhardy innocents come to challenge the desert, only to find that our challenge was ignored.

And then, at last, when the season seemed practically over, the rain came —the real rain. It started one afternoon in early March, slowly at first but steadily. Gradually it picked up and became a driving rain, unrelenting, and it continued determinedly throughout the evening. The whole landscape seemed drenched, the sky and the earth blended in the soggy mist. The satiated soil began to ooze with water, and large puddles formed on the plain. Still there was no flooding in the wadis, and later in the evening the rain slackened. Was this, too, a false sign?

But the air was different this time, the clouds hung heavier and darker. The frequent flashes of lightning foretold more. The earth lay chastised, submissive, expectant. The next spurt of rain, the consummating rain, came shortly after midnight. A mighty thunderstorm rolled in from the northwest, rumbling over the mountains and descending onto the plain like an angry beast of prey, pouring its wrath upon the vulnerable, quenched earth. Myriad heavy drops pounded and flailed the slaked mud, tearing at the surface, trickling off the slopes into tiny rivulets of churning, boisterous, frothing currents, lapping up the earth in gulleys, joining into channels, gathering momentum for the roaring rush down the wadi. The heavy storm lasted less than 20 minutes, but it turned the entire surface into a shiny sheet of flowing water.

This was it, we knew as we stood in the thin drizzle that lingered after the squall. Then we heard the distant rumble, a low, ominous growling. The flood! We ran blindly in the dark toward the wadi, slipping and sloshing in the mud, falling and running again, stumbling on invisible shrubs. There was nothing unusual at the first terrace, nor at the second and third, save for a few glistening puddles. But the roar was near, and coming nearer.

We met the flood at the eleventh terrace — a dark, foaming wave of liquid mud, gathering and filling the wadi and overflowing the terrace spillways. In the dim light of the impending dawn we witnessed the terrible sight of the dragon flood as it crested. Rising and lunging forward, the massing river melted our earthen dikes and broke our spillways, scattering the stones we had spent many months so laboriously fitting into place. We ran alongside the flood as it cascaded from terrace to terrace, wreaking havoc as it rushed down the wadi, until we could no longer keep up with its furious pace. And there we stood, exhausted and awed and humbled in the face of the sudden destructive power we had witnessed so helplessly. What we had longed for had come, but it was beyond our expectations.

Overwhelmed, we knew that we had been defeated by the pent-up power and onslaught of a formidable foe, that this deceptively placid desert is a slumbering giant never to be underestimated. And yet in our disappointment lay the joy of knowing that the rain and the flood are real, not to be doubted, for the desert had indeed given forth water. However impetuous and mighty, the flood carried infinite promise, the promise of water enough to fill cisterns, to irrigate fields, to sustain life.

In the wake of the flood — a freshness, an awakening, a dreary lethargy broken at last. The miracle of spring in the desert. Glorious weeks of new warmth, new life. A drabness suddenly turned green. Thorny, stunted shrubs sprouting delicate, succulent foliage, then blossoming with exquisite flowers. The plain, long barren and dull, now painted green with patches of dwarf grass. The depressions, once brown with the scorched and shriveled growth of yesteryear, newly carpeted with crowded seedlings. The wadis, those winding strips of wilted shrubs and dead undergrowth, suddenly beds of mud drying into caked crust, now transformed into verdant rivers of waving grass. All that lay dormant beneath the dry, seemingly lifeless surface now came to life. Busy insects in a fever of activity, crawling, hopping, flying, buzzing. Birds nesting and chirping among the bushes, now hidden by the foliage, now emerging for a quick flutter. Ancient lizards basking in the young sun.

A flash flood flowing over a paved road in the Negev highlands. The same wadi has on rare occasions exhibited much more powerful floods, capable of breaching the roadway and of capsizing and sweeping vehicles downstream.

Springtime in the desert: so glorious, so hauntingly beautiful and so short.

The amount of runoff generated from the slopes and delivered to the wadis is of course affected by the intensity and duration of the rainstorms and the time of their occurrence, as well as by the infiltrability of the soil. In addition, it is affected by the steepness and length of the slope and by the roughness of the surface or the presence of surface obstructions such as stones or stalks. As mentioned earlier, the loose and unstable loessial soil of the Negev tends to slake under water and to form a surface seal that retards infiltration and, upon drying, becomes a crust. Absence of a protective vegetative or gravel cover, steeply sloping topography, and the presence as surface exposures of large, smooth, and impervious boulders further contribute to high rates of runoff. According to our observations, a rainstorm exceeding 10 millimeters (0.4 inch) and with an intensity exceeding 10 millimeters/hour (for at least short spells) will generally cause runoff and result in some localized wadi flooding. A rainstorm of at least twice that size and intensity is generally required before significant, catchmentwide or region-wide floods can be expected.

As with most rules of thumb, however, this one can have many exceptions. For example, a storm of the size and intensity mentioned may produce no runoff at all if it falls upon a particularly dry soil early in the season, whereas a much smaller storm may cause considerable flooding later in the season if the

A flash flood in Wadi Zin, plunging into the deep gorge at Ein Ovdat. (Courtesy of S. Buchbinder of Sdeh-Boker)

soil is already nearly satiated from the cumulative effect of earlier rains. Although wadi floods cannot be predicted, it appears that there is at least one flood per season in most years in most of the wadis, and that as many as six (or even more) may take place in some unusually wet years. A single flood, lasting several hours, can wet a loessial wadi bed to a depth of nearly a meter; and if the floodwater is detained, or impounded, behind earthen or stone dikes, a single flood may suffice to wet the soil to a depth of several meters, in which several hundred millimeters of water may be stored for subsequent plant use.

The reservoir of soil water available to plants depends on the amount of infiltrated water, on the depth of root penetration, and on the retentive properties of the soil profile. However, the available-water storage capacity of the soil does not necessarily limit the amount of water usable by plants in any particular year, since the soil reservoir may be replenished more than once during the season, depending upon the rainfall pattern. A better measure of the

A profusion of ephemeral wild flowers (including poppies, daisies, and chrysanthemums) growing on the banks of a wadi in springtime.

amount of water used seasonally by plants in different habitats is given by the seasonal "water balance." For any relevant volume of soil (say, for any definable rooting zone of a known plant community), the total amount of water added during a given period must equal the amount of water withdrawn plus the change in soil moisture storage. This is expressible in the form of a simple equation:

$$W_z = P - R - D - E - T$$

in which W_z is the change in water content of the root zone to depth z during a specified period, P is total precipitation during the same period, R is the amount of surface runoff, D is the amount of water lost from the root zone by deep percolation (beyond the reach of roots), E is direct evaporation from the drying soil surface, and T is the amount of water drawn from the soil by plant roots and transpired by plant leaves.

The water balance of habitats in the Negev varies greatly from season to season, but I shall attempt to give approximate, average figures (Hillel and Tadmor 1962). The sole moisture supply to the slopes and the plains is the seasonal precipitation. There is the problem, however, of determining what fraction of that precipitation fails to penetrate the soil and runs off the sloping surface of the land. Runoff is difficult to measure without elaborate gauging devices. Estimates can be obtained from indirect measurements of soil infiltrability, gully discharges during floods, and runoff-runon area ratios in places where the runoff is impounded either naturally or artificially. The available evidence leads to estimated runoff values of 10 percent to 15 percent of average seasonal rainfall for slopes, and of 15 percent to 20 percent for loessial plains.

Studies of depth of rooting and of moisture penetration show that the amount of moisture lost through deep percolation is negligible on the slopes and plains, except perhaps in extraordinarily wet seasons, which are very rare. In general the entire amount of water entering the soil is returned to the atmosphere either by direct evaporation from the drying soil or through extraction by roots and transpiration from plant canopies. Thus, there is hardly any significant recharge of groundwater by direct percolation of rainwater over most of the land area. The groundwater that does exist regionally is, in essence, "fossil" water, the result of earlier and more humid periods in the distant geologic past of the region. Some of this water can perhaps be tapped by modern methods of deep drilling, but energy costs, as well as the brackish nature of fossil water, may limit or preclude economic use even at present.

The water regime of wadi beds is completely different from that of hills and plains. Here the amount of water accumulating as "runon" and infiltrating the soil can exceed the annual rainfall severalfold, and deep percolation below the rooting depth of the native vegetation can be considerable. Wadis, especially those with gravelly beds, thus constitute the principal medium of ground-

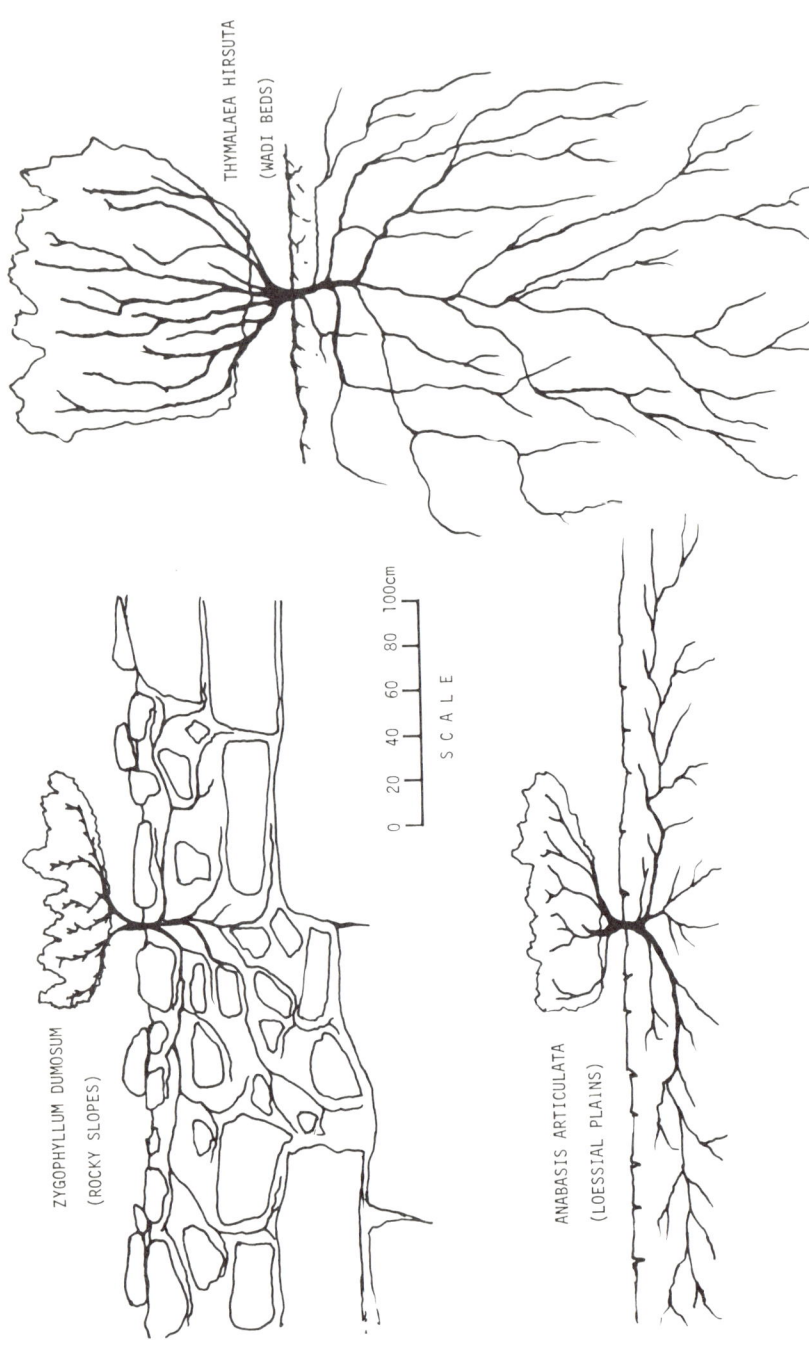

Characteristic root systems of typical shrubs growing in the principal plant habitats of the Negev highlands. Note the shallow depth and wide lateral spread of the roots of *Anabasis articulata* growing in loessial plains, the deeper penetration of roots of *Zygophyllum dumosum* growing under the surface stones on rocky slopes, and the very deep penetration of the roots of *Thymalaea hirsuta* growing in wadi beds.

The root system of *Thymalaea hirsuta*, bared by gully erosion in a loessial wadi bed.

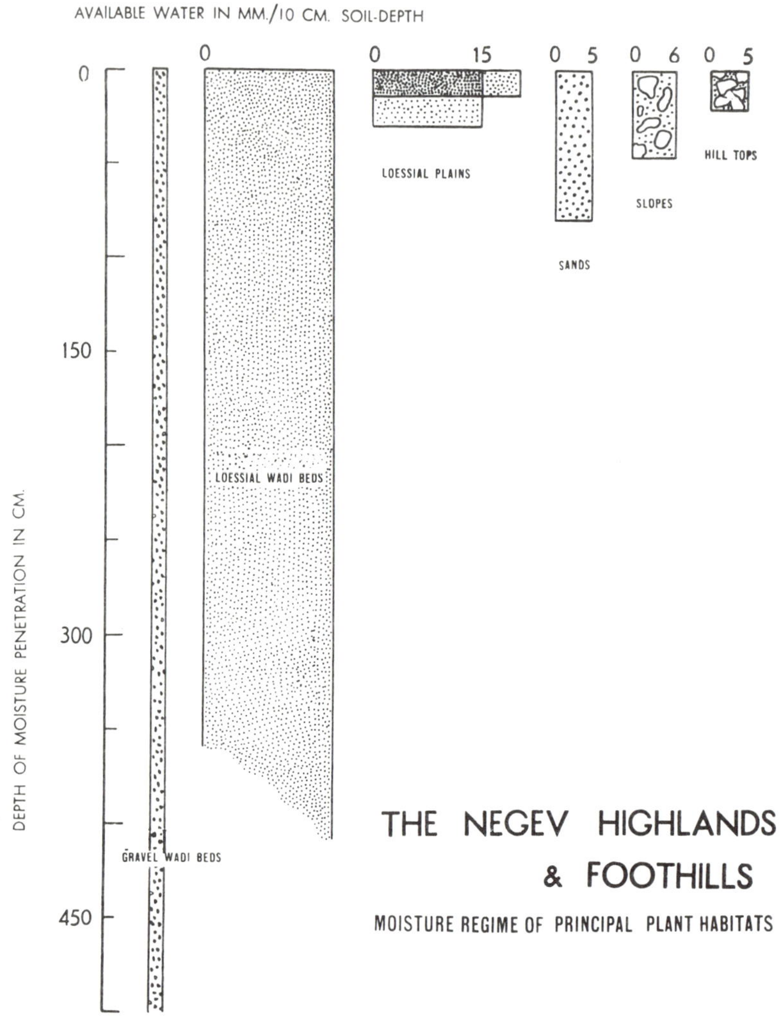

THE NEGEV HIGHLANDS & FOOTHILLS

MOISTURE REGIME OF PRINCIPAL PLANT HABITATS

Availability of soil moisture for plant growth in the principal habitats of the Negev highlands. The amount of water available depends on both the depth of water penetration (and of rooting) and the amount of water retained per unit depth of wetted soil.

water recharge. In areas underlain by impervious strata, perched water tables can form, and the shallow groundwater fed by wadi-bed percolation may give rise to springs or be easily tapped by shallow wells. Though on a regional basis the amounts of water involved are small, they can be important locally.

Quantitative estimates of evapotranspiration in the various habitats can be derived from data on soil moisture changes and from microclimatic measurements. The difficulty arises in trying to separate the amount of water transpired by plants from that evaporated from the soil, since the two processes are not mutually independent. Where the greater part of the soil surface is bare, however, as it is in the slopes and plains, we can estimate soil moisture evaporation by monitoring the wetness changes at the soil surface. Such an estimation leads us to conclude that over half the infiltrated water evaporates directly from the loessial soil of the plains, and that somewhat less than half evaporates from slopes. The reason for the difference is that the latter soil is stony, so that the same amount of precipitation tends to penetrate more deeply (because less of it is retained in the surface zone, where it is more readily evaporable). Not only does the deeper penetration of water in the slope soil (as compared with the generally stone-free soil of the plains) reduce evaporation, but the presence of stones over the soil surface further serves to mitigate the action of sun and wind, and thus helps to conserve soil moisture. Coupled with the effect of stones to increase infiltration and obstruct runoff, even a seemingly slight reduction of evaporation can cause the slopes to be a moister habitat than the loessial plains.

We can now summarize our estimates of the water balance for a "typical" season as follows: In the loessial plains, assuming an average precipitation of 100 millimeters, we find runoff to be on the order of 15-20 millimeters, evaporation about 45-50 millimeters, and transpiration about 30-40 millimeters. On the slopes, with the same rainfall, runoff is 10-15 millimeters and evaporation is 35-40 millimeters, leaving about 45-55 millimeters available for plant use (transpiration). The difference between the estimated 35 millimeters of net available water for plant growth on the loessial plains and the 50 millimeters on the slopes may not seem very significant to the casual observer. Indeed, both the plains and the slopes are extremely dry habitats in which the typical plants are desert xerophytes. However, the rocky slopes can be a visibly more humid habitat than the loessial plains, and may contain a few species of plants not normally found in dry deserts, particularly in pockets of relatively deep soil that may receive spot runoff from adjacent protruding boulders.

The difference between the more arid loessial plains and the somewhat more humid rocky slopes is most pronounced on north-facing slopes, on which solar radiation is less intense and potential evaporation is lower than on south-facing slopes, as well as in the slope-bottom talus, where the soil is deeper and more fertile than on the upper reaches of the hillside. The plains themselves may afford more humid growing conditions where soil texture is sufficiently

Desert shrubs and geophytes growing in gravelly talus (slope-bottom) material.

coarse (sandy or gravelly) to permit greater infiltration and deeper penetration (and hence less evaporation) of water.

Agricultural crops cannot be grown economically on the rocky slopes because of the steepness of the land, the shallowness of the soil, and the numerous obstructing boulders that make cultivation practically impossible. The loessial plains, on the other hand, make excellent agricultural soils once provided with water for irrigation and after being leached of their initially high concentration of salts. The problem is that not much water is available for irrigation other than floodwater, which requires the development of a specialized system of irrigation called runoff farming.

Throughout this exposition I have used the term "precipitation" as synonymous with "rainfall," thus implying that other forms of precipitation are unimportant or even negligible. Snow can occur in the Negev highlands, but it is too rare to be considered part of the normal water regime. Dew is a much more frequent occurrence, and in some places it is highly visible. The desert surface, heated during the day, loses heat by emission of radiation during the night. The air in immediate contact with ground is cooled, and as it becomes denser, it sinks from the higher ground into the depressions, where it condenses its moisture and can be seen in early morning as low-lying cushions of dense fog.

However striking it is in appearance, and notwithstanding the many claims regarding the contribution of dew to the water economy of desert plants, we have seen little evidence that dew generally constitutes a significant component of the ecological water balance affecting any of the habitat types we have studied. And while there is indeed evidence to suggest that certain specialized primitive plant associations, such as desert lichens growing on rock surface, are sustained by dew, this does not apply to higher plants growing in soil. The total condensation of dew in parts of the Negev highlands has been estimated to be the equivalent of some 20 millimeters per season, and while that amount may seem appreciable in comparison with the estimated seasonal available water of, say, 50 millimeters, we must remember that little dew occurs on the high plains and slopes (most of it being in the depressions, which are endowed with much greater amounts of water from runoff). Moreover, the amount of dew condensed per night is usually a fraction of a millimeter, just enough to moisten the surface of the ground, which then dries out soon after the sun rises.

The three habitat types elucidated thus far (rocky slopes, loessial plains, wadi beds) occur in close association in the Negev highlands, in an intricate yet characteristic topographic pattern. Quite a different edaphic environment exists in sandy areas. Such areas occur as enclaves on the western and northern fringes of the region described. Though not very prevalent in the Negev highlands, areas of sand are quite extensive in neighboring desert regions (Sinai, the Eastern and Western deserts of Egypt, and the Arabian Desert).

People who come from semihumid regions, where areas of sand constitute the driest of habitats owing to the land's excessively rapid drainage and failure to retain sufficient moisture and nutrients, might expect this to be the case in the desert also. Here, however, the opposite situation generally prevails, with sandy soils offering more favorable moisture conditions for plant growth than do finer-textured soils (Hillel and Tadmor 1962; Hillel and van Bavel 1976). This is because of the sand's higher permeability to rain and, hence, greatly reduced runoff losses. Moreover, since sand retains less moisture per unit depth than do finer-textured soils (silts, loams, and clays), less moisture remains near the soil surface, where it might be subject to subsequent evaporation. In the desert, rainfall is generally so scant that no appreciable percolation takes place beyond the reach of plant roots.

So, with practically total absorption of rain, no runoffs, and little evaporation or percolation loss, it is no wonder that sand is more efficient in storing moisture and making it available to plants, and that the vegetation of sandy areas tends to be more dense and lush than that of neighboring loessial plains. This is provided, of course, that the vegetation of sand dunes has not been destroyed by overgrazing. Where the sand is denuded of its vegetative cover, the wind takes over, and what was once green with grass soon becomese a rippled surface of moving dunes. Such was the case in the sands of Halutzah and of the Yamin Valley when we first began our observations there in 1951. Subsequent restriction of grazing, however, has resulted in considerable regeneration and fixation of the dunes by clumps of sand-loving grasses and shrubs.

The water-balance data for the different habitats described above were derived from systematic and laborious measurements that the late N. Tadmor and I began in the early 1950s and continued into the 1960s. The work involved staking out observation quadrates in representative locations where repeated and frequent observations and measurements could be made of vegetative activity and of the soil-water regime in relation to seasonal climatic changes. I carry fond memories of my indefatigable friend "Kofish" (the funny nickname by which Tadmor was known to one and all, even after he became a venerable professor) crawling on hands and knees over the sharp stones of a steep hillside, trying very hard to avoid disturbing the natural order of things while sampling ("nondestructively," he would say) the soil and plants in each quadrate.

Our measurements included layer-by-layer soil moisture content, stoniness, texture, salinity, and temperature, as well as plant roots, foliage, and physiological activity. In the process we had amassed more data than we knew what to do with. And yet we continued to collect more data, for that seemed so much easier (despite the physical exertion) than having to draw conclusions and set them down in writing. Years later, when we finally sat down to summarize all those carefully recorded measurements in all those frayed notebooks, we discovered, to our consternation, that we had taken altogether too many measurements of one kind and not nearly enough of another. *C'est une vie de chameau!*

Une vie de chameau? Perhaps I ought to explain the expression. It was from the title of an old booklet (*La vie du chameau*) written by a former officer of the French Foreign Legion. I had discovered it, tattered and dusty, in an abandoned ruin in the old quarter of Beersheba. When some of us conceived the idea of setting up a camel-riding patrol to survey and maintain security in the territory, I asked Barbara to help me translate that book. Barbara was a graduate of the University of Neuchâtel, a very clever and attractive young woman of 22. She was one of only two women in our group of a dozen, the other being an older and much tougher woman named Judith who had been through the Holocaust in Europe and had fought with the partisans during the Second World War. Barbara was amused at the idea of the camel patrol, and applied the book's title in a self-deriding, humorous way to characterize our bungling effort to "go native" and raise crops and livestock in the desert. Skeptical though she was, Barbara gave her life to that effort.

One fateful day in late September 1952, I enlisted the help of Eytan to examine the root systems of plants in the Star, a beautiful valley located some 5 kilometers west of Sdeh-Boker and so named because of the confluence of several large wadis there. As we drove our mule-drawn cart through the winding mountain pass called the Gap, we saw Barbara down in the wadi, standing waist-deep in the brush and surrounded by our small flock of sheep and goats. Barbara the Shepherdess—how incongruous she seemed in that role! Physically delicate and culturally refined, she belonged in the literary salons of Europe rather than on the rough frontier of the Negev. But she played her role with courage and determination, tempered by her somewhat sardonic sense of humor. "C'est une vie de chameau," she would say quietly, and smile as she tried to round up the capricious goats, or milk the bucking fat-tailed sheep, or comb the inevitable caked dust out of her flowing auburn hair.

We waved to Barbara, and she waved back and smiled. That wonderfully mischievous smile that somehow blended innocence and sophistication, faith and disbelief, youth and maturity, joy and sarcasm; the smile of a girl-woman who knew the absurdity of what we were doing, the anachronism and unreality of our trying to relive the Bible in the midst of the twentieth century—knew it and laughed at it, loved it and gave herself to it unreservedly. She waved and smiled, and her smile bespoke the barely audible words "C'est une vie de chameau."

It was the last time we saw her alive. Two hours later, as we dug at the eroded embankment of the wadi in the Star, picking out the roots of some overhanging shrubs, we heard a shot, and then another, coming from the direction of the Gap. Puzzled, we gathered up our tools and rifles, and drove our cart back through the pass. We found Barbara lying in the dry grass, shot dead in broad daylight, almost within sight of our camp. She probably never saw her assailants. The Bedouin marauders who had ambushed her without warning drove away the flock, and simply vanished into the desert.

Years later, after many exhortations, friendly Bedouin finally revealed the assassins' identity and their reason for the attack. Some time earlier an army contingent had driven off Bedouin who had been grazing in a nearby area without authorization, and the soldiers had confiscated some of the Bedouin's flocks. The contingent then stopped briefly at our settlement on its way back north, and although we had nothing to do with the incident, the Bedouin suspected strongly that we had received and accepted their sheep. Unfortunately, too, Barbara was dressed in khaki trousers and wore a cap. To the Bedouin she looked like a man, and a soldier at that. According to the law of the desert, she was fair target.

Inadvertently and unaware, we were thus caught up in the grim, ancient rivalry over possession of grazing land and water rights, a rivalry as old as the history of man in the desert. Witness, for example, the story of Isaac as related in the Book of Genesis:

> And Isaac dwelt in Gerar [in the northern Negev]. And Isaac sowed in that land, and obtained in that year a hundredfold, and the Lord blessed him.

A Bedoui woman and her child, seeming as lonely and forlorn in the empty desert as Hagar and Ishmael were more than three millennia ago.

... And he had possession of flocks, and possession of herds, and a great household, and the Philistines envied him. Now all the wells which his father's servants had digged in the days of Abraham his father, the Philistines stopped them, and filled them with earth. ... And Isaac's servants digged in the nahal [the Hebrew word for a creek or wadi] and found there a well of living water. And the herdmen of Gerar quarreled with Isaac's herdmen, saying: "The water is ours!" And he called the name of the well Esek [contest] because they contested with him. And they digged another well, and they contested over that one also. And he called the name of it Sitnah [hatred]. And he moved from thence, and digged yet another well, and they contested not over it. And he called the name of it Rehoboth [meaning spaciousness] and he said: "For now the Lord hath made room for us, and we shall be fruitful in the land. And he went up from thence to Beersheba . . . and pitched his tent there; and there Isaac's servants also digged a well. (Genesis 26:6, 12–23, 25.)

Nowhere is the importance of water in the desert expressed more succintly, except perhaps in the poignant story of the banishment and loneliness of Hagar and Ishmael:

> And Abraham arose early in the morning, and took bread and a container of water, and gave it unto Hagar, putting it on her shoulder, and the child, and sent her away; and she departed, and strayed in the wilderness of Beersheba. And the water in the container was spent, and she cast the child under one of the shrubs. And she went and sat down opposite a good way off . . . for she said: "let me not look upon the death of the child." And . . . she lifted up her voice and she wept. . . . And God opened her eyes, and she saw a well of water; and she went, and filled the container with water, and gave the lad to drink. And God was with the lad, and he grew; and he dwelt in the wilderness of Paran, and became an archer. (Genesis 21:14–20).

The Negev was a harsh and hostile country of thirst and heat and fatal rivalry even then. To live rather than perish, on the thin edge of survival, Ishmael had to become an archer.

13

Tides and Ebbs of Civilization

> With the ancient is wisdom
> And in length of days understanding.
> Job 12:12

The history of human habitation in the Negev is a long sequence of tides and ebbs. Civilizations, one after another, rose and fell, blossomed and then withered, developed and later declined or were destroyed. A new and growing civilization would establish villages and towns. It would learn to manage its environment, to husband land and water, to mine and utilize minerals, to raise and graze livestock, to provide a livelihood for its people, to maintain security against invaders, and to engineer and build appropriate structures.

Then, its apogee reached, the civilization would sink back. Perhaps, its energy or innovative vitality spent, the civilization would succumb to internal decay. Perhaps some unforeseen internal contradiction—social, political, or religious—would weaken its fabric. Possibly, too, mismanagement of resources would gradually bring about self-destruction. The decline might also result from some totally uncontrollable change in external circumstances or, as has happened altogether too often in the course of human history, from some sudden disaster wreaked by hostile forces.

Whatever the reason, states and cities would be abandoned, temples and monuments would crumble, marketplaces would decay, populations would disappear. Where multitudes once gathered, stillness would reign, and the dust of decades or centuries would accumulate. Yet, even during the ebb, a new force would gather to begin the cycle once more, to build anew, and perhaps on a higher level, on the foundations of the old.

The tidal sequence of rises and descents has governed the course of civilization in the Negev, it seems, since history began. One important factor was the existence, or lack, of centralized control over the region as a whole. As long as a civilization could maintain an organized authority, the Negev could be inhabited by a stable, sedentary population, and it could be made productive. Whenever central authority was disrupted, however, nomads from the surrounding deserts would swarm in and seize the land. Undisciplined and mindless at first, they would destroy, or neglect to maintain, the vital works of soil and water conservation built by their predecessors. Their flocks would overgraze and abuse the land, and the region would revert to a state of desolation. In time the nomads would be driven out or, as happened repeatedly, they would become sedentary, learn the ways of husbandry, and become industrious enough to establish a more or less stable new civilization. Yet even these nomads-turned-settlers would eventually succumb, perhaps centuries later, to new invasions by empire builders from afar or by desert hordes from nearby.

Viewed graphically, the history of the Negev forms a saw-toothed line of steep rises and even steeper descents representing the passing parade of successive civilizations. Each had the vitality to thrive for a while in the austere desert, and the good fortune to be allowed to do so in relative peace. And each was, in its turn, reduced to heaps of ruins testifying mutely to past glories and sad endings.

Since time immemorial the Negev has been a crossroads of trade and traffic between continents. The advantages of controlling the region, however, were often offset by the disadvantages. The very routes that made possible profitable trade and opened up the cultivable areas of the Negev to civilized settlement in times of peace were the ones followed by warring invaders. It is obvious, therefore, that only a strong authority that could preserve peace throughout the region could develop the Negev's resources. Thus, to the difficulties posed by the lack of water, the erodible soil, and the destructible vegetation was added the requirement of constant vigilance against the ever-present danger of encroachment by hostile forces.

Six millennia or more have passed since the dawn of human civilization in the Negev. Was the region always the same? Were the periodic rises and declines of civilizations always and entirely due to human factors, or were there changes in climate that might have made the Negev less arid and more hospitable at certain eras than at others? Climatic changes have been postulated by some popular writers to explain the alternating course of the Negev history. However, the assumption that climatic changes during the course of the Negev's civilized history were of such severity and duration as to make the maintenance of continuous civilization impossible provides an easy but largely unsubstantiated explanation of historical events.

To be sure, climatic changes or fluctuations do occur in desert regions as well as elsewhere. Periods of relatively abundant rainfall often alternate with periods of drought lasting perhaps several seasons. The Bible makes repeated and frequent references to periods of hunger and periods of plenty ("lean" years and "fat" ones). Apart from the random seasonal variation of rainfall, there may have been long-term cyclic changes. The mere absence of exact data does not permit us to rule out the possibility that such climatic cycles may have had some bearing on history.

Meteorological records are still too recent to indicate the possible existence of long-term cycles of rainfall, though these records do show appreciable variations. Annual rainfall in Jerusalem at the turn of this century appears to have been consistently higher than at midcentury. Indirect evidence has also been sought in the fluctuations of the Dead Sea shoreline. The Dead Sea has in fact contracted considerably in recent decades, its water level having dropped by several meters, but this is partly, and perhaps primarily, the result of the increased use of irrigation water in the streams feeding that lake (that is, the Jordan River and its tributaries). Tree ring studies made in California on ancient sequoias reveal evidence of some long-term fluctuations in ring width (presumed to correspond to rainfall fluctuations), but similar studies attempted on local trees or woody shrubs do not carry us back sufficiently far to resolve the problem of the Negev's climatic history.

It appears to us that such climatic fluctuations as must have taken place in historical time were, in all likelihood, of a minor nature. While it is true that in a marginal region even small changes in rainfall can be important, the overwhelming body of evidence indicates that there has been no fundamental change in the climate of the Negev in the last two or three millennia. The region we know today seems to be essentially the same as it was in the days of Abraham and Moses, the Nabateans and the Byzantines. The landscape features and the desert climate are permanent in the historic (though certainly not in the geologic) scale of time.

The remnants of dikes, conduits, and cisterns testify that the settlers of the Negev in ancient times had to contend with a water shortage as acute as that which we know at present (otherwise, they would not have had to devote such an enormous amount of effort to the construction of elaborate water conservation works). In fact, where ancient diversions and dikes have been restored in recent years, they have proved to be as functional now as they must have been originally. Modern archeological techniques, based on the identification of pottery fragments, have made possible the dating of ancient sites with a fair degree of accuracy. Accordingly, many sites were found to have flourished during the very period when other sites nearby lay unoccupied (the latter often showing evidence of violent sacking by enemies). If a diminution in the regional rainfall had caused agriculture to fail at some sites, how could the land continue to sustain crops at neighboring sites within the same climatic zone?

On balance, therefore, it appears that forces that shaped the history of civilization in the Negev, as elsewhere, were more often related to changes in the human, rather than the strictly physical, environment. The human drama is a primary determinant of the fortunes and misfortunes of history. Economic, social, religious, technologic, military, and ethnographic changes brought about in the course of the incessant internal striving of each tribe and nation, and their mutual cooperation or conflict, shape the history of whole countries and regions, and alone provide sufficient reason for the rise and fall of entire societies.

The long procession of civilized human history in the Negev begins, as far as we can discern most readily, during the late Chalcolithic Age, toward the end of the fourth millennium B.C. (between 3500 and about 3150 B.C.). The Chalcolithic, which followed the Neolithic Age and preceded the Bronze

One of numerous rock drawings found in the Negev highlands. The figures were scratched into the dark manganese oxide coating ("desert patina" or "varnish") of an exposed limestone boulder. From the secondary development of desert varnish on the drawings, one can judge the drawings to be many hundreds of years old. This drawing depicts a hunting scene in which two hunters shoot arrows at a herd of fleeing ibexes, which are simultaneously being chased by spirited dogs.

Age, was characterized by the use of both copper and stone tools. The people of the period lived in villages of mud houses and were definitely sedentary cultivators and herders. The excavations conducted by Jean Perrot near Beersheba unearthed a Chalcolithic settlement in which fired pottery and carved ivory figures, in addition to copper tools and weapons, were found. The copper industry that existed in the Beersheba area was most probably supplied with ore brought from the Arava Valley or the mountains of Edom. The Chalcolithic dwellings in the Beersheba area were mainly dug into the loessial ground. (Similar subterranean dwellings, incidentally, have been used by Bedouin until quite recently.) The Chalcolithic Negevites stored their grain in plastered pits and apparently kept flocks of sheep.

The Beersheba Plain appears to have been the most densely populated subregion during the Chalcolithic Age, though small settlement sites of the period have been identified in the central, as well as the northern, Negev. We know little about the type of desert agriculture that the people of this period practiced, because the remnants of their constructions, if any, evidently were obliterated by subsequent agricultural civilizations. In the Beersheba area itself, they may have practiced a form of extensive, if somewhat marginal, rain-fed farming. In the highlands, however, we may only surmise that they grazed, and perhaps cultivated, the wadi bottoms.

We do not know exactly what brought an end to the Chalcolithic civilization in the Negev. In any event, there seems to have ensued a lapse in the history of civilization in our region that lasted for much of the third millennium B.C. The next stage in the settlement of the Negev belongs to the Early Bronze II period, approximately 2900 to 2700 B.C. A fairly large city, extending over an area of about 10 hectares (25 acres), was established in Arad. The city was fortified by a semicircular wall with protruding towers, and the water supply was based on the collection of rainwater into a central pool. Numerous storage structures indicate that the inhabitants engaged in agriculture, and the presence of Egyptian pottery (in addition to the local product) suggests either trade with Egypt or Egyptian rule over the region during this period.

A new civilization arose, primarily in the northern highlands, between the twenty-first and nineteenth centuries B.C., a period known as Middle Bronze I (abbreviated MBI). Numerous settlements of this period have been discovered. Typically they are circular enclosures built of stone that apparently served to shelter humans, who might have lived in tents, as well as animals (probably sheep and goats). Nelson Glueck, in his book *Rivers in the Desert*, equates the MBI period with that of the Hebrew patriarchs (Abraham, Isaac, and Jacob). The Book of Genesis describes the seminomadic lives of the patriarchs in fascinating and vivid detail. It depicts the northern Negev as a land where large flocks were grazed, wells were dug, and grain was sown and harvested. Glueck further speculates that the destruction of this period's settlements was due to the aggressive incursion of the kings of the East, as related in the fourteenth chapter of Genesis. However, Yochanan Aharoni, in a more recent publication (1979), disputes Glueck's hypothesis.

The next period of habitation in the Negev is that of the Hyksos (Middle Bronze II), during which fortified emplacements were built in the coastal area and in the western Negev, which apparently served to control the northern approaches to (and from) Sinai and Egypt.

The Negev comes into prominence in the Bible once again in connection with the wanderings of the tribes of Israel, after their exodus from Egypt (during the thirteenth century B.C.). Unable to take the short route along the coast of the Mediterranean because of the mighty fortifications there (which the Bible attributes to the Philistines), the Israelites under Moses tried to penetrate northward through the central Negev. The Book of Numbers, chapter 13, relates how Moses sent spies to gather intelligence before attempting to penetrate the Promised Land. Ten of the dozen spies were so intimidated by the mighty cities they saw that they advised against any campaign of attack; their advice, alas, went unheeded. The Israelites suffered a humiliating defeat at the hands of the Canaanite king of Arad, and their hopes of gaining quick entry into the Promised Land were shattered. They were forced to retreat into Sinai and the southern Negev, the regions surrounding Kadesh Barnea (now generally acknowledged to be Ein Kudeirat, a perennial spring just west of the present-day Sinai-Negev border).

Eventually the Israelites bypassed the northern Negev completely by circling around it, through the southern Negev, the Arava Valley, and alongside the Kingdom of Edom, finally gaining entry into Canaan by crossing the Jordan River near Jericho. By all biblical accounts the wandering tribes of Israel must have spent some years in the southern Negev, and very probably in the central Negev as well, both of which subregions were apparently unoccupied by any sedentary population at the time. (The Amalekites, with whom the Israelites waged a bitter and protracted war, were, like them, nomads.)

The Israelite settlement of the Negev began during the Late Bronze Age, apparently after their conquest of Canaan, under the leadership of Joshua, in the latter part of the thirteenth century B.C. Extensive remains indicate that the Israelite settlements of this period were denser than those of all preceding periods, and included a network of strategically located fortifications. Of these, the large fort found at Beersheba is the most noteworthy. Its length was 50 meters, and it had a double wall. The northern and central parts of the Negev were then in the domain of the tribe of Simeon. This tribe is often portrayed as being too weak to have survived independently, and to have been assimilated into the stronger tribe of Judah. In the light of recent findings, however, the tribe of Simeon now appears to have been both vigorous and industrious.

It seems that the conquest of Canaan did not happen all at once, nor perhaps in a single generation. The Israelites, divided as they were into separate

Jebel Musa, believed by some to be Mount Sinai, viewed from below.

(and often squabbling) tribes that only seldom united for concerted action, had difficulty subduing the strong Canaanite cities controlling the fertile valleys in the north. Hence the Israelites were relegated for some time to the marginal lands in the Judean, Samarian, and Galilean hills, as well as in the northern and central Negev. To those who came out of the utterly desolate Sinai, those parts of the Negev may not have seemed so forbidding.

The Israelite occupation of the Negev became much more intensive during the Iron Age, corresponding to the period of the Judean Kingdom (end of the tenth century to the beginning of the sixth century B.C.). King David occupied the Negev, but it was his son and successor, Solomon, who really turned his sights southward and made the occupation effective. The Judean kings maintained villages, fortresses, and trade routes throughout the Negev, and linked Judea with the copper mines of the Arava Valley and with the seaport of Elath (Etzion Geber) on the Red Sea. During the Judean period the principal sites were strongly fortified with massive stone walls, sloping revetments, and guard towers, and were located strategically on commanding hilltops, at major crossroads, and near the main sources of water supply.

The traditional archenemies of the Israelites were the Philistines in the west and the Amalekites in the south. The Philistines apparently originated in the eastern Mediterranean islands, and invaded the southern coast of Canaan from the sea. They had already entered the Iron Age while the peoples of Canaan (including the Israelites) were still in the Bronze Age. With their overwhelming technical superiority, based on the use of iron tools and weapons, even chariots (the ancient equivalents of tanks), they terrorized the tribes that

A tel (mound), one of several sites of ancient cities in the northern Negev.

dwelt in the lowlands and foothills. The Israelites therefore retreated into the rugged mountains of Judea and Samaria, where the horse-drawn chariots were ineffective and where skill in archery and cunning use of the steep terrain gave the mountaineers (which the Israelites had perforce become) an advantage over the plainsmen.

Nevertheless, the Philistines kept the upper hand as long as they were able to maintain their metallurgical advantage. The First Book of Samuel, chapter 13, tells the story:

> Now there was no smith found throughout all the Land of Israel, for the Philistines said: "Lest the Hebrews make them swords or spears." So all the Israelites had to go down to the Philistines, to sharpen every man his plowshare, and his spade, and his axe, and his mattock. And the price of the filing was a pim for the mattocks, and for the coulters, and the forks with three teeth, and for the axes, and to set the goads. So it came to pass in the day of battle that there was neither sword nor spear found in the hand of any of the people that were with Saul and Jonathan (Samuel I 13:19–22).

The predicament of the Israelites ended when the Philistines' monopoly and their power were broken in the days of King Saul's Judean successors, David and Solomon. Nevertheless, it is interesting to note that the Kingdom of Judea, even after subduing the Philistines, never controlled the Mediterranean seacoast effectively. No Judean seaports were active there (except Jaffa, in later times). This was in marked contrast with the Judeans' northern neighbors, the Phoenicians, whom the Bible called the Tyrians and Sidonites (after their principal cities, Tyre and Sidon). Instead of turning westward to the Mediterranean, the Kingdom of Judea, as if obeying an ancestral call, turned itself southward, toward the Negev and the Red Sea. Solomon, who built the Red Sea port of Elath and may have exploited the Aravah Valley copper deposits, would have had to establish firm control over the entire Negev to keep travel and trade routes open and secure. Several of his successors, including Asa, Jehoshaphat, and Uzziah, took a continuing interest in the Negev. Of the latter king, the Second Book of Chronicles mentioned as a major achievement that he "built towers in the wilderness and hewed out many cisterns."

The First Book of Kings tell us that Jehoshaphat "made ships to go to Ophir for gold; but they went not, for the ships were broken at Etzion-Geber." To this day that same place (modern Elath) is noted for its sudden and treacherous northerly winds, which make sailing there most hazardous, particularly by those who are not experienced seafarers. An even more interesting story concerning Jehoshaphat described the sudden appearance, seemingly miraculous, of flash floods in the desert (II Kings, 3):

> Now Mesha the king of Moab was a sheep-master, and he paid tribute to the king of Israel the wool of a hundred thousand lambs, and of a hundred thousand rams. But when Ahab died, the king of Moab rebelled against the king of Israel. And King Jehoram went out of Samaria at that time, and mustered all Israel. And he beseeched Jehoshaphat the king of Judah, saying: "The king of Moab hath rebelled against me; wilt thou go with me against Moab to do battle?" And he said: "I will go up; I am as thou art, my people as thy people, my horses as thy horses." And he said: "Which way shall we go up?" And he answered: "The way of the wilderness of Edom." So the king of Israel and the king of Judah and the king of Edom went, and they made a circuit of seven days' journey, and there was no water for the host, nor for the beasts under them. And the king of Israel said: "Alas! for the Lord hath called these three kings together to deliver them into the hand of Moab." But Jehoshaphat said: "Is there not a prophet of the Lord?" . . . So the kings went to the prophet Elisha. . . . And Elisha said: "Bring me a minstrel." And when the minstrel played . . . he said: "Make this stream bed abound with water holes. For thus said the Lord: Ye shall not see wind, neither shall ye see rain, yet that stream shall be filled with water, and ye shall drink together with your beasts." And it came to pass in the morning . . . that, behold, there came water from the direction of Edom, and the country was filled with water.

There follows a description of a terrible battle, in which the cruel wrath of the victors was wreaked as much upon the land, its vegetation, and its water resources, as upon its inhabitants.

The Judean-age fortresses in the Negev were constructed of heavy, rough-hewn stones, and were often located above fertile creek beds in which terrace remains are clearly discernible. Though it is difficult to establish incontrovertibly the correspondence between these fortresses and the nearby agricultural works (since there are no exact dating criteria for agricultural structures, and often the works of one period are found superimposed upon those of an earlier one), it is unreasonable to assume otherwise.

We cannot doubt that the Judean-age settlements practiced desert agriculture based on techniques for channeling and utilizing runoff water, since there could be no other way to sustain so extensive a network of settlements. The fortified emplacements were probably surrounded by open villages of mud houses or tents, the inhabitants of which withdrew into the fortified confines when an attack was imminent. Unlike the sites of earlier civilizations, the Judean constructions were not confined to the vicinity of springs or of shallow groundwater sources that could be tapped by wells. Rather, they occurred in many locations that could only have been supplied with water from cisterns — that is, artificial reservoirs filled periodically with water collected from the slopes or diverted from a creek.

We do not know just when the techniques of runoff utilization were invented. Such innovations as cistern excavation and wadi-bed terracing were quite obviously decisive in the history of the Negev, yet we cannot date them precisely. The early cisterns were undoubtedly crude and inefficient. Building efficient cisterns became possible only with the use of watertight plaster (which is difficult to make in the Negev, owing to lack of fuel for "burning" lime), the identification and location of suitable rock formations, and the proper construction of channels to collect and divert overland flow (surface runoff) during the infrequent rainstorms.

In any case, it is clear that these techniques were already fairly well developed by the time of King Uzziah, if the biblical account of his having "hewed out many cisterns" is at all believable. The evidence suggests that it is. Without cisterns many of the Judean settlements in the Negev would not have been possible. Springs, and proper locations for shallow wells, are few and far apart in the Negev highlands. Though used as settlement sites whenever possible (as in the case of Kadesh Barnea), they were not available in most places.

As mentioned earlier, the development of the Negev was not possible without a strong centralized authority able to maintain security and communications. The Kingdom of Judea fulfilled this function for nearly four centuries. It came to an abrupt end with the conquest of Judea and the destruction of Jerusalem by the Babylonians early in the sixth century B.C. The situation in the Negev during that desperate period is depicted in the letters written to and about Eliashiv, the Judean commander and administrator of the Negev at the time. These letters, found in Arad, were inscribed on small tablets of clay. They include a particularly poignant note from the Judean king, probably King Jehoachaz, calling upon the garrison in the Negev to mobilize. These extraordinary documents were described and interpreted by Aharoni (1979).

I remember, on one hot summer day in the late 1950s, while on a field excursion with Aharoni, taking issue with him over the apparent role of the Judeans in developing the techniques for collecting and utilizing runoff in the Negev highlands. The prevalent view had been that the invention of these techniques was due almost entirely to the later Nabatean civilization. Aharoni was the first to discover the Judean antecedents, which were associated with houses, cisterns, and agricultural terraces, together constituting integrated units. I had the greatest respect for Aharoni, and yet the nationalistic implications of his discovery aroused my skepticism. Considering myself to be a consummate amateur archeologist (the only people in the Negev at the time who were not consummate amateur archeologists were the professional ones), I argued with him rather strongly. Aharoni, however, forgave my temerity and proceeded most patiently to show me the evidence. We visited three sites that day: the first at Mishor Haruach (Sahel el-Hawwa, "The Windy Plain," as the high plateau just north of the Ramon Crater was called by the Bedouin), the second at Ramat Matred (west of Ovdat), and the third on the Halukim Range (near Sdeh-Boker). In each case he showed me the characteristic Judean potsherds, and the incontrovertible association between the stone houses and the adjacent terraced farmland.

After the destruction of the Kingdom of Judah by the Babylonians, the Judeans were led into exile and their land was laid waste. Less than a century later some of the exiles returned to reestablish their state, but they were not strong enough to regain control of the Negev. The region remained outside the domain of the Judeans even after the rise of the Hasmoneans and the extension of Judean power over the territories east of the Jordan. Alexander Jannaeus (103–76 B.C.) penetrated south as far as Mampsis at the northern edge of the Negev highlands, but otherwise the Judean state of the Second Temple Era reached no further south than the foothills of the Hebron range.

The Negev, however, did not remain desolate for long. A new nation arose, seemingly out of nowhere, to build a magnificent civilization, the achievements of which excite the imagination and admiration of visitors to the Negev to this day. The new masters of the desert were the Nabateans ("Nabatu" in their own inscriptions), people who began as nomadic traders and in time became superb architects and engineers, as well as expert hydrologists and diligent cultivators. The Nabateans left few historical records, and we are thus dependent mainly on the descriptions of Greek and Roman writers. The earliest of these descriptions is by Diodorus (circa 300 B.C.), and it tells how Antigonus (one of the Greek generals who, after the death of their leader Alex-

The Qumran caves, where the Dead Sea Scrolls were discovered. The scrolls were written by the Essenes, a monastic Jewish sect that lived in the desert during the last century B.C. and the first century of the Christian era.

ander the Great, vied with their erstwhile comrades in arms over portions of the great new empire that Alexander had bequeathed them by his conquests) set out to plunder the country east of the Jordan. The Greek army penetrated the mountainous territory of the Nabateans, who hid their property and families on a "certain rock" (*petra* in Greek), probably the same place where the Nabateans later built their fabled capital, which came to be known as Petra.

We do not know for certain from whence the Nabateans derived. The early records refer to them as Arabs, suggesting that they came out of the Arabian Peninsula and seized control of the lands of Edom and Moab east of the Arava Valley. From there they expanded westward to the Negev and Sinai, and northward toward Syria. From aimless nomads the Nabateans became traders, then regular travelers through the Negev, then sojourners, and finally permanent colonizers.

The Nabatean domain lay astride the important ancient trade routes between Arabia in the south and Syria in the north, and between the Orient, including India, and the Mediterranean world. These were the routes along which camel caravans transported spices and silks, ivory and incense, myrrh and medicinal herbs—commodities as prized and as valuable in antiquity as

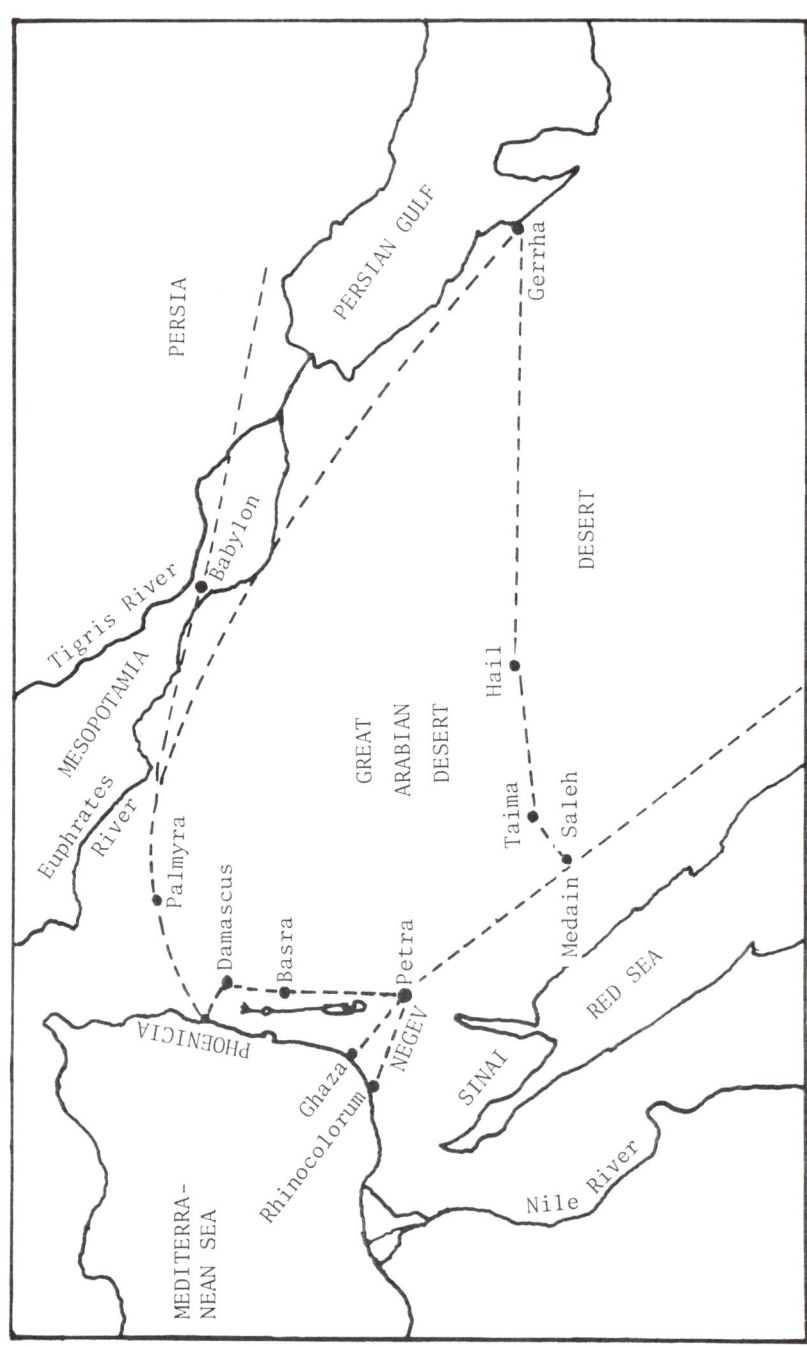

The main overland trading routes of western Asia in antiquity. The southern routes, through which spices and medicinal herbs of the Orient were conveyed to the Mediterranean, were controlled for several centuries by the Nabateans.

are perfumes, cosmetics, and drugs today. Spices were in fact even more highly regarded then than now, not merely because our taste in food has become blander than that of our forebears, but primarily because refrigeration and other means of food preservation that we take for granted were then unknown, and food could quickly become inedible without a heavy dosage of spice. In addition to the commodities listed, the Nabateans were reported to convey asphalt from the Dead Sea (called Mare Asphaltum by the Romans for the lumps of the material that were found floating on this lake from time to time) to Egypt, where it was used in the embalming process.

Two major alternative avenues of east-west commerce existed in antiquity, the northern and the southern; when one became insecure and declined, the other rose in prominence. The northern avenue linked Mesopotamia, through Palmyra, to Syria, Asia Minor, and Phoenicia on the Mediterranean coast. The southern avenue connected the Persian Gulf and southern Arabia, through the Negev, with the southeastern coast of the Mediterranean and with Egypt (via Sinai). It was this latter route that the Nabateans controlled and that, during their heyday, brought them great wealth.

Caravans passing through the desert needed stopping places where they might rest and obtain water and other provisions. To secure and supply their trade, the Nabateans therefore had to establish and maintain regularly spaced bases along their main routes, at important crossroads and convenient sources of water. These bases eventually grew into permanent, self-supporting villages and even towns, and the Negev became more densely populated than ever before. The principal Nabatean-established centers were Ovdat (Arabic name, Abdeh), Halutzah (Elusa), Shivta (Subeita), Mamshit or Mampsis (Kurnub), Nitzana (Nessana), and Rehovot (Ruheiba).

A population of many thousands, in several large centers and numerous small villages scattered throughout a large region, obviously could not be sustained, in the long run, solely by importing and transporting all vital commodities (including so voluminous and perishable a commodity as food). And thus, in addition to their trading and defensive tasks, the Nabateans perforce began to develop agriculture in order to ensure a livelihood for their people. In this task they were undoubtedly aided by the example of their predecessors, the Judeans. But the Nabateans excelled all previous efforts, and indeed developed the science, and art, of desert agriculture and of desert living in general to a degree that we find astonishing even today.

The glory of the Nabatean kingdom can be seen not only in the ruins of Petra, with its monumental facades of intricately carved sandstone, and not only in the foundations and ruins of the many towns they built throughout the Negev and the territories east of the Arava and the Jordan River, but also — and perhaps more impressively — in their extensive, carefully and expertly engineered and laboriously constructed, soil and water conservation works.

A partial view of ancient Petra, the Nabateans' capital, in the Idumean mountains (in what is today southern Jordan). The Nabateans carved ornate temples and palaces in the red sandstone cliffs, and many of these remain remarkably well preserved.

A detailed description of the Nabateans' political history, and of their architectural remains, was given by Israeli archeologist Avraham Negev (1972; 1979), who excavated several of their towns (including Ovdat and Mamshit) and made several important discoveries that have shed light upon their civilization. The story is interesting and rather complicated, and we need mention only a few of the details. The earliest Nabatean inscription, found by Woolley and Lawrence at Elusa, pertains to the period of King Aretas I, early in the second century B.C. The history of most of that century is obscure, but we know that the Nabateans at that time enjoyed friendly relations with the emerging Hasmonean dynasty of Judea. About 110 B.C., however, Aretas II became king of the Nabateans and began to press northward, toward the fertile region of southern Syria, a move that brought him into conflict with the Judean ruler, Alexander Janneaus. When the latter conquered the seaport of Gaza (a Nabatean trading outlet) and invaded 12 cities in the Nabatean-controlled province of Moab, the conflict became a war.

In 93 B.C. a decisive battle was fought between Alexander Janneaus and the new Nabatean king, Obodas I, in which the latter emerged victorious. This stopped the Hasmonean expansion to the east and opened the way to further Nabatean expansion northward. There ensued battles between the Nabateans and the Syrian Greeks then ruling Damascus, until another Nabatean victory was achieved under King Aretas III Philhellenos (87-62 B.C.). He conquered northern Trans-Jordan and southern Syria, and became ruler of Damascus at the request of its inhabitants. The title Philhellenos ("Lover of Greeks") was earned by Aretas III after he deliberately exposed his kingdom to Hellenistic culture, which eventually came to influence every branch of Nabatean art.

Their extraordinary synthesis of Greek and Semitic cultures may be part of the secret of the Nabateans' phenomenal success. Prior to the Greek influence, the Nabateans, who emerged from ancient Arabia and continued to worship their ancestral gods, quickly adopted the Aramaic script and language that was then the lingua franca of the entire region. Following the conquest of the region by Alexander the Great and his successors, the Nabateans accepted Greek writing, art, and science, and identified their ancient gods with those of the Greeks. They thus assimilated a new culture while retaining and enhancing their distinctive nationality. This adaptability to new influences, and eagerness to accept and apply the benefits of the science and technology of their times to their own special needs without losing their identity and separate ways, may have been a source of their strength and success, as is the case with the Japanese today.

Toward the middle of the first century B.C., the Romans arrived in the region. In 62 B.C., Scaurus, Pompey's general, devastated the surroundings of Petra, the Nabatean capital, but could not take this natural stronghold. However, the Nabateans were forced to pay tribute, and came under the hegemony of Rome. After their conquest of Egypt (25 B.C.), the Romans sent an expedition to seize the Nabatean trade routes in Arabia. They made the mistake, however, of inviting the wily Syllaeus, then minister and adviser to Nabatean King Obodas III, to serve as their chief guide. He deliberately led them astray, and those of the 10,000 Roman soldiers (including a contingent of Judean archers) who did not perish of thirst and disease in the desert straggled back empty-handed. For thus betraying the Romans to serve his people, Syllaeus was taken to Rome and executed.

Still another war was fought between the Nabateans and the Judeans, this time under the leadership of King Herod, in which the Nabateans were defeated. Their fortunes improved once again under King Aretas IV, who is described on coins and in inscriptions as "he who loved his people." According to Negev (1979), it was under Aretas IV that the Nabatean kingdom reached its zenith, economically as well as in architecture, sculpture, painting, and pottery. The decline set in during the reign of Malichus II (A.D. 40-70), with the loss of Damascus. So great, by now, was the enmity between the Judeans and the Nabateans that Malichus II actually sent an army to help Roman general Vespasian and his son Titus to quell the great Jewish insurrection and to destroy Jerusalem.

The ruins of a Byzantine church at Shivta. The Nabatean and Byzantine constructions are particularly remarkable for the extremely sparing use of mortar. Their artisans learned to shape and fit the stones together, and to employ arches, so as to build beautiful wall facings, behind which the wall space was filled with a mixture of rough-hewn stones and mud.

The loss of Damascus was less devastating to the Nabateans than the discovery by the Romans, some time in the first century of the Christian era, that the seasonal monsoon winds made it possible for them to sail through the Red Sea to India and back. They were thus able to trade directly for the coveted spices and aromatics, and to break the Nabatean trade monopoly. Soon after, as misfortune would have it, the Nabateans were invaded by another wave of nomads from Arabia, who destroyed Ovdat and the forts on the Petra-Gaza road.

Now the Nabateans had to face their greatest test of survival. Their lucrative role as caravan stations lost, were the Nabatean settlements in the Negev viable on their own? The last Nabatean king, Rabel II (70-106), is described on the coins and in inscriptions of his day as "he who brought life and deliverance to his people." This gives rise to the hypothesis (Negev 1979) that he earned his distinction by subjugating the invading Arab tribes and, even more important, emphasizing the improvement of desert farming practices, by which alone the Nabatean civilization could continue to thrive in the Negev. The Romans' annexation of the Nabatean kingdom (which they renamed Provincia Arabia), and their shift of the capital from Petra to Bozrah, did little to change the basic condition of the populace. Certainly there was no ethnic change, nor a significantly altered economy. To the Romans the Negev was merely a frontier province, but to the inhabitants (most of whom were Nabateans) it had become home, the very center and crux of a unique desert civilization. In the early part of the second century, Emperor Trajan ordered the construction of a new road from the Gulf of Aqaba to Syria, with a branch leading through the Negev to the Mediterranean. The same period also witnessed the construction of new monuments in Petra.

After the division of the Roman Empire in 330 and the establishment of Byzantium, the entire eastern realm of the empire, including the Negev, enjoyed great stability and prosperity. Strong central power and uniformity of religion and language eventually prevailed. The Christian Church became preeminent. Major churches were built in the towns, and monasteries were established in numerous locations, some far out in the desert. The Negev became even more densely populated, and the high technical achievements of the era surpassed even those of the Nabateans when they were independent. Yet, though they lost their traditional distinctiveness, the descendants of the first Nabateans remained, and continued to constitute the greater part of the populace. The principal towns and villages established by the original Nabateans remained intact through the Roman and Byzantine eras.

The grand scale and magnificence of the Byzantine constructions (churches, walled fortifications, bathhouses, dams, diversion dikes) are still very much in evidence; in some cases they have remained in a remarkable state of preservation. In other cases, alas, these structures have been dismantled and the stones carried off to serve in the construction of newer projects (for example, Gaza and Beersheba under the Turks), so that only the foundations remain. The Byzantines, in their day, were no more respectful of archeology. They, too,

A view of the partially restored ruins of Ovdat.

An ancient winepress.

cannibalized and nearly obliterated many of the structures of the earlier Nabateans, as the latter, in their own time, had done to the remains of the structures of their predecessors, the Judeans.

The eclipse of the Byzantine Golden age in the Negev came very abruptly in the seventh century. The rising tide of Islam swept over the entire region, submerging all in its wake. Following the Moslem conquest in 636, the tenacious desert cultivators tried to hold on to the way of life created by their ancestors. But within a few generations, with the disruption of the old order and of commerce, the population dwindled. Desert nomads (Bedouin) took over, and ushered in a long period of retrogression and poverty. Where thousands once prospered, a few hundred now eked out a bare subsistence. Magnificent monuments were pried apart, or crumbled gradually into haphazard heaps of stone, and thin black goats grazed among the ruins. Great cisterns were choked by dust, and strongly built dikes were loosened by time and left unrepaired in the face of destructive floods. Complete farm systems that needed only to be maintained, to be repaired when occasional damage occurred, were left untended and allowed to disintegrate. Overgrazing of the wadi bottoms caused erosion, so that some of the once-wide bands of watered land became narrow, gouged-out gullies. Terraces once green with crops were left high and dry while torrential floods rushed uncontrolled through breached dikes and scoured creeks. Thus, the sustained effort and experience of generations, and the excellent works of an ingenious and diligent people, were wasted by neglect and abuse born of ignorance or indifference.

The casual visitor to the Negev finds it difficult to understand how the ancients could have developed a civilization on such a grand scale in the midst of such barrenness and desolation and under such austere circumstances. Only a careful study of their techniques reveals how such large permanent communities could indeed live prosperously in such a region. That the Bedouin failed where their predecessors succeeded proves once again that only an organized society possessing great cultural and energy resources, as well as technical and administrative ability, can overcome the privations of the desert and triumph over seemingly insurmountable difficulties.

14

Catching and Storing Runoff

> Behold, I will do a new thing,
> Now it shall grow, shall ye not know it?
> I will even make a way in the wilderness,
> And rivers in the desert . . .
> To give drink to My chosen people
> Isaiah 43:19-20

The story of how the people of the Negev contended with their ungenerous environment is not a simple one. There never was a magic key, a simple formula, to draw water from the rock and make the desert blossom. Rather, it was by the cumulative experience of generations, based upon trial, error, careful observation, and antlike diligence that selected sites were made fit for and by self-sustaining communities. There were and are many different ways to gather, conserve, and utilize water in the desert, and those who made it their home were — as, indeed, they had to be — versatile. They employed every means at their disposal to ensure and increase their supply of water, and were undeterred, it seems, by the amount of labor involved.

The major source of water in the Negev, as we have already pointed out, has always been the surface runoff of winter rains. Runoff can be gathered in either of two ways: directly — by intercepting and concentrating the water trickling off the slopes, before that water reaches the natural creek beds and accumulates to form a flood; and indirectly — by trapping or diverting the natural floods after they have formed.

The use of runoff for the irrigation of crops will be elucidated in a subsequent chapter. In the present one we shall describe the collection and storage of runoff in cisterns, which are artificially constructed reservoirs of potable water, filled by directing surface flows during rainstorms.

Cisterns are a common and time-honored means of supplying water to humans and livestock throughout the Near East. The city of Jerusalem, for instance, was sustained for many centuries by underground cisterns, hewn in the bedrock and fed by runoff from roofs, courtyards, and streets. Though cisterns were not unique to the Negev, they were, nevertheless, absolutely essential there. Without cisterns the establishment of numerous and dense settlements along the trade routes and throughout the Negev highlands would have been impossible, and the region could not have been made to sustain tens of thousands of permanent inhabitants together with their livestock. In many of the ancient villages and towns, some of which were built on hilltops and quite far from any perennial sources of water (springs or wells), there was a cistern in nearly every house. While many of the ancient cisterns are choked with debris and have not been used for centuries, the surprising fact is that some have remained serviceable to this very day, and apparently have been in continuous use for something like 2,000 years.

The earliest cisterns were probably imitations of natural waterholes, which are hollows in the beds or banks of wadis where small pools or puddles of water remain after each flood. The desert dwellers must have discovered quite early that they could obtain some water, at least for a short time, by simply digging or chiseling small pits or depressions in places where runoff accumulated naturally. Such cisterns were obviously inefficient, because they were subject to rapid seepage and evaporation losses. In time, therefore, the inhabitants of the Negev had to learn how to line the walls and bottoms of their artificial water holes with close-fitting stones, plastered watertight with lime. We do not know exactly when such watertight cisterns were developed, though it is known that the technique of "burning" lime to make cement and plaster was discovered as early as the fourth millennium B.C.

Among the earliest of the cisterns found in the Negev are the open-pit cisterns. Apparently dating back to the time of the Judean kings, these were built by digging a roughly hemispherical pit in the soft marl to a depth of 4-5 meters, then lining it with stones and constructing steps leading down to the bottom. Water was directed off a hillside via a single channel or several converging ones to a stilling basin, where some of the silt would settle out, allowing the partly cleared water to enter the cistern. Big boulders were arranged around the lip of the cistern to form a protective circle and to prevent the sediment-laden "fresh" runoff water from flowing directly into the cistern without depositing at least some of the sediment in the stilling basin, which needed to be cleaned out periodically. To prevent pollution, minimize evaporation, and maintain safety, it must have been necessary to cover the open-pit cisterns with some sort of roofing. However, whether planks or branches or cloth forming a tent (we do not know for sure), such roofing could not have been very effective. Nor could the simple procedure of lining the bottom and sides with stones, and plastering over them with lime, form a truly seepage-proof seal.

The next advance in cistern construction involved the technique of cutting and quarrying into bedrock. Nearly all of the ancient cisterns in the Negev that are still serviceable were excavated sideways into the exposed rock formations of the hillsides, their roofs, walls, and floors formed of the bedrock itself. Wherever possible, the cistern makers of antiquity shunned the fissured, hard limestone formations, in which quarrying was difficult and repeated heavy plastering was necessary to seal the cracks. Instead, they chose the soft chalk and marl formations, easy to cut into and naturally impervious. In the process of learning how to build cisterns, they had to study the geology as well as the hydrology of their region.

Some of the ancient cisterns, cut in bedrock, are very well preserved and amazing to behold. They vary in capacity from several cubic meters to several thousand. The larger ones are huge underground halls, perfectly dimensioned, with smooth walls and with pillars to support the overburden of the rock ceiling above. Crawling into a rock-hewn cistern through one of its narrow openings, the visitor is immediately made aware of the extreme difference between the sun-seared, dry, hot exterior and the dim, dank, cool interior.

An early cistern, probably of the Israelite period.

Catching & Storing Runoff

The floor is often covered with a thick mantle of silt that the Negev dwellers of old must have had to clean out periodically.

To minimize evaporation, each cistern was generally given only two openings: one for water to enter and one for water to be withdrawn. Runoff was directed to the cistern via collection channels, which often led to a stilling basin, the overflow of which entered the cistern proper. The opening for the withdrawal of water was often marked by grooves, cut into the stone facing of the hole by the repeated friction of the sliding ropes that served to raise brimming jars of life-giving water.

Where cisterns were situated along the rim of a natural watercourse, they were filled directly with the floodwater, rather than with runoff collected from the slopes through constructed channels. In some places one can still find the ancient water troughs, rock-hewn, where caravans and flocks quenched their salt-aggravated thirst and washed off the desert dust. Hillside cisterns are clearly discernible landmarks. A typical one resembles a giant necklace, with the glistening white pile of excavated rock hanging as a pendant from the two collection channels which ring the hill and curve down its sides from opposite directions, like strings of beads.

To the parched traveler of old, to whom these cisterns would beckon from afar, no sight could be more gladdening.

In the early years of Sdeh-Boker, we sought ways to develop the desert range by flood-irrigating and reseeding the bottomlands, and to pasture livestock on the improved range. Because of the sparse and seasonal nature of the vegetation, and its spotty rather than continuous spatial distribution, it was obvious from the start that each flock or herd would have to wander many miles from home base. Hence, we wished to prepare secondary bases in a number of possible grazing centers, complete with corrals for livestock and camping facilities for the herdsmen. The first requirement, obviously, would be water, which must be available at each camping site and within each section of the territory to be grazed.

We therefore undertook to survey the old cisterns and to renovate as many of them as possible. Aided by aerial photographs, we walked the hills and valleys in search of usable cisterns, and were able to locate about 40 within a radius of 10 kilometers from the settlement. Some could be seen from afar and were easy to identify, while others were so well blended into the landscape that they could be identified only at the site itself. Most were rather small cisterns, but a few were very large and resembled the pillared halls of some legendary underground kingdom. Hardly any of the cisterns we found held water, and many were choked with a deposition of dust and silt. To restore the old cisterns, we would have to clean them out, repair their collection channels and stilling basins, and plaster their cracked walls. It would be laborious, we knew, but worthwhile, for the total capacity of the cisterns in the vicinity of

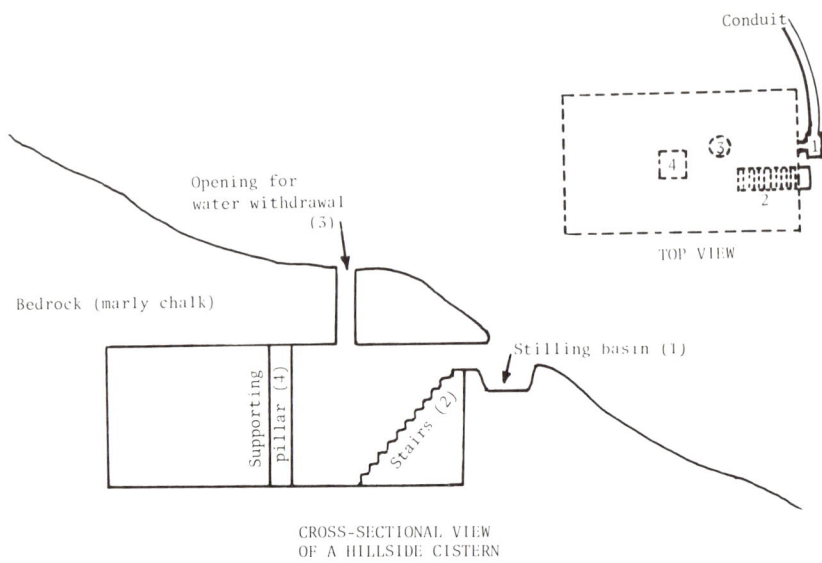

Schematic cross-sectional plan and top view of a hillside cistern. The excavators used hand chisels and pickaxes, marks of which can be discerned on the walls of ancient cisterns. A central pillar was often left intact (or built) to help support the cistern's roof.

our settlement could suffice for all our foreseeable needs, if indeed we were to live on the land and raise livestock as originally envisaged.

So a team of us began to clean out and repair the ancient cisterns. Day after day we hauled ladders, buckets, ropes, and shovels from one cistern to another. We crawled into the dark and dank interior of a long-abandoned cistern, unvisited by man for perhaps a thousand years or more, and spent the whole day digging out the accumulated debris of all those years, layer by layer. From time to time, we surprised a family of bats, or caught a snake that had fallen into the cistern's narrow opening. It was in the course of this work that I first caught specimens of two highly venomous snakes, until then not known to be present in the Negev highlands (namely, *Walterinnesia aegyptiaca*, a relative of the cobra, and the smaller but even more dangerous *Atractaspis engeddensis*).

Unfortunately, our work was stopped by an unexpected and seemingly unrelated event: the decision by Israel's founding father, Prime Minister David Ben-Gurion, to resign from the government and join Sdeh-Boker. He evidently intended to participate in our settlement's original task, which was to discover, develop, and subsist on the region's own resources. His presence, however, changed the character of the settlement. An out-of-the-way and out-of-mind frontier spot suddenly became the focus of great attention, and the

A channel leading runoff water to a series of cisterns hewn into the chalky bedrock of the hill on the left.

country's institutions vied for the privilege of lavishing their favors upon it. Was water a problem? The Water Authority was now only too willing to supply water by pipeline from the north. Never mind the great distance or the cost.

Soon the tractors came. Across the hills and valleys, regardless of obstacles, they dug a trench and laid a black pipe within it. And lo, within a few months water was a problem no more. Where a small container was once the sole source of water and the precious fluid was used ever so sparingly, faucets could now be turned on at will. No longer did the territory and its wadis and cisterns seem to matter so much, and the back-breaking task of restoring old cisterns became irrelevant. Eventually the settlement, inside its fenced confines, was planted with ornamental trees, shrubs, and lush lawns, and became isolated from the surrounding bare desert, which now served only as a picturesque backdrop.

The misgivings came only later. At the time the arrival of the pipeline seemed an unqualified blessing, a true cause for celebration. So we invited our good neighbors, the friendly Bedouin, to share in our joy. The climax of the ceremony was to be the turning of the tap to start the sprinklers. At the crucial, dramatic moment, the sprinklers burst forth with glistening jets of Jordan River water brought from incredibly far away, shooting it into the clear desert air "for the first time" (as the Israelis never tired of joking) "in two thousand years."

An old Bedoui sheikh, befuddled at all the strange gadgetry, deaf to all the highblown speeches, was suddenly caught in the swirl of water. And there he stood, amid the streams flying all about, his beard and nose dripping and his flowing robes drenched; there he stood, sheepishly, not knowing how to evade the missiles of water shooting at him from all directions. Finally the hapless old sheikh mustered a resigned and kindly smile as he blurted out: "W'Allah el Azim, hada'l mattar min el ard!" (Great God, this rain is coming up from the earth!). We all laughed together then, and in an instant we plunged in to stand there with him, clapping hands and dancing to the rhythm of the pulsating water in a display of joyful amity.

If the use of cisterns as a major source of water in the Negev seems—for the moment, at least—to have been superseded by the importation of water pumped and piped from afar, there still remains the proven fact that the old cisterns can, if necessary, be made operational just as they were in ancient times. And what with the increasing pressure of population and economic development, and the increasingly acute shortages of water and energy, the principle of storing runoff water in cisterns remains a sound one that may yet become economically feasible once again. More is involved than a few hundred quaint old water holes—more, even, than the development of a specific region. The ultimate global question is whether runoff collection and storage in cisterns can be practiced on a wide scale in various arid regions.

If we were to build new cisterns in an arid region, we would certainly wish to benefit from the experience of our predecessors, yet chances are we would employ different methods. Finding the appropriate rock formation, then excavating into it by hand, no longer seems practical. A modern cistern may bear little resemblance to the old ones. It may consist of a large basin, either natural or artificially formed by earth-moving machinery. The sides and bottom of such a basin can be lined with plastic sheeting to prevent seepage. The more difficult problem in the desert is the prevention, or at least substantial reduction, of evaporation. Monomolecular films, formed from such substances as hexadecanol, though much touted some years ago, are easily broken by wind and become ineffective on extensive open bodies of water. Floating rafts or beads of styrofoam have been tried, and various other techniques are under investigation. For the time being, however, the simplest answer seems to be filling the reservoir with coarse gravel or stones. This will effectively minimize evaporation—but also reduce the storage volume by as much as 60 percent. Perforated pipes can be laid at the bottom of the reservoir, and water can be drawn either by pumping or by gravity, depending on the topography.

Such ideas await implementation not only in the Negev but also in many other drought-stricken regions, such as the Sahel in sub-Saharan Africa.

15

Harvesting Runoff from Hillsides

> As cold water to a thirsty soul,
> So is good news from a far country.
> Proverbs 25:25

In the Negev highlands 80 percent to 90 percent of the area consists of bare, rocky hills. During intense and heavy downpours the fraction of rainfall trickling off the slopes as runoff may be as high as 30 percent, but such events are rare in the desert. As a "normal" seasonal average, natural runoff yield does not generally exceed 15 percent of total rainfall, and in seasons with small rainstorms it may be less than 5 percent. We use the agricultural term "yield" deliberately, since the desert dweller of ancient times actually harvested his supply of water from the slopes, depending almost entirely on runoff to fill his cisterns and to irrigate his terraced fields, which were invariably located in bottomlands and wadi beds. But with rainfall so sporadic and variable, how could runoff be a dependable source of water for a large population?

We know that, at least by the time of the Nabateans and Byzantines, the Negev dwellers did more than merely gather natural runoff—they actually devised an ingenious method to induce more of it, by clearing the stones off the slopes and thus smoothing the surface and exposing the finer soil to facilitate the formation of a self-sealing crust (Tadmor et al. 1958; Hillel 1959).

Among the most conspicuous, and for a time most puzzling, of the ancient remains in the Negev are the countless heaps, mounds, and strips of gravel found on many hillsides, particularly in the vicinity of the old towns of Shivta, Ovdat, and Nitzana. Aerial photographs show that the areas with gravel mounds are extensive, covering many scores of square kilometers. In places the strips and mounds are arranged to form regular geometric patterns. Too numerous and widespread to have been merely ceremonial, they must have had some economic significance. Ask the Bedouin, and they will tell you that the mounds are very old indeed, even predating the time of the Prophet, by which they reckon. They also believe that the mounds served somehow for the growing of grapes, and hence name them *tuleilat el-einab* (grapevine mounds) or *rujum el-kurum* (vineyard stone heaps).

Palmer, who first described these mounds in his book *The Desert of Exodus* (1871), accepted Bedouin lore literally. He supposed that the gravel mounds supported the grapevines rooted under or within them, and that heat emission from the dark gravel hastened the ripening of the grapes. Since Palmer's day additional speculations concerning the function of the mounds have been proposed, some quite fantastic and completely unsupported by scientific evidence. (Not that the lack of sound evidence would ever deter speculators; it merely gives freer rein to their unfettered imagination.) One of the most popular and persistent of the speculative hypotheses presumed that the gravel mounds were "aerial wells," designed to condense dew at night and so to irrigate the roots of the grapevines.

I began to study these intriguing mounds in 1952, with the aid of Naphtali Tadmor. We dug through and under the mounds, and found the soil beneath to be undisturbed desert earth, very saline, shallow, gravelly or marly, and highly calcareous—altogether thoroughly unsuitable for any agricultural crops. The spaces among the stones in all the old mounds were completely choked with soil material, and could not serve to condense dew. New mounds of stones constructed on metal pans and on virgin ground, observed for two full years, neither collected dew nor improved the water regime of the soil below to any significant degree.

Kedar (1957) offered another hypothesis. He suggested that the mounds were built to increase the rate of erosion from the hillsides and to hasten the deposition of soil in the bottomland terraces below. This hypothesis seems to overlook the obvious principle that water, not the amount of cultivable soil, is the factor limiting crop and pasture production in the Negev. Moreover, it is irreconcilable with the fact that gravel strips and mounds are found on slopes that drain into cisterns, even though silting is a distinct disadvantage in the operation of a water cistern. Finally, many of the natural terraces and plains into which the mound-covered slopes drain have a soil depth of at least 3–4 meters, and nothing could have been gained by adding more silt.

If not "grapevine mounds" or "aerial dew wells," and not "accelerated erosion," then what could have been the purpose of the gravel mounds and strips so laboriously constructed by the Negevites of old? The answer seems entirely obvious: they served to enhance runoff.

The hillsides of the Negev are covered with loose stones and gravel fragments partly embedded in soft soil, the exposed tops of the stones and

Runoff from Hillsides

Close view of a desert pavement, an almost continuous cover of gravel (in this case, fragments of black flint) on the surface of the ground.

fragments constituting an almost continuous surface called "desert pavement." This natural gravel mulch increases the infiltrability of the soil and slows the overland flow of water down the slope, thus hindering runoff. When the loose gravel is removed, the fine, loesslike soil beneath is laid bare and subjected to the influence of pelting raindrops. Being an unstable soil, the loesslike material slakes down to form a surface seal that markedly reduced the rate of water absorption (that is, the soil's infiltrability). Those who husbanded land and water in the ancient Negev must have learned by experience that clearing a slope of its stone cover can cause its runoff yield to be greater than that of an uncleared slope.

If, as the result of greater runoff, the amount of erosion is also increased, this is merely an incidental consequence of the method, generally undesirable but probably unavoidable. In time, the accelerated erosion causes the stone-cleared surface to revert to its original state: the finer soil material, exposed by removal of the original gravel pavement, gradually washes away during rainstorms and blows away during windy dry periods, until the stones intermixed with it reappear on the surface to re-create the desert pavement. We

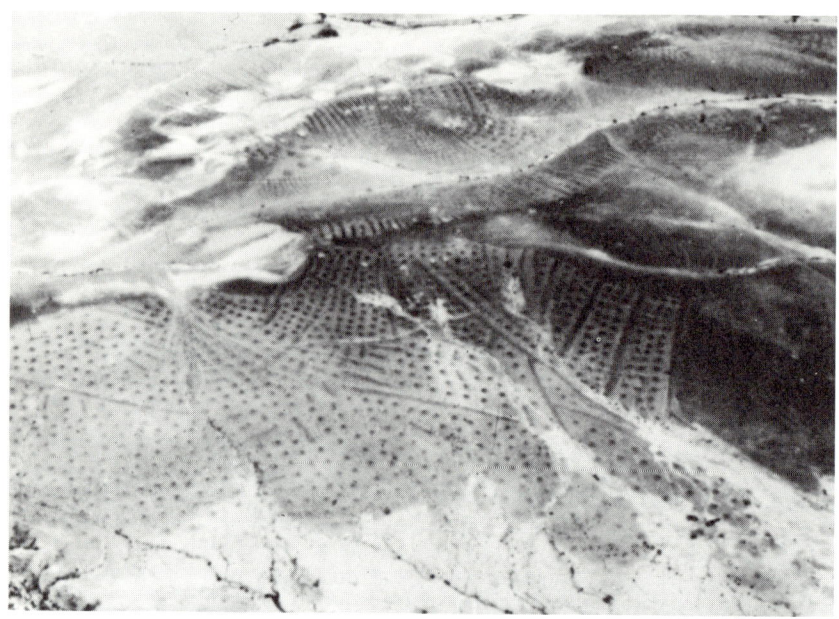

An aerial view of a sloping area in which, in ancient times, the gravel of the original desert pavement was gathered into gravel mounds and strips. Such areas are quite extensive in the northern Negev highlands and foothills subregions.

have evidence of this process of reversion in the fact that the ground surface between the ancient mounds is now nearly devoid of soil material and almost as gravelly as the undisturbed slopes found nearby. Yet this process appears to be rather slow, so the benefits of clearing stones were likely to have persisted for many years, perhaps even generations. Furthermore, that act of clearing stones and of smoothing and compacting the surface could have been repeated from time to time.

The key to the hypothesis that clearing stones can induce runoff is the surface-sealing tendency of the Negev loess when it is exposed to raindrop action. This self-sealing or crusting effect was the specific topic that I had chosen for my doctoral research. The fact that the soil of the Negev tends to slake down spontaneously when wetted and to form a crust upon drying had long been known qualitatively. However, the quantitative aspects of this phenomenon and its influence on such processes as infiltration, evaporation, and germination had not previously been measured. I began to make such

The ancient gravel mounds as they now appear on the ground. Erosion by water and wind during the centuries since they were collected has carried away the finer soil once exposed between the mounds.

measurements during the course of my investigation of the water regime of Negev habitats.

While measuring the infiltration rates in each of the various habitats, I noticed an unexpected effect. I had a priori expected that the natural stone pavement of the rocky slopes would contribute to high rates of runoff, since the stones were impervious and covered roughly 80 percent of the surface. Hence, it would stand to reason that removal of the stones should enhance infiltration into the porous soil beneath. Testing this experimentally, however, I discovered the very opposite. As long as the stones were present, the unstable soil was protected against the beating and slaking action of the raindrops. Once exposed, it quickly succumbed to this action and formed a surface seal. As early as 1953, Naphtali Tadmor and I speculated on the possible connection between this phenomenon and the ancient Negevites' clearing the hillsides to form the famous stone mounds. My good colleague later developed the idea to its logical conclusion and wrote the definitive paper on it (Tadmor et al. 1958), including me among his coauthors.

In 1962, I designed an experiment to test the quantitative effect of clearing stones and smoothing the surface on slope runoff in the Negev highlands. The experiment compared the following treatments (all simple enough for the Negev dwellers of antiquity to have practiced with the means at their disposal): "control" — the surface was left in its original state, undisturbed; "mounds" — the surface was raked and the stones gathered into mounds: "bare" — the surface was raked and the stones were completely removed from the experimental plot; "mounds, rolled" — the stones were raked into mounds and the bared surface was then smoothed, wetted, and compacted by means of a roller; "bare, rolled" — the stones were removed and the entire surface was smoothed, wetted, and compacted.

I personally performed these treatments, with four replications on slopes varying from 10 percent to 20 percent, in the Hebrew University's experimental station at Ovdat. The bounded runoff plots, engineered by Leslie Shanan, drained into tanks in which the amounts of runoff and erosion could be measured after each rainstorm. The results of the experiment were later reported by Evenari et al. (1971). Over a period of five seasons, the raking of the surface to form mounds increased runoff by about 8 percent (over the "control"), and the raking followed by smoothing and compaction increased runoff by about 20 percent. Along with the runoff, the cleared plots delivered more erosional sediments, but at a rate low enough to leave the plots practically unaffected for some years.

I subsequently embarked upon a long-term investigation, supported by the U.S. government, to test new techniques for runoff inducement in arid lands. This project was based on the proposition that modern technology offers the promise of surpassing the achievements, however excellent, of our predecessors who lived so long ago. Though we may lack their patience, diligence, and accumulated experience of generations, we do have at our com-

Experimental plots designed by the author to test surface treatments for runoff inducement and for evaporation control

mand powerful slaves, called machines, and formerly unimagined tools in the form of chemicals (including plastic films and sprayable waterproofing agents).

If merely clearing, smoothing, and compacting the surface can increase runoff significantly, then the additional impregnation of the exposed soil with materials that can both seal and waterproof the surface against infiltration, and stabilize it against erosion, may do much more. Even at best the desert dwellers of old could not harvest, on an average, much more than, say, 25 percent of the seasonal rainfall as usable runoff. Perhaps, with our modern magic, we can double or treble or quadruple that yield. We may even be able to approach getting 100 percent of the rainfall as induced runoff. Recall that 100 millimeters of rainfall on just 1 square kilometer (less than half a square mile) constitutes 100,000 cubic meters (nearly 30 million gallons) of water of the highest quality!

Quite a different question is whether we can induce and store runoff economically. There can be no universal answer to that question, since the economics of one region or country differs from that of another. The imperatives of future settlement in desert regions are likely to change our economic outlook, and what seems prohibitive today may become feasible tomorrow. In some desert regions, especially in high-altitude plateaus far from the sea, even allowing for the cost of land preparation and surface treatment, the inducement and collection of runoff is already far more economical than the desalinization and conveyance of seawater, once held to be the ultimate solution to the problem of water supply in arid regions.

The importance of runoff inducement (known variously as "water harvesting" or "milking the hillsides") is greater than the mere increase in runoff yield that it may produce. The practice can also lower the "runoff threshold," the minimal rain (in terms of intensity and duration) needed to start runoff. This decrease of the threshold correspondingly increases the probability of obtaining sufficient runoff (for domestic human use as well as for industrial or agricultural purposes) a sufficient number of times during the season even from small rains, and thus it decreases the effective frequency of drought. We must remember that one of the greatest drawbacks to desert settlement has always been the drought hazard—that is, the number of seasons in which practically no effective rainstorms occur.

Perhaps the simplest approach to runoff inducement is to cover the surface with an impervious apron of plastic, metal, or concrete. The problems encountered with such an approach are how to make the covering materials adhere permanently to the soil surface, which may be irregular and have jagged protruding stones; and whether such materials can resist weathering. An alternative approach is to cause the soil itself to shed, rather than absorb, the rain. In general it is possible to classify soil treatments for runoff inducement as follows: mechanical treatments, such as clearing stones and

A rainfall simulator and experimental soil-filled containers designed to screen treatments for the stabilization and hydrophilization of soil surfaces. The purpose is to induce runoff while limiting erosion.

Runoff from Hillsides

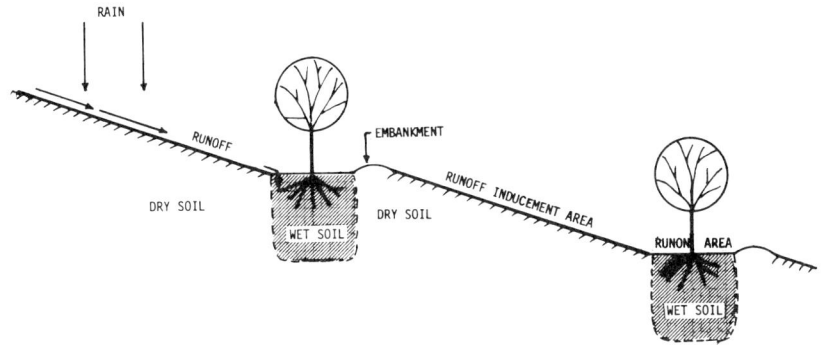

Runoff inducement and utilization on sloping land, by a series of alternating contour strips: runoff-contributing strips, treated to enhance runoff; runon-receiving strips, serving as cropland (for example, for fruit trees, as shown).

smoothing and compacting the surface; dispersive treatments, to enhance the self-sealing of the soil surface; hydrophobic treatments, to reduce the wettability of the soil surface, the way fabric raincoats are treated to make them water-repellent; surface-binding treatments, to permeate and seal the soil with an adherent material that can cement the loose soil into a firm matrix; various combinations of these treatments.

Preparing experimental plots to compare surface treatments for runoff inducement. The late N. Tadmor supervises the effort from atop the vehicle.

The results of comprehensive studies by the author (Hillel 1967) and by others have proved the effectiveness of the following methods for treating arid-zone soils to collect runoff: eradication of vegetation and removal of surface stones, to reduce interception of rain and obstruction of overland flow, and to permit the formation of a continuous surface crust; smoothing of the land surface, to obliterate surface depressions and prevent water retention in puddles; compaction of the top soil layer, to reduce its permeability, by means of a smooth roller at optimal soil moisture content; dispersion of the colloidal clay that is present in finer-textured soils, by means of sodic salts, to cause self-sealing and self-crusting of the soil surface; impregnation of the surface with sealing, binding, and hydrophobic materials, the most promising of which are solutions or emulsions of asphalt and of silicone water-repellents. These methods are listed in order of increasing complexity and cost. Which of them, alone or in combination, will be most suitable in any particular area will, of course, depend upon local conditions, requirements, and alternative possibilities.

16

Farm Units and Small Watersheds

> As a tree planted by the waters,
> That spreadeth out its roots by the stream,
> And shall not see when heat cometh,
> But its foliage be luxuriant;
> And shall not be anxious in a year of drought,
> Nor cease from yielding fruit.
> Jeremiah 17:7-8

Although rainfed farming has long been practiced in the northern Negev, and irrigated farming with imported water is now carried out in the northern Negev and even in limited locations in the Negev highlands, it is a fact that in historical times practically all farming in the latter subregion has depended on runoff utilization. This is a fundamental fact that bears repeating, for it implies far-reaching corollaries. In this type of agriculture, runoff water from winter rains falling on adjacent slopes was gathered and directed to bottomland fields for periodic flooding, in order to accumulate and store sufficient moisture in the soil to produce crops. Although the average winter rainfall in the Negev is only about 100 millimeters, the settlers were able to gather sufficient runoff from the barren slopes to develop intensive agriculture in the depressions and bottomlands.

This ingenious type of desert agriculture has been called runoff farming. Whereas the farmer in more humid lands aims to soak all of the rain into the soil and thus prevent runoff, the desert runoff farmer of old worked on the opposite principle; his aim was to prevent the rain from penetrating the soil on the slopes so as to produce the maximum possible runoff. He then collected this runoff from a large area of slopes and directed it to a small cultivated area in the bottomlands. In this way he was able to raise crops even under adverse desert conditions.

The cultivated area was usually divided into small fields, which had to be leveled and terraced to ensure efficient spreading of water as well as both soil and water conservation. The oldest version of runoff farming probably consisted of simple terracing in the small wadis. This had the effect of transforming the entire length of the wadi into a continuous stairway, with stairs perhaps 10–20 meters wide and 20–50 centimeters high. The terrace walls were designed to spread the flood and to prevent erosion. The slowed-down flow of the flood from one terrace down into the next could thus irrigate the fields sufficiently for a crop to be grown. Distinct groups or series of terraced fields having definable catchment areas and surrounded by stone walls constituted integral units that could be called "runoff farms." Such farms consisted typically of, say, one-half to several hectares of cultivated land.

Hundreds of such farm units are spread throughout the Negev highlands, most commonly and typically in the environs of the principal ancient towns. Well-defined runoff farms have been found that date back to the tenth century B.C. As the main form of the region's sedentary agriculture, runoff farms were probably maintained in the same locations by successive civilizations until the end of the Byzantine era. But because the later farm units are superimposed upon the earlier ones, it is extremely difficult to determine the exact extent and character of runoff farming during each era as distinct from the preceding and following eras. The development of these units seems, however, to have reached its highest stage under the Byzantines, whose stable and secure regime enabled settlers to build and maintain their farms in the open country, even many kilometers from the region's ancient cities.

Detailed observation of typical ancient runoff farm units reveals that each unit was served by a particular and well-delineated portion of the watershed. An elaborate system of conduits was constructed to collect runoff from specific sections of the adjacent slopes, not merely for each farm or set of fields, but indeed for each terraced field within the farm. The complete farm unit thus comprised both the slope catchment (the runoff-contributing area) and the bottomland fields (the runoff-receiving area). Fields could be made productive only if associated with a catchment from slopes, since the meager rainfall alone could not normally sustain a crop. The larger the catchment, the greater the expectable water supply and the corresponding area that could be irrigated.

The runoff farmers, therefore, understandably sought to extend their water-collecting conduits to the plateaus above their fields, in an effort to maximize the water supply. Long conduits, in some places exceeding a kilometer in length, were extended, where feasible, even beyond the limits of the natural watershed serving the wadi in which the farm was located, so as to invade and divert water from an adjacent watershed. No farmer, however, could extend his conduits arbitrarily without eventually interfering with his neighbor's catchment. Clearly delineated catchment areas, allocated to serve particular farm units, necessarily constituted "water rights." Typical farm units, consisting of 0.4 to 4 hectares of fields, included 10 to 100 hectares of sloping catchment.

To manage a runoff farm, given the vagaries of rainfall in the desert and the unpredictable nature of the water supply pattern within and between seasons, a farmer would be required to maintain operational flexibility and to be able to make quick adjustments to varying circumstances. In wet years the farm as a whole would probably experience an excessive supply of water, and it would be necessary to discharge the surplus downstream while preventing erosion. In dry years the amount of runoff collected could be insufficient for all the fields on the farm, so the operator would have had to decide how to utilize the limited amount of water available most efficiently. The strictly equal allocation of a small amount of water to all fields on the farm may not be the optimal allocation. Providing water to some fields while denying it to others may be a better strategy, depending on the selection of crops. Perennial crops such as fruit trees, for instance, must be irrigated sufficiently every season without fail, whereas the part of the land allocated to annual crops could be sacrificed if water were insufficient for all the fields. Far from being automatic, the operation of a runoff farm required great knowledge, alertness, skill, and diligence.

Indirect evidence of the indissoluble link between a section of cropland and its catchment can be found in the papyrus documents discovered by the Colt expedition in Nessana (now called Nitzana) in 1936. Originally intended to be an exploration of the ruins of Shivta, this American expedition, initiated by H. D. Colt, was diverted to Nessana by chance circumstances. The reason for this change of plans was, appropriately enough, a matter of water availability: Shivta's cisterns went dry owing to drought and neglect, while Nessana had well water. However, the reluctant selection of Nessana was, in the words of Colt, "amply rewarded by the discovery of papyrus documents" in two ancient Byzantine churches. The documents, written in the Greek language prevalent during the Byzantine era, do not deal directly with water supplies or agriculture, but these vital aspects of life in the Negev are inevitably referred to. Legal contracts and deeds to farmland include listings of fields, cisterns, and associated water channels (Kraemer 1958; Mayerson 1959). At least one of the documents refers explicitly to land "with all the rights of access and of conducting water."

Measurements made by Shanan et al. (1958) of the areal ratio of runoff-contributing catchment to runoff-receiving cropland in the ancient farm systems of the Negev highlands revealed this ratio to vary from 17:1 to 30:1. That is, each hectare of cropland required on average about 25 hectares of catchment to ensure a supply of water sufficient for adequate irrigation in most years. By an interesting and perhaps not entirely fortuitous coincidence, this ratio is very nearly equal to the actual areal ratio of slopes and plains to wadi-bed bottomlands. We can use this ratio of runoff to runon areas to obtain an independent estimate of the average runoff water yield obtained from the slope catchments.

Present-day agricultural experience has shown that at least 250 millimeters of water (equivalent to 2,500 cubic meters per hectare of cropland) are required, over and above the average precipitation of 100 millimeters, to ensure a successful winter crop in this region. For 25 units of catchment to provide 250 millimeters of water, each unit must yield about 10 millimeters, or 10 percent of its seasonal rainfall of 100 millimeters. To be sure, the foregoing is only a rough estimate, but it accords with, and helps to reinforce, our earlier estimate (based on the water regime) of 10–15 percent runoff from the slopes.

The use of conduits to divide the sloping ground into subcatchments had the practical effect of preventing runoff from accumulating to form uncontrollable flash floods. Instead, each conduit, collecting water from a section of slope not much greater than 1 hectare, delivered a small stream of water that could be handled and, if necessary, diverted from one terrace to another or directed to individual trees, by one or two operators using hand implements. The conduits themselves had a cross section on the order of 0.05 to 0.1 square meter and sloped at no more than 1 percent. Constant vigilance was required to prevent the embankments of these conduits, built by hand from loose stones and soil, from being breached. Any damage that did occur was to be repaired prior to the next rainstorm. The uncemented structures within the cultivated part of the farm (weirs, dikes, and spillways) also required frequent, and prompt, repair.

Even with all the alertness, ingenuity, skill, and diligence they could muster, the runoff farmers operated a risky business and had to face new uncertainties each season. It is all the more remarkable, therefore, that they were able to cope with all the difficulties and to sustain a viable agricultural economy on such a scale. That scale is worth emphasizing: During its period of maximal development in the Byzantine era, the system of runoff farming encompassed practically all of the usable land in the northern Negev highlands, and numbered many hundreds of farm units.

As we mentioned, the cultivated area of each farm unit was sub-divided into terrace fields. Each field was defined along its lower (downstream) edge by a level, steplike retaining wall, or dike, partly embedded in the ground and protruding about 10 centimeters above the soil surface. The function of each dike, built at right angles to the natural gradient of the wadi bed, was to spread and impound some of the floodwater on the field, where the water could soak into the ground and be retained in the soil in a form available for subsequent use by crops, and to allow the excess water to flow downstream in a controlled manner.

The dikes were built of several level tiers of stone blocks, averaging perhaps 20 × 20 × 40 centimeters and weighing roughly 30–40 kilograms, about as much as a man can readily handle. Each successive tier of stones was tapered back slightly from the tier below to enhance stability and to allow the overflowing floodwater to cascade down in stepwise fashion, thus dissipating some of its kinetic energy and erosive power. Where the vertical drop from terrace to terrace was greater than, say, 50 centimeters, a double wall was sometimes built, with downstream and upstream facings and the space between filled with gravel. Construction was facilitated by the natural blocky cleavage of the stratified limestone outcrops in the Negev; upon weathering, the rock splits into roughly rectangular blocks that can often be pried out of the exposed bedrock and then fitted together in a dike with a minimum of artificial shaping.

While in most cases each dike served as a spillway, allowing the floodwater to overtop its entire length, in other cases where the wadi bed was especially wide, and the dikes unusually long, special spillways were constructed at regular intervals along the dike. In either case every effort was made to prevent the floodwaters from concentrating and forming destructive gullies. The art of runoff management on the land thus consisted of spreading the floodwater on as wide an area as possible, a technique known in the American Southwest as "waterspreading." The silt-laden floodwater tends to deposit some of its sediment whenever the water is slowed down or impounded. Gradual silting of the terraced fields apparently required adding a tier of stones from time to time to raise the spillway level. Over the years a considerable amount of silting occurred in some places, and many of the dikes that may appear to be only 50 centimeters high actually extend a meter or so below the present ground surface. In addition to terrace dikes and spillways, some of the farm units show remains of weirs and dividing conduits designed to give the runoff farmer better control over the distribution of the flowing water within the farm.

The runoff farms generally had high, solidly built stone fences delineating the cultivated area. The principal function of these fences was probably to prevent strangers from entering, and especially to keep stray goats from trampling and grazing in the fields. In some places the fences served two additional functions: to prevent erosion and to provide the lower embankment of conduits collecting runoff from the slopes. The remains of a house, cistern, or watchtower may be found within or alongside the fenced boundaries of the runoff farm. The houses were usually one or two stories high. A cistern was generally under the floor of each house or in close proximity to it. It was fed by a special conduit, and the surplus water was directed toward the fields just below.

Though some of the runoff farms were located not in wadis but on plains adjacent to slopes, the vast majority of them were set in the wadi beds proper.

An ancient farm system reestablished. In the foreground is a series of reconstructed terraces and cropped fields, managed by a Hebrew University research team (Evenari et al. 1971). In the background, on a hilly eminence, looms the ancient city of Ovdat, its acropolis partially restored.

The reconstructed runoff farming system near Ovdat. The runoff collecting conduits are on the hillside in the background, and the runoff-irrigated terrace fields are in the foreground.

In fact, many of the farms units were arrayed in series, one below the other along the entire course of a wadi, so that the whole natural watershed was utilized. Such an arrangement of course required the close cooperation of all of the watershed's farmers in alerting one another to the coming flood, regulating water rights, and maintaining structures. Each farmer would depend on the one above him, since dike failure on the higher farm could result in a sudden rush of the flood onto the lower farm and in a disastrous chain reaction all the way down the wadi.

Notwithstanding all the care and skill of the Negev's runoff farmers, occasional disruptions of the dikes certainly did happen, as they happen today, caused by the scouring action of running water. If a breached dike were left unrepaired, the cancer of gullying could quickly propagate and cut into the level fields. Once gullies had formed, the floods would no longer spread gently in a thin sheet over the whole terrace, but would concentrate destructively and become an ugly, snaking stream capable of gnawing at and lapping up the soft earth, wreaking practically irreparable damage. Numerous formerly productive but now badly scoured wadis stand in mute and tragic testimony to the

Local runoff impounded behind an earthen dike sustains a grove of ornamental and fruit trees in the middle of the desert.

subsequent neglect and mismanagement of the splendid but fragile works of the Negevite runoff farmers of ancient times.

Two of the ancient farm units, one at Shivta and one at Ovdat, were reconstructed in 1959 by a Hebrew University research team, and have been in continuous operation since 1960. A detailed account of these farm units and of the agricultural experiments carried out on them was given by Evenari et al. (1971). An effort was made to remain faithful to the original plan of the ancient runoff farms and to collect water from the same catchments. Various species of annual crops (such as winter barley and summer sorghum), as well as perennial grasses and fruit trees, were grown successfully with locally intercepted runoff and without supplementary irrigation.

The fact that the ancient methods have proved to be workable today does not mean, however, that we should necessarily copy them without change. Recently reawakened interest in the utilization of storm runoff water in arid regions has led investigators working in several countries to apply present-day technology to improvement of the old techniques. As I have already pointed out, runoff rates can now be increased severalfold by means of various mechanical and chemical treatments of the catchment. Where rainfall alone is insufficient for crops but the soil is otherwise arable, it is possible to utilize the land in a modern system of runoff farming, in which a section of the land is shaped and treated for runoff inducement while another section receives the runoff so produced. Runoff irrigation may be carried out either immediately, with runoff water flowing directly onto the section serving as cropland, or water can be stored for future use in reservoirs. Although the former method is less expensive, it is also less flexible because irrigation is applied immediately following precipitation, regardless of whether the root zone can effectively retain all the water applied.

Several systems have been tried with respect to size and arrangement of the contributing area in relation to the water-receiving area. A small natural watershed can be treated in its entirety so as to provide the maximal amount of water that can be conveyed to irrigated fields. On a smaller scale, sloping land can be divided into more or less parallel contour strips, with alternating pairs of strips treated to shed runoff and to receive it, as illustrated on p. 163. Microwatersheds are the third possible approach, wherein each tree or small plot of a crop is associated with an individually tailored, artificial separated catchment (Aase and Kemper 1968; Shanan et al. 1970; Fairbourn and Kemper 1971). A long-term experiment, carried out by the author of this book in collaboration with E. Rawitz at Gilat in the northern Negev, using the contour strip method, proved that in a region of 200 to 250 millimeters annual rainfall, almond trees can be sustained with contributing-to-receiving ("runoff-to-runon") area ratios as low as 3:1 (Hillel 1974).

17

Harnessing the Floods

> "Who hath cleft a channel for the waterflood,
> And a pathway for the lightning of the thunder;
> To cause rain on an uninhabited land,
> In the wilderness, wherein there is no man;
> To satisfy the desolate and waste ground,
> And cause the tender herbs to grow?"
>
> Job 38:25-26

The preceding chapter dealt with utilization of runoff from small watersheds, generally no larger than, say, 1 square kilometer. Flows from such watersheds can be handled by relatively simple means in runoff farm units located in small wadis. The small wadis described are generally tributaries to what we might call "medium-size wadis," which typically drain synclinal valleys with watersheds of up to 100 square kilometers and which, in turn, discharge into the large regional wadis that drain hundreds or even thousands of square kilometers. This hierarchy of wadi types is, of course, somewhat arbitrary, since in reality we can find a continuous spectrum of watershed sizes; nevertheless, it is a convenient way for us to categorize wadis with respect to their flood-producing potential. The medium-size wadis produce torrential flash floods, often hundreds of thousands of cubic meters per season, that cannot be regulated by individual farmers, and require large-scale works if they are to be harnessed and utilized.

A bad mistake we made at first in Sdeh-Boker was trying to take on a medium-size wadi directly, brashly expecting to tame the floods along its lower section, instead of starting with the small wadis that constitute its headwater tributaries and working our way gradually downstream. The transverse earthen dikes and alternating left-right stone spillways we built across the wadi were designed to slow and spread the flood, and to impound some of the water to irrigate a strip of land several-score meters wide. The very first flash flood breached these dikes, and we had to spend several seasons rebuilding and reinforcing them until we finally realized the futility of challenging so unpredictable a force of nature without first regulating and taming it upstream.

The surface hydrology of medium-size subregional watersheds differs from that of the small catchments described in chapter 16. In the latter, runoff may begin after a small amount of rain (5–10 millimeters) has fallen, whereas a threshold rainstorm of at least 10 millimeters is typically required to cause a general flood in the former. This is partly because of the spotty and variable nature of desert rainstorms, which seldom occur evenly over a large watershed. Flash floods in a fair-size wadi may in fact result from a localized downpour causing flow in a few tributaries while others remain dry. Furthermore, there are considerable seepage losses in the permeable watercourses themselves, and the greater the path of flow (that is, the larger and longer the wadi), the greater these losses. Thus, while the runoff from a small catchment

A flash flood in a subregional wadi.

Two silt-choked storage dams at Mamshit. The ancient dam is in the background, the modern one in the foreground.

may be as high as 10–15 percent of the seasonal rainfall, the corresponding amount flowing from a large watershed rarely exceeds 5 percent. Thus, it is clear that the occurrence of wadi floods is less frequent than that of runoff from small catchments. However, when floods do occur in the large wadis, they are often of such magnitude and violence as to endanger all but the sturdiest structures along their path.

What can be done with these wadi floods?

One possibility is to construct storage dams to retain the water for subsequent use in irrigation. This, however, is not often practical. Successful damming of wadi floods requires a particularly auspicious, and hence rare, combination of hydrologic, topographic, and geologic conditions. In most locations, even where stable dams could be constructed to withstand the unpredictable torrents and peak floods, seepage and evaporation losses might soon deprive the engineers of the water they seek to retain. We should, therefore, not be surprised that in the entire Negev, with all the intensive development carried out during so many centuries by highly skilled civilizations, only a single storage dam of any size was found. This is the Roman-period dam at Mamshit, the foundations of which can be seen today under the superstructure rebuilt by the British in the 1940s. It could not have been a successful venture, as recent experience has shown. The ponding basin behind the dam is so completely silted up that it resembles a large terrace. The periodic removal of the great bulk of sediments that gradually deprive a dam of its storage capacity is a costly and cumbersome operation even with modern earth-moving equipment, let alone with baskets and camels. At Mamshit the rate of silting proved to be so rapid that the British engineers found it expedient to go below the original dam and build a completely new one, using the former only as a silting basin for the latter. Even so, they gained little for their double effort because the rate of seepage into the sandy bottom, underlain by fissured limestone, was so great that little water was retained after just a few weeks.

The task of sealing the bottom to render it impervious is problematic even with today's technology; it was well nigh impossible in ancient times. We may add in passing that, in nearly thirty five years, engineers in the State of Israel, though bent strongly upon the development of water resources in the Negev, have found it feasible to construct only one sizable storage dam in the Negev highlands—the one at Yerokham. Even there, despite the nearly ideal topography of the ponding basin and the presence beneath it of a layer of naturally watertight marl, the seepage rate proved excessive and an expensive grouting operation (the injection of cement into the substratum) had to be carried out. In addition to the silting and seepage problems, a storage dam in the desert incurs considerable evaporation losses.

Although the Negev dwellers in ancient times had no practical way to tame and utilize the entire flood capacity of a medium-size wadi without undue risk or cost, they did not leave such wadis entirely unutilized. Rather, they developed elaborate methods to divert measured portions of the floods for use on adjacent fields.

Aerial and ground surveys have revealed a number of large diversion systems along the subregional wadis near the principal ancient towns. All were laid out on an exact and complex engineering plan that had to be surveyed and measured for accurate interpretation. In order to bring out the main technical features of such large developments, three diversion systems in widely different areas were studied in detail by Shanan et al. (1961). These are located along the Lavan, Ovdat, and Mamshit wadis. They are by no means the only such ancient systems in the Negev. In many cases, however, the meandering watercourses have so affected the topography of the alluvial plains that it is difficult to decipher the original extent and form of each system, particularly because later systems were often superimposed on earlier ones. A schematic illustration of an ancient diversion system is shown above. Such a system must have begun with a stone overflow-type diversion dam designed to raise the floodwater to a level higher than the downstream banks of the wadi. However, the diversion dams themselves have long since been destroyed by the rushing torrents, and only a few remnants can still be seen.

From the point of the diversion dam, a canal was built to lead the water

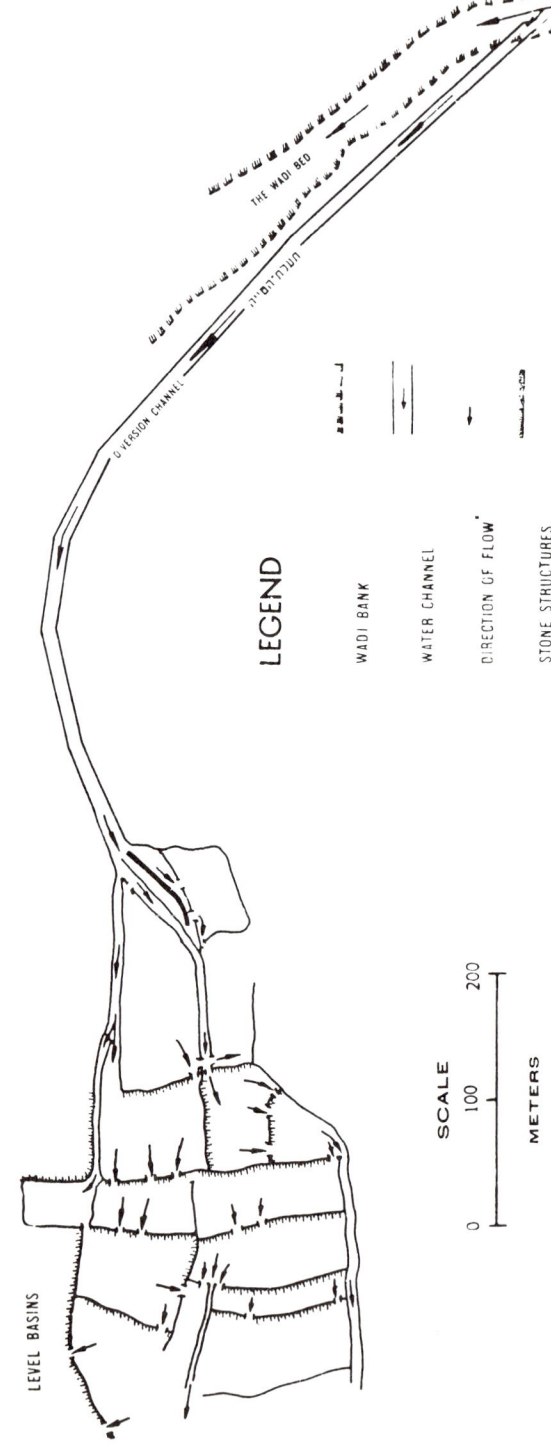

AN ANCIENT WATER-SPREADING SYSTEM

An ancient diversion system from a subregional wadi in the northern Negev foothills subregion.

A cascading spillway allowing the excess water from an upper terraced field to flow into a lower field without scouring the soft loessial soil.

onto the plain, where the water was introduced into a series of broad terraced fields. Many of these fields are still well preserved. They are more or less level in the transverse direction, but have a slight gradient (typically 2 percent) in the direction of the water flow. This arrangement would have enabled the farmer to irrigate his crops either in large basins or in small plots. The excess water from each terrace flowed to the next lower one through well-constructed drop structures, usually tiered, cascading spillways built of stone.

Typically the total area of cultivated terrace fields in one of these ancient diversion systems was about 10 hectares. Since modern experience has shown that 2,500–4,000 cubic meters of water must be applied per hectare per season in order to ensure a crop, a diversion canal designed to irrigate 10 hectares must have supplied 25,000–40,000 cubic meters a year to the cultivated terraces. This would represent about 1 percent of the 100-millimeter hypothetical annual rainfall of a medium-size watershed of, say, 25–40 square kilometers. In principle, therefore, along its course a subregional wadi could supply water to more than one such diversion system. However, suitable places for diversion systems are not found everywhere along the course of a typical wadi.

Handling the larger flows of a diversion from a subregional wadi required

Flood scouring of a loessial wadi bed. (Courtesy of S. Buchbinder)

greater skill and sophistication than the operation of small runoff farms. For example, failure to repair and maintain the system at the very first sign of damage could at once start the insidious process of accelerated gully erosion, which, given the large and potentially erosive flows, could quickly transform a fertile water-spreading plain into a barren, gully-incised badlands.

The largest, most elaborate, and most striking of the ancient diversion systems found in the Negev is that of Nahal Lavan, near the old town of Shivta, at the point where the subregional wadi, draining about 50 square kilometers on the western side of the northern Negev highlands, emerges onto the plain. The wadi bed at this point is cut into the white chalky bedrock, which accounts for its name, "White Stream." As it continues through the plain, its banks reveal numerous remnants of massive ancient walls, terraces, and spillways. Some of the spillways have crest lengths of 30–60 meters, capable of handling flows in the range of 10–30 cubic meters per second. However, there are also many smaller spillways, 3–8 meters wide, and many that are less than 1 meter wide. The total terraced area is about 200 hectares, but it is highly doubtful that all this land could have been cultivated at the same time. Rather, it is a complex of many superimposed systems, each built and operated at a different time. Potsherds found nearby date as far back as the Judean period, as well as to the late Nabatean, Roman, and Byzantine periods.

Contrary to the impressions of some authors who regard floodwater diversion as the principal method of ancient desert farming, the fact is that all the diversion systems in evidence account for but a small fraction of the total area of land cultivated in the small runoff farms described in chapter 16. The diversion system was used only in restricted areas with special topographic conditions. Moreover, it could not have been a stable system, because the progressive deepening of the wadi and silting of the terraces eventually necessitated its discontinuance.

According to Shanan et al. (1961), typical diversion systems along subregional wadis reveal a three-stage history associated with the divergent processes of erosion in the wadi bed and silting in the terraces. The first stage is that of floodplain development. Apparently the wadis originally were wide and shallow depressions in the alluvial or eolian plains. Cultivation of these depressions necessitated the construction of transverse stone dikes in order to stabilize the cultivated fields. These dikes were subsequently extended so as to spread the water over larger sections of the floodplain. Examples of such floodplain development can be found in the plains of Matred and Haruakh, and date back to the Judean era (circa 900–800 B.C.).

At a certain period the floodplain waterspreading systems were apparently abandoned and allowed to deteriorate through lack of maintenance. Consequently the wadi gouged a gully, perhaps 1–3 meters deep, through the floodplain. We come now to the second stage, in which the next settlers in the area, unable to repair the breach and spread the water over the width of the floodplain, developed the technique of diverting water from the channel to a part of the floodplain. During this period the wadi continued to erode, and silt from the eroding upstream banks and from the lengthening gully was deposited in the terraced fields.

This silt raised the level of the fields until the terrace walls had to be raised by yet another tier of stones. At a later stage a new canal and diversion structure higher up the wadi were required to ensure the gravity flow of floodwater onto the fields. As the silting process continued, it eventually raised the level of the beds by a meter or more. The maintenance of these systems became increasingly difficult. The wadi bed at this stage was already several meters below the floodplain, often narrowly channeled between heavy stone walls. Any break in the walls would have caused serious damage to the whole system.

The construction of all the structures described required a thorough working knowledge of both hydrology and hydraulics. Thus, the period in which these diversion systems were in operation must have been one in which the science of land and water engineering was well developed. Furthermore, this period must have been one in which a central governing body controlled

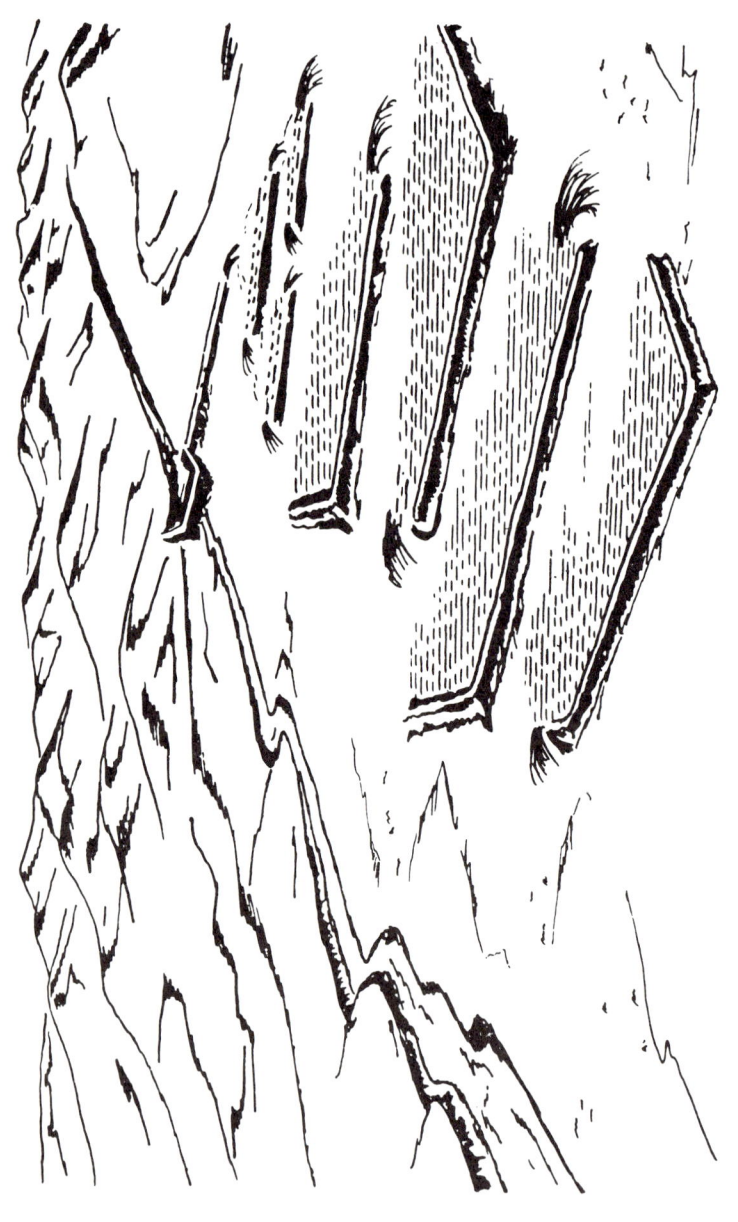

WATER SPREADING BY EARTH DYKES

Two general methods of water spreading by diversion from an intermittent stream (a wadi).

A. Diversion of an uncontrolled volume of water over the unleveled land by means of a zigzag series of earthen dikes. This system is prone to erosion, and is therefore suited only for soil-conserving, close-growing perennial vegetation (such as grass pasture).

B. Diversion of a controlled volume of water by means of a detention dam. The water is led into a series of level basins with concrete- or stone-lined spillways, to prevent erosion and allow cultivation of annual or orchard crops. (After Tadmor and Hillel, 1956b)

WATER SPREADING IN LEVEL BASINS AND CONCRETE SPILLWAYS

The construction of a detention dam on Nahal (Wadi) Haroah, near Sdeh-Boker.

the whole watershed and had the legal authority to distribute the water equitably throughout the length of the wadi during each short flood period. The Romans and the Byzantines possessed both the technical engineering skill and the central authority, and the Roman potsherds found in the area probably relate to these diversion systems.

The third and final stage in the history of the diversion systems in the Negev followed a period in which the area was abandoned, either for extraneous reasons or because the system itself became unmanageable. The next users no longer attempted to divert water from the main wadi, but reverted to the collection and utilization of local runoff from small watersheds adjoining the cultivable land.

This complex interaction of historical and physical factors that has governed the course of civilization in the Negev undoubtedly has its parallels elsewhere. Yet it seems that nowhere can the agricultural history of a desert civilization be studied and illustrated more vividly than in that microcosm of deserts, the Negev.

Modern engineering offers another possibility for the control and utilization of runoff from medium-size wadis: the construction of dams designed not to retain the floods, but merely to detain and regulate them so as to provide farms located downstream from the dam with controlled flows. Such dams, called detention dams, are built across a wadi in order to temporarily impound the entire flood. A large-diameter open pipe is laid through the dam to permit downstream flow at a predetermined rate, as through the drain of a bathtub. Thus, a flood lasting perhaps several hours is temporarily impounded and

An aerial view of the then newly built detention dam and level fields at Sdeh-Boker. At the top of the picture are the earthen dam across the wadi bed and the delta-shaped ponding basin behind it. An open pipe drains a controlled volume of water through the dam into a channel, and then to a system of dike-enclosed level terrace fields, located on the plain alongside and above the old wadi bed (seen curving at left). Notches in the dikes are concrete-lined spillways. The excess water, if any, is allowed to flow back into the wadi at the lower end of the system.

Controlled floodwater flowing from terrace to terrace over a concrete spillway.

A panoramic view of the same system of leveled fields below the detention dam at Sdeh-Boker, about ten years after its completion. An established fruit-tree orchard is being flood-irrigated. (Courtesy of S. Buchbinder)

Supplementary dry-season pipeline irrigation of fruit trees that are flood-irrigated during the rainy season.

made to flow through the pipe and into the field for perhaps several days. The field dikes can be built economically and safely to withstand known flood intensities, and farming operations can be planned to handle the floods.

An example of an operating detention dam system is the one we built in 1955 on Nahal Haroah, a couple of kilometers north of Sdeh-Boker. An aerial

The failure of an earthen dam in Nahal Boker. The high dike was scoured and breached by water running down its steep face and, perhaps, by the "piping" of percolated water.

photograph of the system shows the earth dam built straight across the wadi, the inverted V-shaped ponding basin above it, and the narrow channel leading water from the open pipe draining the dam down to the leveled fields with their contour dikes. At first we grew forage crops in these fields, but later put in fruit trees, which have been growing successfully on a combination of floodwater and supplementary pipeline irrigation for what is now about 25 years.

On the other hand, a poor example of a detention dam is the one built several years later at Nahal Boker, another synclinal wadi, about 5 kilometers west of Sdeh-Boker. This dam was breached by the floods shortly after it was built. Not only did it fail to fulfill its intended purpose (to provide a controlled irrigation to leveled fields on the alluvial plain alongside the wadi) — worse yet, it seems to have done more harm than good. By concentrating the flood and funneling it through the unrepaired breach, the dam has apparently increased the flood's erosive power. The result has been an accelerated rate of scouring and gullying in the once-wide and beautifully vegetated floodplain downstream of the dam site. Thus, we see that even a sound concept can lead to failure if carelessly implemented, and if improperly maintained.

It should be obvious by now that the construction and operation of a detention or diversion system in any given wadi are affected by upstream watershed conditions (size and character of catchment, amount and pattern of rainfall) and, in turn, affect water-supply conditions downstream. It is therefore possible to utilize wadi floods efficiently only on an integrated basis. Wadi development cannot be carried out in isolated spots, but must be coordinated in an overall watershed management program. In all except the smallest of wadis, such a program requires regional coordination and administration.

18

Tapping Groundwater

> For the Lord thy God bringeth thee
> into a good land, a land of brooks
> of water, of fountains and depths,
> springing forth in valleys and hills.
> Deuteronomy 8:7

An assured water supply, both to satisfy direct human requirements and provide secondarily for livestock and crop requirements, is obviously the primary and crucial factor in the settlement of a desert. Some desert regions are the fortunate recipients of "exotic" water, originating from more humid regions. Exotic waters may arrive as rivers, such as the Nile (which draws its waters from the tropical regions of east-central Africa), the Indus (deriving its water from the western Himalayas), the Tigris and Euphrates (originating from northern Persia and eastern Anatolia), the Jordan (from Mount Hermon), the Colorado (from the Rockies), and the San Joaquin and Sacramento rivers (from the Sierras).

Waters originating elsewhere may also enter a desert area as groundwater flowing in aquifers, which are porous rock strata capable of carrying usable supplies of water. In some cases the water contained in an aquifer may derive from an earlier and more humid geological period, and, while usable, is irreplaceable under the present climatic regime. Such "fossil" water is known to exist in large quantities in the Sahara and Sinai, and to some extent in the sandstone formations underlying the Negev as well. However, these deposits are generally hundreds of meters deep, and in many places of rather poor quality (brackish), so that their utilization, even given our present-day technology, is questionable. In prior times it would have been unthinkable.

Since the Negev is not fortunate enough to receive an exotic river, nor any significant infusion of groundwater from afar, we are reduced to considering the region's own surface and underground water resources.

I have already indicated that over much of the land area of the Negev, seasonal rains wet only the surface zone of the soil, which again dries up by direct evaporation and by the extraction of natural vegetation. Below the seasonally wetted zone the soil conducts practically no water. Thus, over the greater part of the Negev there is no significant replenishment of groundwater by the direct downward percolation of any excess of rainwater over evapotranspiration. The situation is very different in wadi beds, however. Here, considerable percolation into and through the permeable gravel takes place during floods. In places where the underlying rock is relatively impervious, the percolating water may accumulate to form shallow perched water tables that can be tapped by means of wells. In places these waters even emerge as springs and form oases.

Surface runoff is fresh water and so, generally, is the water found in perched water tables along wadi beds. Where groundwater percolates through saline strata, however, it dissolves salts and becomes brackish. Groundwater flow sometimes ends in shallow depressions or valleys, where the water level comes close to the ground surface. In these places evaporation causes the progressive concentration, and sometimes the precipitation, of salts. Such is the situation in the "salines," which are salt marshes (called playas in America, *takyrs* in central Asia, *kavirs* in Iran, and *sabhas* or "mamlakhas" in the Near East) that occur in many deserts. In the Negev there are several salines, mainly along the Arava Rift Valley. There, recharge of the shallow water table occurs through seepage of floodwaters into the gravelly wadis that originate in the highlands and descend into the Rift Valley from both the eastern (Edom) and western (Negev) sides, forming alluvial fans that culminate in saline basins at the bottom of the valley.

Places where readily usable groundwater occurs are relatively few, and the amounts of water that can be tapped are scanty. Yet in antiquity the inhabitants of the Negev were able to locate many of these places, and to find the means to tap them. That they were successful even without tools of modern hydrologic and geologic exploration is a source of amazement, not least to contemporary scientists and engineers, who meet with great difficulty in their own search for water in the desert. Surely the achievements of the Negev dwellers in antiquity were partly the result of trial and error, pursued incessantly over many generations by tenacious people undeterred by repeated frustrations. But the remarkable fact that they found so many of the spots where perched water tables exist in the Negev gives us pause. It could not have been by random, unguided trial and error alone. They must have possessed a basic and practical knowledge of the sciences that today we call hydrology and geology.

The simplest way to search for underground water in the desert is to dig

Tapping Groundwater

in the large wadi beds. We have the Bible as evidence that "the servants of Isaac dug in the nahal [wadi] and found there a well of living water." The practice persists to this day among the Bedouin of the Near Eastern deserts, who call these shallow wells *tamilat*. It is, however, a hazardous practice. Though the search for promising sites can be aided by the presence of indicatory phreatophytes (plants that draw their water from a shallow water table), such as reeds and tamarisks, most holes are likely to be dry or of ephemeral seasonal yield only. Furthermore, holes dug in the wadi floor are subject to damage by periodic floods, and the loose earth walls oozing with water inside the well can collapse at the most inauspicious moments.

In time the dwellers of the Negev learned to line and reinforce their wells, and to locate them on higher ground alongside the wadi rather than in the stream bed. Such wells, tapping shallow groundwater recharged by floodwater, are found in a number of locations in the Negev. An outstanding example is the well at Yerokham, which even in summer provides enough water to allow the use of a motorized pump. Here the gravel bed of a large wadi is underlain by a tight layer of marl (a mixture of chalk and clay) at a depth of 10 meters or so. Wells of this sort, however, yield only slight amounts of water in most cases, and users may have to wait hours until an emptied hole refills. Following a succession of droughts, or even a single drought, a shallow well may go completely dry.

In some places the seepage from the wadis may be sufficient to permeate porous rock formations that can serve as aquifers. In such places deeper wells can be drilled into the bedrock, and the supply obtainable is likely to be perennial — that is, more steady and dependable and less affected by seasonal variations of precipitation. Wells of this sort are fairly common in the northern Negev, and several ancient ones can also be found in the central Negev. Two outstanding examples are the wells at Rehovot (Ruheiba), first described by Woolley and Lawrence and found to be over 100 meters deep, and the well at Ovdat, which is nearly 70 meters deep. These wells, choked with the dust and debris of centuries, were hardly discernible. When cleaned out, however, they proved to be living wells, flowing with water at apparently the same depth and rate as when first constructed.

The story of the Ovdat well is worth telling in detail. The well is located at the foot of the hill on which the ancient town was built, several hundred meters from the large wadi known as Nahal Zin. Alongside the well stands a Byzantine bathhouse. Above the mouth of the well are the massive foundations of a structure that apparently collapsed into the well, and that might have served to house the winch or windlass device by which the water was originally drawn out. A British-led crew in 1936 excavated the site and attempted to clean out the well. They stopped short, however, at a depth of about 35 meters, having apparently run out of patience, time, equipment, or funds. And so, for nearly

20 years, there remained this gaping round hole, 3 meters wide at the opening, to puzzle all visitors. Some claimed that it was a giant, deep cistern, while others conjectured that it must have been a well, or at least an unsuccessful attempt at one.

In the early years of Sdeh-Boker, we had all assumed that importing water from nothern Israel to the Negev highlands would be an economic impossibility. Our task, therefore, was to develop the local water resources. Quite naturally we attempted first of all to create a surface reservoir by damming up a wadi. So we built an earthen dam across the wadi in the Gap, just west of the settlement. When the first flood came, the reservoir was indeed filled to capacity. The scarred earth scraped by the machines behind the dam was submerged under a smooth, shining pond of quiescent water. And there was water enough, we figured, to supply our needs for the coming summer; enough for our livestock, too; even enough for us to pump out and irrigate a small tract of land where we might plant some fruit trees. It is hard to describe the elation we felt, and the pride, knowing that our dam had withstood the onslaught of the flood, that it was strong and stable, and holding water. Jubilantly we jumped into the cold, muddy water and swam in it, fully clothed. Alas, ours was an ephemeral and illusory success, for the water soon seeped away, several feet each day, into the underlying gravel. And there we stood, helplessly watching the shrinking of our pond and of our hopes, as what had seemed like a veritable lake became a bed of sticky mud that soon began to cake and crack as it dried, retaining not a drop of water.

So the water had infiltrated into the gravel under the dam. Might it remain there, and could it be tapped and recovered? So thinking, we decided to pursue the water on its underground course. We set up a makeshift, hand-operated drilling rig in the wadi just below the dam, and drilled laboriously through several meters of gravel, sand, and silt, only to arrive at the solid bedrock without finding any of the lost water, which had evidently escaped irretrievably into the fissured rock below.

We next turned our attention to the old well at Ovdat. I, for one, was convinced that it was indeed a well. My conviction was based on the presence, several kilometers away, of small and highly picturesque springs (Ein Ovdat and Ein Mor), which flow out of the same Eocene limestone formation in a deeply incised gorge at a level corresponding to less than 100 meters below the top of the well at Ovdat. Although a good 8 kilometers from Sdeh-Boker as the crow flies (or 12 kilometers along the winding road skirting the edge of the Chasm, as we called the canyonlike Valley of Zin), Ovdat was, from the start, a focus of great interest to us. There, on a prominent hilltop, in splendid and lonely eminence, stood the proud old city, defiant of time, its glories undiminished—indeed, enhanced—by the state of its dust-choked, half-hidden ruins. There were remnants of temples and fortresses on the hilltop, of catacombs and cave dwellings on the hillside, and of ancient farm systems

A spring flowing out of the Eocene limestone at the bottom of a canyon leading to the Valley of Zin. Though somewhat brackish and meager, a living perennial spring in the midst of the barren desert is a sight to gladden the heart of a weary wanderer in the desert.

complete with terraces, spillways, dikes, and conduits in the valley below. There we spent days on end, rummaging through the remains, our mind's eye probing the distant vistas and faraway times, our fantasy reviving the city in all its glory and busy commerce. And it was there that we first conceived the plan to reconstruct the old city and its associated farming systems, and to test whether the latter can be operated as in the days of yore. In time all these things were done, and the first among them was the revival of the old well.

In the summer of 1954, we were finally able to organize a team of well drillers to probe the bottom of the old well until they reached either the original floor or water. They set up a sturdy tripod of steel and a pulley to lower the diggers into the well and withdraw the excavated debris. The job had to be done by hand, and with the greatest care, to protect and recover whatever archeological treasures might be hidden inside. Men working in the pit loosened the fill with pickaxes and spades, and sent it up in barrels. From time to time they encountered a large stone or boulder, and worked for hours to pry it loose with steel rods. As the initiator of this project, I felt bound to take part in the work personally, and it was hellishly uncomfortable. The air at the bottom of that hole was dank and stagnant, and hazy with a sticky, chalky dust that caked in our eyes and mouths, and the walls of the pit felt slimy. Standing down there, gazing upward through the mist at the circular spot of light high above, examining the ancient chisel marks of the original excavation on the vertical walls, tracing the labors of long gone and nameless, yet strangely familiar, men of old, we felt an almost eerie sense of communion with the earth and with the past. The deeper we got, the narrower became the circular shaft containing us and the smaller the spot of light above. And our respect grew for the skills and endurance of our long gone predecessors.

At 65 meters the slick walls began to exude water that trickled onto the soggy bottom. A couple of meters, and the solid floor of the old well appeared, and soon we were standing in a pool of clear, cool water, apparently at the original level, still marked as a ring of faint green (dead algae) on the circular rock wall. Even more striking was the fact that the water level in the well matched the level of the nearby spring. A test of the water showed it to be slightly brackish, though still drinkable, with the same concentration (about 900 parts per million of chlorides) and quality as the spring water of Ein Ovdat and Ein Mor.

Of the remains of ancient wells in the Negev, none are more interesting than those of the "chain wells" in the Arava Valley. Known as *karez* or *qanats* in Iran and as *foggaras* in North Africa, chain wells are long, nearly horizontal underground tunnels designed to tap the groundwater at some higher elevation (generally at the foot of the mountains) and lead it to an outlet in the valley. Chain wells are found throughout the Near and Middle East, most typically in Iran, where for countless generations they served as the principal method of supplying water to villages and towns. They consist of one or more mother wells drained laterally through a gently sloping tunnel that emerges at ground surface some distance (perhaps many kilometers) away from the source.

To provide access to the lateral tunnel, as well as ventilation and a way to dispose of the excavated material, there are vertical shafts dug from the surface to the tunnel at regular intervals. These shafts not only facilitate the initial construction of the tunnel, but also allow the later removal of blockages that may result from the occasional collapse of the unsupported sides or top of the tunnel. The surplus excavated material is deposited around the mouth of the shaft, typically forming a circular mound. At the surface the whole system looks like a long chain of hollow mounds running down to the valley floor. The mother wells may be over 100 meters deep, and the upper part of the tunnel, below the water table, serves as a seepage gallery, often with many side branches to increase the volume of water tapped.

Qanats are of Persian origin and date back more than 2,500 years. Herodotus, in writing about the wars in Persia, described the way towns could be subdued by filling in their wells, thus plugging their supply tunnels. Nowadays, lines of *qanat* mounds may lead to nothing but abandoned old wells; many *qanats* had dried or clogged, and the system became unusable. The extraction of water from the desert earth, by means of *qanats* as well as ordinary single wells, has always been a chancy enterprise. Even at best, *qanat* systems require maintenance, and prolonged neglect leads to eventual failure.

When I first visited rural Iran in the late 1950s, there were operating *qanat* systems everywhere, and I had the chance to observe the *qanat* diggers at work. They were a special breed, an ancient caste proudly practicing their exclusive and hazardous craft that had been passed from father to son for countless generations. Into the shafts and tunnels and secret passageways they would crawl and burrow, molelike, with nothing more, it seemed, than a rope, a basket, a hand spade, and the fatalistic courage and skill of generations to serve them inside the lonely depths. Twenty years later, when I revisited Iran, most of the *qanat* systems appeared to have been abandoned, victims of the modern motorized pump and the illusion of cheap petroleum fuel. And what happened to those formerly indispensable and proud members of the ancient order of *qanat* diggers? Deprived of their traditional livelihood and mission, had they simply gone to the city, there to blend with and vanish into the amorphous lumpenproletariat of the brave new industrial society?

Qanats are limited to sloping lands, usually alluvial fans of gravel outwash at the foot of a mountain range, where the seepage of floodwater forms a

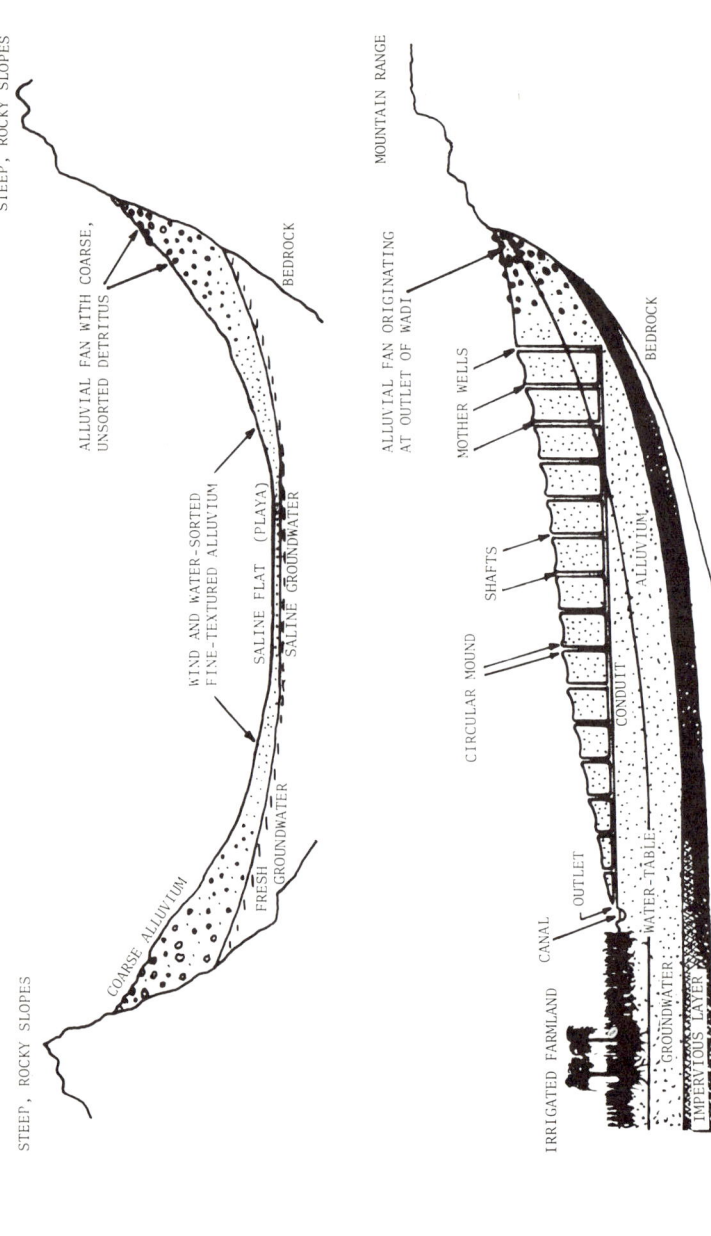

Groundwater in the desert.
A. Cross section of an intermontane basin in the desert.
B. Cross section of a *qanat* system. The fresh groundwater is intercepted in the alluvial fan (where the stream emerges from the mountains into the basin) by means of "mother wells." The fresh water thus tapped is conveyed by gravity through a gently sloping tunnel, which emerges at the valley floor and delivers water to irrigable farmland.

Tapping Groundwater

Runoff-irrigated terraces planted to deciduous fruit trees at Sdeh-Boker. In the dry season the trees are irrigated by means of a pipeline. (Courtesy of S. Buchbinder)

perched water table in the porous sediment resting on a relatively impervious bedrock. The perched groundwater drains slowly toward the valley floor, where a saline marsh often forms. As the groundwater drains toward the valley, it approaches the surface until it becomes exceedingly shallow. At the focal center of the drainage basin, the water tends to be nearly stagnant and highly mineralized owing to evaporation, though at its source, the upper wadi alluvium, the water is normally fresh. The purpose of the *qanat* system is to tap the fresh water and convey it by gravity to irrigable land above the valley floor rather than depend on the naturally emerging, saline water at the bottom of the valley.

Such *qanats*, or chain-well systems, have been found near at least three oases in the Arava Rift Valley: Yotvata (Ein Ghadian), Evrona (Dafieh), and Ein Marzev (Zureib). The ones described by Evenari et al. (1959) range in length from several hundred meters to about 4 kilometers, with remnants of vertical shafts spaced 15 to 25 meters apart. Attempts to excavate a few of the mother wells revealed the present water-table level to be about equal to what the original level must have been in order for the same system to be operational. Since these systems, long abandoned, have been partly obliterated by floods and wind-blown sand, they are difficult to discern. It is likely that a thorough investigation of both sides of the Arava Valley will reveal many more than are known at present. Their importance derives from the fact that the oases they served (or even created) were situated on the highroad linking the Red Sea port of Eilat, via the Negev, with the populated regions to the north and northwest (including the Mediterranean coast).

Thus we see how versatile the ancient desert civilizations were in adapting to the potentialities of each location, and in learning to find and utilize groundwater even where it is scarcest. Over the greater part of the Negev, however, it is runoff rather than groundwater that constitutes the principal source of water for people, livestock and crops.

19

Crops and Cropping

> A land of wheat and barley, vines, fig trees and pomegranates, a land of oil olives and honey; a land wherein thou shalt eat bread without scarceness, thou shalt not lack anything in it.
>
> Deuteronomy 8:8–9

Thus far we have concentrated mainly on the physical and technical aspects of ancient desert agriculture and its modern extensions. But of course dikes and conduits, wadi diversions and spillways do not themselves supply food. They are only the elaborate and ingenious means to achieve the practical aim of food production. The mere fact that the Negevites of ancient times engineered such intricate and extensive hydraulic systems in the desert is interesting in itself. However, the character and degree of their activity in the desert is not fully understandable to us unless we know something about its ultimate utility. Interpreting the way old installations functioned technically does not provide the whole answer. The economic potential of these installations lay in the crops they were designed to produce. In short, a consideration of ancient desert agriculture in its total context requires knowledge of the end sought and achieved, as well as of the means employed. That end was to sustain and feed a stable populace of many tens of thousands in a desert where normal (rainfed) cropping was impossible.

What crops did the ancients raise in their terraced fields, and how well did these crops justify the great effort invested in creating the systems needed to irrigate them? The answer, perhaps surprising, is that, to the best of our knowledge, the desert farmers of antiquity produced on their flood-irrigated land the very same crops that were produced in the more northerly and humid regions of the country and were common throughout the Mediterranean realm. Of course we cannot know exactly, since crops do not leave remnants comparable with those of stone structures. But we have considerable evidence on which to base our conjecture.

In the first place, we have the practices of the Bedouin to go by. The Bedouin are today's runoff farmers, and they have been farming in the Negev in much the same way, practically unaffected by changes elsewhere, throughout the many centuries since they replaced the descendants of the Nabateans after the seventh-century Moslem conquest of what was then a Byzantine province. That conquest did not bring immediate destruction of the ancient farming communities. For a few generations after the Byzantine eclipse, these communities were maintained. Only gradually did the change in overall economic circumstances cause abandonment of the old towns and neglect of the old installations.

The Bedouin who took over the land from their sedentary predecessors also adopted some of their basic methods. The main pursuit of the traditional nomadic Bedouin is grazing the desert range. But an important secondary activity of the Bedouin who became seminomadic or semisedentary has been the cropping of flood-irrigated land, or runoff farming. Although the greater number of the old systems lie abandoned and the installations used by the Bedouin were not nearly so extensive and efficient as those of the ancient farmers, they employed the same principles of runoff collection and, in places, even wadi diversion. We have no doubt that they learned these principles and methods from the technically more advanced settlers who had preceded them, and that likewise they copied some of the predecessors' cropping practices. Thus, the Bedouin have continued to raise seasonal field crops as well as fruit trees in numerous patches of runoff-receiving land. To this day one can find scores of Bedoui *boustans* (small orchards) in the Negev highlands and foothills, usually hidden in narrow wadis. Planted behind earthen dikes sometimes 2 meters high, such *boustans* may be less than a tenth of a hectare in size. Yet in them one may find, intermixed, such varied trees as almonds, apricots, figs, olives, and pomegranates, grapevines, and occasionally date palms. Chancing upon such a plantation during the fruiting season and savoring its delicious, sun-ripened fruits is an experience never to be forgotten. Just resting in the cool shade of such trees, in the midst of the sunbaked barrenness of all around, perhaps after an arduous exploration of a tortuous wadi, is a memorable and special delight.

Although the perennial fruit orchards of the Bedouin are small and few, their seasonal fields of annual crops are numerous and extensive. The principal winter crop is barley, but occasionally the Bedouin plant wheat or legumes (peas). After the first effective rains of the season, in late autumn or early winter, the Bedoui seeks a wet spot where runoff has accumulated. He may test the depth of wetting by probing the soil with a stick. If the soil appears sufficiently wet, and it is sufficiently early in the season, the Bedoui will scatter seed over the earth, then hitch his camel to the ancient chisel plow and scratch the soil to mix in the seed. Within the corrugated shallow furrows the seeds may germinate even if no subsequent rains come. Once planted and germinated, a grain field requires little care (though it is vulnerable to stray goats and camels), and the Bedoui may wander off for many weeks — being certain, however, to return in time for harvest. The unwritten law of the desert forbids any man to harvest what has been planted by another.

If the rains are delayed and the first effective ones do not come until it is too late for a winter crop, the Bedoui may prepare the land for a summer crop, to be planted in the spring, by plowing to eradicate the weeds and to conserve soil moisture. Before the time for planting summer crops, one can ascertain the amount of moisture accumulated in the soil by the winter rains and their resultant runoff, and on this basis decide whether indeed to plant a summer crop, and which one. The most common summer crops are grain sorghum, various cucurbits (such as melons), and tobacco (the latter being a relative newcomer from the New World, unknown to the ancients).

To the sure, the ancient Nabatean or Byzantine farmer was not like his Bedoui counterpart. He had permanent tenure over his land and its installations, and was a member of a more highly organized and technologically advanced society. Nevertheless, we may gain some insight into ancient farming by observing Bedoui ways. If the Bedouin are successful in producing crops in the Negev, we may assume that the ancients were at least equally so.

Something needs to be said at this point in defense of the Bedouin. They have been stereotyped as thoughtless and uncaring exploiters of the desert ("the sons of the desert who quickly become the fathers of the desert wherever they go," as some harsh critics have written). In fact, the Bedouin do understand their environment, and harmonize with it as best they can. Given the constraints of their traditional situation, they could scarcely do much better. One constraint was the lack of land tenure. Why would any rational person invest the great effort necessary to construct an elaborate runoff farming system if he did not own the land and could not protect his handiwork? It was while living among the Bedouin in the mid- and late 1950s, and learning their language and lore, that I began to perceive how very much they know about the ways of the land and its water regime, and how clever they are at the art of survival in the desert without the benefits of land tenure, recognized water rights, and a benevolent central authority, all of which were essential to the success of earlier civilizations.

In the 25 or so years since then, many of the Bedouin of the northern Negev have become sedentary, and are now living in permanent houses and even townships. Anything but slothful, many of them earn good wages as diligent workers on farms, in factories, and on construction projects. Young Bedouin attend secondary schools, and some go on to higher education. Health and longevity have improved. Bedouin now own tractors and operate farm machinery. And all of this revolutionary metamorphosis has taken place in the course of a single generation. Surely, this is progress! Why, then, do I have a sense of regret over the progressive disappearance of that age-old and honorable way of life, so rapidly being blended into that homogenized modernity that submerges us all?

We can derive more direct evidence concerning crop production in ancient times from the papyri found at Nessana in 1937 (Kraemer 1958). These papyri date from the sixth and seventh centuries—the end of the Byzantine Christian and the beginning of the Arab Moslem eras. Many of the papyri were fragments of books, mostly religious. Of the nonliterary papyri, which include documents in Greek and Arabic recording various economic and legal transactions, about 25 percent make some reference to agriculture and mention reservoirs, water channels, fields, gardens, vineyards, and crops of wheat, barley, aracus (apparently a legume), olives, grapes, figs, and dates. Among the most interesting of these documents, studied by Mayerson (1959), is an account of the amounts of wheat, barley, and aracus sown and reaped. It seems to indicate that wheat was a more common crop than barley (though nowadays the reverse is true in the Negev), and that grain yields were as high as those reported in ancient and medieval documents for regions having much greater rainfall than the Negev: seven or eight times the amount planted. Similar yields are still obtained by the Bedouin in satisfactory or good seasons.

Modern farming in the northern Negev (rainfall 250-400 millimeters per annum), using improved varieties and fertilizers, produces much greater yields (over twenty times the amount planted), but this is not comparable with ancient runoff farming. In our second full winter season at Sdeh-Boker, the winter of 1953/54, we grew both wheat and barley in a shallow depression where runoff collected from the loessial plain. Though with 89 millimeters of total rainfall this was a somewhat drier season than the "average," three well-distributed rainstorms totaling 51 millimeters were effective in producing runoff: one in mid-December, the second in mid-February, and the third in early April. Our yields were 1,210 kilograms of wheat and 1,540 kilograms of barley per hectare, which are slightly over eight and ten times, respectively, of the quantities of seeds planted. Considering our inexperience at the time, we held these to be satisfactory yields. However, David Ben-Gurion, who had resigned from the government to become a member of our settlement, complained that our yields were a far cry from the record hundredfold yield purportedly gathered 3,500 years earlier by Isaac (Genesis 26:12).

On the basis of indirect evidence, Mayerson (1959) calculated that the annual wheat production in the Nessana district may have been nearly 200 tons—enough to feed some 1,000 habitants. (Kraemer [1958] estimated the population of Nessana at no more than 1,500.) The ancient population of the central Negev subregion, at its peak, may well have exceeded 30,000; we cannot, however, simply extrapolate the Nessana figures (themselves only rough estimates) to cover the whole region.

The Nessana papyri also attest to the cultivation of vineyards. Other documents record the tax demands for oil (almost certainly olive oil) at about 5 percent of the total yield, which would suggest that the community of Nessana may have been self-sufficient in oil as well. There is irrefutable evidence of grape and olive production in the archeological findings of presses for wine and oil at several of the Negev's ancient sites. Kraemer (1958) has estimated from the analysis of two papyri that in one year over 2,500 baskets of dates were sold to traders in Nessana. This, together with the fragments of palm branches that had been used in the mud-wattle roofing of a room, would seem to prove that date palms were grown at Nessana, a rather surprising fact in view of their high water requirements.

Some seeds were discovered with the papyri in one of the time-sealed rooms of a monastery in Nessana. Most of the seeds were identified as weeds, but some were of the crops mentioned in the papyri. In addition, seeds of pomegranate, almond, peach, and walnut were found. While these fruits may have been imported, it seems more probable that they were grown locally.

Recent experiments with these species, as well as with others, conducted under runoff irrigation conditions in the northern and central Negev, proved that these trees can indeed thrive locally, and produce satisfactory yields. Peaches, almonds, figs, and pomegranates are particularly noted for their drought-resistance and hardiness. An experimental orchard of peaches, apricots, plums, and almonds, planted in a terraced section of Nahal Haroah near Sdeh-Boker in 1953, developed beautifully for several years; however, it had been provided with some supplementary irrigation. In 1956, unfortunately, the orchard was cleared to make room for a new commercial planting of apricots and peaches grown under full irrigation. Later experiments with some of the same species of fruits, grown in the reconstructed runoff farms at Shivta and Ovdat, were largely successful, as reported by Evenari et al. (1971).

Certain considerations are inevitably involved in crop cultivation under runoff farming, as the Negevites of antiquity were undoubtedly aware. Efficient runoff inducement and utilization could probably ensure a minimally adequate supply of water in most (though not all) seasons. But no amount of engineering ingenuity could control the anomalies of the weather, and the ancient farmer could not know ahead of time what each season held in store. The rains often started late, or ended early; there might be only one effective (runoff-producing) rain, or even (though rarely) none. In seasons of several effective rains, the latter might all be clustered in the early or late part of the season, or they might be evenly spread throughout the season.

All this made the growing of annual crops highly hazardous, while the growing of certain perennial crops, such as winter-dormant fruit trees, was less so. Perennials are generally deeper-rooted and, if assured of a thorough wetting at least once each season, they can thrive even in a relative drought. The problem of the initial establishment and early growth of tender young plants, encountered each season with annuals, is less acute with perennials. Individual saplings could be given limited supplementary irrigation with cistern-stored water to ensure their establishment during the first season or two, after which they would be expected to survive on the basis of collected runoff alone.

The production of annual crops tends to aggravate soil erosion. The act of plowing the land early each season loosens the unstable surface soil and makes it even more vulnerable to the erosive action of raindrops and of running water. This hazard exists in the perennial plantations as well (where occasional plowing is necessary to help eradicate the weeds), but to a lesser degree. The ancients quite evidently took great pains to avoid erosion in the fields, by controlling flow rates in conduits and by constructing sturdy terrace dikes and spillways.

My measurements of the soil-water regime in cropped fields have shown that the medium-textured and relatively stone-free arable loessial soils of the Negev highlands retain, after being thoroughly wetted, about 250 millimeters of water per meter depth of soil. That is, if all the retained soil moisture were extracted from under a unit area of soil having a depth of 1 meter, and if this water were impounded over the same unit area, the water depth would be 250 millimeters. This is equivalent to 2,500 cubic meters per hectare. Of this amount I found that about three-fifths is available for subsequent plant use. If a field had been wetted by floodwater in the winter season to a depth of, say, 2 meters, and if, moreover, the planted summer crop were deep-rooted, then it would have available to it a reservoir of extractable soil moisture amounting to three-fifths of 500 millimeters — that is, 300 millimeters. This amount would be sufficient to sustain a drought-tolerant crop such as grain sorghum even without replenishment of soil moisture by late-season rains or floods. Such replenishment would, however, enhance yields.

At Sdeh-Boker we were successful in growing several species of summer crops in the wadi bed of Nahal Haroah even after the drought winter of 1952/53, entirely on the strength of that season's single flood, which had occurred in early March. We did still better during the following two summers, as the detailed published accounts (Hillel 1954; 1955) show. The summer crops grown successfully on winter floodwater irrigation included grain sorghum, sunflowers, corn, watermelons, other melons, squash, cucumbers, and even tomatoes. Unfortunately, this work has not continued after the pipeline made possible summertime irrigation with imported water. Later experiments with winter and summer crops grown on reconstructions of ancient runoff farms were reported by Evenari et al. (1971).

20

Grazing the Desert Range

> For the mountains I will take up a weeping and wailing,
> And for the pastures of the wilderness a lamentation,
> For they are so scorched.
>
> Jeremiah 9:9

The desert regions bordering the Fertile Crescent have been the domain of nomadic and seminomadic herders since time immemorial. The Bible refers repeatedly to the Midianites, Amalekites, and the other "Sons of the East" who dwelt in the desert, and at one point (Exodus 3:1) tells us that "Moses was keeping the flock of Jethro his father-in-law, the priest of Midian, and he led the flock to the farthest end of the wilderness and came to the mountain of God, unto Horeb." (The name Horeb, incidentally, implies both desolation and dryness.)

The Negevites of antiquity likewise engaged in animal husbandry, in addition to crop production. The Nessana papyri mention camels explicitly. These were used by the imperial (Roman and Byzantine) troops garrisoned in this frontier province, as well as by the local inhabitants, for riding and as beasts of burden. Stables for horses were discovered at Mampsis (Negev 1979). It is certain, also, that flocks of goats and sheep were kept. There is abundant (albeit indirect) evidence of this in the fact that a high fence surrounded each runoff farm, and in the numerous remains of stone corrals of various ages. The presence of hundreds of laboriously constructed cisterns, at sites remote from the urban centers and from the main trade routes, attests to the extensive grazing of the desert range practiced by the ancient civilizations of the Negev.

During intervals between periods of sedentary occupation, grazing by seminomads was undoubtedly the main source of subsistence. Even during periods of the most intensive settlement, however, considerable tracts of wadi land remained unterraced, or at any rate uncultivated, especially at some distance from the principal ancient towns. Although for many centuries the region has been overgrazed by the Bedouin, the wadi beds still support a highly pasturable vegetation composed of a mixture of annual and perennial grasses and legumes, of shrubs and occasional trees. The grazing potential, or carrying capacity, of the uncultivated wadis in the Negev highlands was in all probability great enough to support many thousands, or even scores of thousands, of sheep and goats. Nor was grazing confined to wadi beds. Then, probably more than at present, the vegetation of the extensive slopes, though sparse, provided considerable grazing value.

The present-day carrying capacity of the northern Negev highlands and foothills subregion has been estimated (Tadmor 1965) at about 50,000 sheep. This figure includes large tracts of wadi land that in antiquity were cultivated and unavailable for grazing, so it might seem too high to serve as a basis for estimating the conditions prevailing then. On the other hand, cultivated fields could be grazed at certain times (such as after harvest), and the present-day natural vegetation is undoubtedly much poorer and much below its potential grazing value, owing to the effects of overgrazing and erosion (especially in some of the wadis that were once shallow depressions abounding with pasture and are now deeply incised, gravelly gullies). So perhaps the available carry-

An overgrazed tributary wadi. Note the ancient terraces, formed by stone dikes.

ing capacity of the region was not much smaller then than it is now, despite the extensive appropriation of wadi land for cultivation practiced by the ancients.

All the evidence at hand leads to the conclusion that the ancients, especially during the Nabatean-Roman-Byzantine epoch, maintained a diverse agricultural economy in the central Negev, with cultivation and grazing carried out simultaneously. Since roaming livestock could devour and trample crops, destroy runoff-collecting conduits, accelerate erosion of slopes, and induce silting and pollution of cisterns, undisciplined grazing has always been a menace to farming. Only an organized and coordinated society could resolve and integrate such potentially contradictory activities as farming and grazing, as well as land and water rights, so as to avoid conflict and damage.

No such coordination existed in the Negev between the seventh-century destruction of the ancient Negevite civilization and the establishment of Israel in the middle of the twentieth century. The tribes of Bedouin that inhabited the region were engaged in internecine and interminable struggles over territorial rights, and none could be certain of long-term land ownership. Hence the careless way in which they treated the land and its vegetation. In good years their well-fed flocks would multiply. In drought years their numbers exceeded the dry range's carrying capacity. In the absence of any feed reserves or supplementary supplies, overgrazing would ensue. A succession of droughts would result in eradication of the most highly palatable plant species, and if the Bedouin were unable to find better pasture elsewhere, their flocks would be decimated and they would be impoverished for years. And the surface of the dry earth of the Negev, deprived of its protective vegetation and pulverized by the sharp hoofs of goats and sheep, would be blown away by winds and washed away by subsequent rains. So desperate could be their plight that the Bedouin, driven by starvation, would invade neighboring regions, where they would tear down fences and descend like locusts upon fields and orchards. No wonder they were regarded with such fear and hostility by their sedentary neighbors, whose crops were in all likelihood suffering the same drought.

The Bedouin's goat, incidentally, has been vilified and condemned before the court of expert opinion as an inveterate and incorrigible overgrazer, a denuder of vegetation and promoter of soil erosion, a cause of desertification, altogether a menace to civilization. It is too much guilt for one small scapegoat to bear. The truth of the matter is that overgrazing is caused by the people who put too many animals for too long on an area of rangeland incapable of sustaining them. With proper grazing management the goat is no special menace, and no worse than its cousin the sheep. However, with heavy grazing, and given no choice, the goat will subsist on anything it can find, including thorny and dry residues, and it will survive long after the sheep has died of starvation. The goat is a remarkably hardy animal, a constant forager, a spirited and whimsical individualist that gives meaning to the word "caprice." Anyone who has lived among the Bedouin, and shared their plight

Bedouin's goats grazing a barren hillside in the midday heat.

in times of drought, cannot but appreciate, even grudgingly admire, this clever little animal and its contribution to the survival of its owners, even though it can become an instrument of great destruction.

Shortly after the establishment of Israel, overgrazing of the Negev highlands range was curtailed. Consequently we had the opportunity to observe the rate at which the indigenous vegetation could regenerate and reestablish itself. Tadmor and I made repeated observations of the composition and density of the vegetation in special, undisturbed quadrates located in the various habitat types. We found, to our great amazement, that the rate of regeneration was higher than had hitherto been supposed. Fastest to regenerate were the sands of Yamin and Halutzah, where seemingly sterile, loose dunes became stabilized with sand-loving grasses within two decades. We watched the wadis regenerate, too, as species of palatable plants that were nearly extinct became increasingly prevalent. The slopes also regenerated, particularly on their north-facing sides and in the slope-bottom taluses. The advent of earth-scanning satellites in the late 1960s revealed the extent of the regeneration that had taken place in the Negev as a whole. In photographs taken from space, the international boundaries are clearly visible in the con-

Caked mud in a flood-irrigated basin, prior to reseeding with pasturable vegetation.

Propagating pasturable shrubs at Sdeh-Boker.

trast between the vegetation-darkened Negev and the bleached, denuded neighboring territories of northern Sinai and the southern Gaza Strip (Otterman 1974).

The natural regeneration can be accelerated by artificial reseeding. This involves widespread dissemination or actual plantings of seeds of selected species and varieties that are particularly nutritious and pasturable, as well as ecologically adapted to the local conditions. Another criterion for the selection of species is their effectiveness in forming a soil-covering and erosion-preventing sod. The surest approach is to identify the best of the local species and to collect their seeds. When we began this work in the early 1950s, however, we could not find enough plants of the desirable species to provide a significant quantity of seeds, since these plants had been selectively decimated and practically eliminated by long-term overgrazing. So we had to embark upon the laborious task of multiplying a small seed stock under nursery and field conditions. In other words, we had to treat our native pasture plants as an agricultural crop, and to produce seeds in a quantity commensurate with the large areas surrounding Sdeh-Boker we had targeted for reseeding.

Further improvement of the wadi-bed range could be effected through selective eradication of the inedible shrubs, such as *Thymalaea hirsuta* (the shaggy sparrow wort) and *Retama roetam* (white broom), that might otherwise compete with the species to be reseeded.

The difficult emergence of seedlings through the dense loessial crust. Seedlings that fail to emerge quickly may lie smothered under the hardened crust, and an entire planting may fail.

The most important of the local species of perennial grasses we selected for reseeding were *Hordeum bulbosum* (bulbous barley grass), *Oryzopsis miliacea* (smilo grass), and a desert variety of *Dactylis glomerata* (orchard grass). In addition to these, we tried to introduce into the region grasses that were not growing there at the time but that we judged to be suitable, including *Phalaris tuberosa* (Harding grass), *Oryzopsis holciformis* (large-flowered smilo grass), *Agropyrum elongatum* (tall wheat grass), and *Panicum antidotale* (panic grass). An important native pasture grass that propagated itself whenever range conditions were improved, and in fact became a weed in our orchards, was *Cynodon dactylon* (Bermuda grass). The local vegetation also included numerous species of palatable annual grasses and legumes that reseeded themselves yearly and needed only to be encouraged to do so. Among these were *Avena sterilis* (wild oats), *Hordeum spontaneum* (wild barley), and numerous species of the genera *Medicago* (medics) and *Trifolium* (clover).

In addition to the grassy plants, we did much to propagate pasturable shrubs. In doing so, we had serveral purposes in mind: to utilize the moisture of deeper soil layers, beyond the reach of the root systems of most grasses; to prolong the effective grazing season by providing green and protein-rich edible foliage even after most of the grassy plants had completed their growing season and had dried out, generally in late spring or early summer; and to provide shade spots within the pasture. The two native species of shrubs we found to be most suitable for these purposes were *Atriplex halimus* (saltbush) and *Colutea istria* (a leguminous shrub). All this work is described in technical detail in a number of publications (Tadmor and Hillel 1956a, 1956b, 1957a, 1957b; Tadmor et al. 1965.)

One interesting problem we encountered in the course of our reseeding work was the characteristically low rate of germination exhibited by the seeds of many of the native plants. Their reluctance to germinate all at once is nature's way to preserve the species: were they to germinate too easily and uniformly after the first rain, the tender seedlings might all die in the long, dry spell that often follows the early rain. As it is, some seeds germinate after a rain, while others lie in wait for a subsequent rain, which may provide still more favorable conditions; some, indeed, remain in the soil for years before a thorough soaking finally brings them to life. The seed coats of desert plants are often waxy and water-repellent, and may contain various germination-inhibiting substances. However, in reseeding operations the low rate of germination is a distinct disadvantage and the problem is exacerbated by the crusting tendency of the soil surface. So we had to bring plant physiologists into the picture, and seek their help in developing pretreatments for seeds to enhance their germinability.

One simple and particularly successful case in point was saltbush, *Atriplex halimus*. It is a highly nutritious shrub (with a leaf protein content well over 12 percent of the dry matter), drought-resistant and salt-tolerant. The seeds,

A grass nursery at Sdeh-Boker, established for the purpose of selecting the most suitable species for reseeding the natural desert pasture.

Rows of *Atriplex halimus* planted across a wadi north of Sdeh-Boker.

however, are rather small, and are encapsulated in a bifoliate sheath that is usually charged with exuded salt. The seeds cannot readily germinate until a soaking removes the salt. Since we were the first to attempt to propagate this plant in the desert (it has since gained wide recognition), we had to devise methods to pretreat the seeds and then either to sow them directly in the field or to sow them in a nursery and then transplant the seedlings to the field (Koller et al. 1958).

In the course of this work, I tried out an interesting idea that, only many years later, proved to have succeeded. The idea was to plant multiple rows of *Atriplex* plants across the wadi beds, at regular intervals. If successful in slowing, spreading, and filtering the floods, such "vegetation dikes" could obviate the need for the laborious and expensive task of building stone dikes in pastured wadis. Moreover, if established at the headwater tributaries of a subregional wadi, the rows of *Atriplex* could serve as a source of seed for the eventual spontaneous reseeding of the entire downstream course of the wadi. The *Atriplex* rows I planted in the 1950s in the upper reaches of the Nahal Haroah, 7 or so kilometers north of Sdeh-Boker, were successfully established and withstood floods, but for some years seemed to have had no visible effect upon the vegetation downstream. It took over a decade for the effect to be

Goats grazing avidly on reseeded *Atriplex halimus* near Sdeh-Boker.

noticeable, and after 20 years it was undeniable. By early 1981 sections of the wadi bed near Sdeh-Boker, where no *Atriplex* at all grew in the 1950s, had become veritable jungles of luxuriant *Atriplex* plants, evidently the offspring of the mother plants established far upstream some 25 years earlier.

Because of the extensive nature of the desert range, being scattered and sparse rather than continuous and concentrated, and because of the great and unpredictable variations in seasonal water supply, the age-old practice of individual herders tending small flocks, trailing them into the hills and faraway tributary wadis, seems as anachronistic as the equally ancient practice of using hand labor, aided by animal power, to cultivate the small and irregular patches of discontinuous and sporadically flood-irrigated arable land. Nowadays we require, above all, "efficiency," by which we generally mean "labor-saving." To graze the desert range efficiently requires fencing of large areas, providing continuously available water in many places, and managing large flocks with minimal handling. No longer does it seem practical to use the desert range to raise milking goats and the traditional Awasi milking sheep, which must be gathered and tended individually twice a day. Instead, meat and wool production, and perhaps the breeding of specialized animals,* seem destined to become the major objectives in utilizing the desert range. The

---

*Perhaps including racehorses, or desert animals for zoos (such as gazelles, ibexes, oryxes).

problem is to establish an appropriate grazing potential, and to provide reserve feed for the eventuality of a drought.

The grazing potential, or carrying capacity, of wadi beds is similar to that of good rangeland in the northern regions of Israel. Improvement of the range by reseeding of desirable species and eradication of undesirable shrubs, together with occasional fertilization and—especially—a proper grazing load and seasonal schedule, can undoubtledly increase the carrying capacity. In normal years green pasture is available for about five or six months (December–May), though the beginning and end of the growing season vary with the rainfall-runoff pattern. For the rest of the year the range consists primarily of dry grass, with some green shrubs and, in seasons with late rains, some green summer grasses (such as native Bermuda grass). Supplementary feeding will be required during the dry season, particularly in drought years. In good years hay can be harvested in the wadi beds and stored on the range. There are periods, such as during germination and early seedling growth, when grazing the wadi beds can damage the pasture by trampling the seedlings and compacting the moist soil excessively. Hence, conjunctive utilization of the wadi beds and slopes must be optimized. The carrying capacity of the slopes is much lower than that of the wadis, but because they occupy roughly 20 times the area of the wadis, their total grazing potential is nonnegligible and may, indeed, significantly supplement the wadi-bed pasture.

In summary, the following principles should guide a contemporary or future settlement attempting to utilize the desert range:

1. Secure tenure to as large a tract of land as possible.
2. Survey the land and assess the grazing potential of the wadi beds and slopes.
3. Divide the area into sections, to be fenced and grazed on a rotation basis.
4. Avoid bringing the herd to a single center every day, and provide facilities in each section for the herd or flock to remain there for days or weeks, until shifted to another section.
5. Locate and improve cisterns and other water supplies at strategic locations in each section, so that the stock can be watered on the range.
6. Prepare and store supplementary feed (hay, silage, and grain) from local sources or from lands in the northern Negev especially designated for this purpose.
7. Improve water spreading in the wadi-bed range, starting as high up the watershed as topography will allow, in order to infiltrate as much floodwater in the soil as possible, as rapidly as possible, in the tributaries, thus minimizing potentially destructive floods downstream.
8. Further improve the wadi-bed range by eradication of undesirable shrubs, reseeding of high-quality species, and, if possible, by fertilization.

Thus summarized, these principles seem almost self-evident. However, there was much trial and error in the process of learning them. At Sdeh-Boker we began with a flock of the local fat-tailed (Awasi) sheep and the local black

Scenes from the early work at Sdeh-Boker
1. Finding water at the Ovdat well — the first pumping test.
2. Preparing to enter ancient, silt-choked cisterns.
3. Cleaning out the accumulated silt inside a large ancient cistern.
4. Exploring the region. Kneeling at right is Eytan.
5. Tadmor examining reseeding trials with pasture grasses.
6. Tadmor with the author in a newly reseeded loessial wadi bed.

goats, planning to milk them daily to produce cheese. This required permanent and proper milking and cheesemaking facilities at the settlement, so we had to take the flock out to pasture every morning and bring it in every evening. Hence there was a limit to how far we could graze and how much grazing land we could command, and the temptation to graze excessively at the near periphery of home was practically irresistible. Soon the trails leading to the various grazing areas were churned and pulverized, and the movement of the flock to and fro was marked twice daily by a dense cloud of moving dust. We could not do it in the way of the Bedouin, who herd small flocks, milk the goats and sheep on the range, and allow the flock to roam over the land and search for pasture wherever it may be found. Instead, we were determined to build a large herd of several hundred sheep so as to operate "efficiently" and at the same time live at the settlement, an approach that tied us to home base. The contradictions and drudgery of this approach eventually led to its abandonment.

Instead of milking goats and sheep, we then tried meat-and-wool sheep of the Corridale breed, imported from Australia. Still we brought them in every evening, because leaving them out on the range unattended at night was impossible for security reasons, and our people were determined to spend their nights at home. When it eventually proved impossible to sustain a large flock on the limited rangeland accessible daily from the settlement, we set up secondary grazing centers with portable corrals and a trailer camp at two locations some kilometers north and west of the settlement. The amenities at these camping sites left so much to be desired that the romanticism eventually faded and our people lost their enthusiasm for the task. We also trailed the flock every summer to the northern Negev, where the sheep could graze and fatten on the postharvest stubble of the vast barley fields. Trailing the flock each way took several days, during which we fancied ourselves to be reenacting Abraham's trek from his native Ur in Mesopotamia to the Promised Land, and the similar trek of Jacob on his return to his homeland with Leah and Rachel.

However romantic, our effort to trail sheep annually from region to region was eventually abandoned. At a time when even the Bedouin were forsaking their ancient ways and adopting modernity, modern Israelis were not about to become Bedouin.

The next attempt was to raise and graze horses in the Negev highlands. This venture had several advantages. One was that the grazing radius was greatly enlarged. Another was that herding horses on horseback seemed more dignified and exciting than herding sheep or goats on foot. However, the economic returns were meager and the horses proved to be less efficient than sheep and goats at utilizing the desert range.

We come finally to the last (or at least the latest) stage. After some years during which Kibbutz Sdeh-Boker seemed to have given up on grazing the desert range and to have turned to economic activities closer to home (pipeline

Grazing the Desert Range 199

irrigation of fruit trees, services to tourists, light industry), the settlement acquired a new flock of sheep. This time, however, the approach was to be different. The rangeland, extending over many hundreds of hectares, was fenced in sections, in which the flock or flocks could be left for days or weeks with minimal attendance. What had been impossible in prior times, because of the area's insecurity and the constant threat of sabotage, now became possible, particularly after the Egyptian-Israeli peace treaty. It is now becoming increasingly doubtful, however, that much of the territory of the Negev highlands will be available for grazing in the future, because of the increasing need for land for what seem like more pressing, non-agricultural uses: airfields, military installations, training areas, industrial centers. Nonetheless, the desert range, if properly developed and utilized, can constitute a very considerable economic resource, in the Negev as well as in many similar desert regions.

How well I remember those treks in the desert, and the intoxicating experience of wandering through the wadis and hills, oblivious to the turmoil of the remote cities, away from the mundane business and busy-ness of what one normally accepts as "ordinary life." For me it was an occasion to commune with the past, to sense the mystery of eternity, to measure my own ephemeral existence and physical frailty against the desert's sweep of time and space.

On a typical desert night the air is heavy with an eerie stillness, and very cold. The landscape, too, assumes a dreamlike placidity, bathed in the luminescence of myriad incredibly bright stars hanging low in a cloudless sky, while a lustrous moon hovers over a distant black mesa. Lie on the ground and submit to the lure of the night, feel the weariness of soul and limb dissipate slowly, and sense your body hovering miraculously in the midst of the desert's infinite beauty. Or turn your attention from the boundless vistas to the immediate surroundings, see the grotesque shadows of the twisted and stunted desert shrubs that seem to glide over the surface, listen to the whispering sounds of a distant owl or a lonely cricket, a fleeting jerboa or a plodding porcupine, the faint but undeniable stirrings of life even in the midst of desolation. Then hear your own breathing and heartbeat blend into the harmony of the universe. Observe, finally, as the eastern sky begins to brighten and streams of light illumine the western mountaintops with a warm reddish glow while the lingering veil of dark shadow gradually fades from the valley.

Or sit on a sloping ledge of bedrock overlooking the wadi in the midday's unlidded hour of unrestrained sunlight and observe the sheep grazing lazily below, almost motionless in the brief shadows of the bushes. Sit still and submit to the merciless sun, let its warmth suffuse your body as it suffuses the universe. Float away in time, to the distant past. Is herding sheep in the desert a part of life in the twentieth century or a return to an ancestral history? Is it real or illusory? Reality and illusion become indistinguishable. The desert casts its magic spell. The fantastic scenery unveils a land everywhere molded by the miraculous: the burning sun, the wheeling eagle, the barren fig tree—all the poetry and imagery of the Bible are here and now. Every mountaintop enshrines its secrets, every cave echoes the past, every protruding rock foretells the future, every ravine resounds with the voice of a prophet.

Inadvertently and momentarily, the mind wanders to a different landscape, to a memory of cheerful green pastures and azure lakes somewhere far away, only to return to the realization that this land is not cheerful, but somber. Here the dried-up streams, the shattered rocks, the crumbling tombs all bear witness, silent witness. It is as if the desert is still dumb with fear, as though having once heard the voice of the Almighty, it has never since dared break the silence.

Eytan was the best man we had on those long treks. Sandy-haired, stocky, powerful Eytan, the most indefatigable on foot, the surest on horseback and camelback. He smiled readily and laughed heartily, and even when he didn't, his eyes sparkled with mischievous humor. Simple and direct in manner and speech, Eytan was a farm-born man of the soil with no particular intellectual pretensions. But while alone he read poetry, and when climbing to the dizzying peak of a cliff, his eyes would betray the rapturous expression of a truly romantic spirit, a free spirit always willing to dare the new and untried.

Once, as we were sitting in the circle of light formed by a flickering fire amid the infinite gloom of an overcast desert night, savoring Eytan's special tealike brew of desert sage, he suddenly invited me to join his secret group of comrades and hike to Petra. Just like that—would you like to visit Petra? Petra the fabulous Nabatean capital, with its glorious temples and palaces carved in the red Nubian sandstone in the remote vastness of the rugged mountains of Edom. There was only one slight problem. Petra lay some 20 kilometers across the Jordanian border. To get there, we would have to start under cover of darkness from the Arava Valley and climb the steep and tortuous Wadi Musa, a rigorous climb even under the best of circumstances and in daylight. Surely this was a crazy plan. So I agreed.

The four other members of the pack were all ex-Palmachniks,* and their leader was Arik, the consummate adventurer, whose exploits were legion and legendary. He led a charmed life, having hiked on foot to the ancient Israelite site of Kadesh Barnea in Sinai, to the summit of Mount Hermon in Syria, and to many other out-of-the-way and dangerous places. Arik and Eytan were a perfect pair of friends: free, fearless, venturesome, wild, earthy—the epitome of their generation of Israeli youth and the antithesis of their ghetto-bred

---

*Members of the Palmach, the commando unit of the Hagannah, the underground guerrilla force that was the forerunner of the Israeli Army.

forebears. This is the generation that had come of age at the most trying and challenging time in their nation's history. They were called upon to serve and sacrifice without measure, and responded heroically. Throughout all their trials they maintained a cheerful faith and a romantic vision of the new state and the new society destined to be the culmination and justification of their struggles. But when the state came into being, there were profiteers who enriched themselves from dealings in real estate and importation of luxury goods, and a flood of unknowing immigrants and uncaring petty merchants selfishly exploited and despoiled land over which their predecessors had shed their blood.

Forgotten by what seemed like an ungrateful society, some of Arik and Eytan's generation had reason to feel disillusioned. Most, however, adjusted to the new life, taking up farming or commerce. Others entered the new state's universities to study a profession, making up for lost time by great diligence and pursuing academic achievement with the same zeal that was their hallmark in times of war. But a few of that generation could not make the transition from the glorious years of living history to mundane existence and ordinary affairs. They yearned to continue the exciting life by seeking great new exploits and high adventure.

The group assembled in Sdeh-Boker to prepare for the secret mission. For two nights we pored over maps and photographs to plan the foray in detail. Then, on the day before our planned departure for the Arava Valley, I received an unexpected radiotelegram. A colleague from the university in Jerusalem asked me to host and guide an international team of arid-zone ecologists intending to tour the Negev over the next couple of days.

I was in a quandary. One part of me was keyed up to go to Petra; the other, eager to receive the professional visitors. Adventure versus science, unfettered freedom versus responsibility, emotion versus rationality. The latter won, and I decided to remain. The trek to Petra could not be delayed because of the particular phase of the moon, by light of which we were to make our way.

The group left without me. I felt that I had lost a great opportunity. But I retained my life. Three days later their bodies were returned by the Jordanian border patrol that had tracked them and found their resting place in a cave above Wadi Musa. They were apparently on their way back when ambushed.

Some 20 years later I happened to be piloting a light plane from Tel-Aviv to Eilat. Flying along the western edge of the Arava Valley and gazing eastward, I noticed the notched ravine of Wadi Musa. Acting on a sudden impulse, I swerved the aircraft leftward and flew across the border and up the gorge to the high plateau. Circling, I caught a glimpse of Petra and its ornate facades all around the hidden valley. I banked sharply, leaned out the window, snapped a picture of the ancient city, then turned back. The entire foray, my private journey to Petra, took only about 25 minutes. Eytan would have loved it . . . or perhaps he would have found it too easy.

21

The Bedouin

> And Lot also, who went with Abram,
>   had flocks, and herds, and tents.
> And the land could not carry them together;
>   for their flocks were so great that they could not dwell together.
> And there was strife between the herdmen of Abram's flocks
>   and the herdmen of Lot's flocks.
> And Abram said to Lot: "Let there be no strife, I pray thee,
>   between me and thee, between my herdmen and thy herdmen,
>   for we men are brethren.
> Is not the entire land before thee?
>   Separate thyself, I pray thee, from me;
>   if thou wilt go leftward, I will turn rightward;
>   or if thou take to the right, I will go to the left.
>
> Genesis 13:5–9

In Arabic, the word *badia* means "desert," and the derived term Bedoui (pronounced *badawi* or *bedawi*) designates quite literally a "desert man" or "desert dweller." The Bedouin (plural of Bedoui) refer to their own tribes, however, simply as "Arab," believing themselves — with some justifiable pride — to be the original Arabs. Anyone studying the Negev, as well as other desert regions of southwestern Asia and northern Africa, cannot but take an interest in the Bedouin, for these remarkable people are the desert's truly indigenous inhabitants. Anyone also interested in history and in the Bible must, moreover, be doubly fascinated by the Bedouin, for here is a living relic of biblical times, a people who have maintained a distinctive culture and way of life almost without change for so many thousands of years. They remind us, too, of the

Israelites who wandered in Sinai and the southern Negev for the legendary 40 years before mustering the strength and courage to enter the Promised Land. The desert was the crucible wherein the Israelites were smelted and transformed from a disarrayed and motley assemblage of hardly freed slaves, aimlessly wandering over the trackless wasteland, into an organized and purposeful force imbued with a sense of destiny. To look at the Bedouin and their ways is to peer through the mirror of time at the ancient Hebrews. In the words of the prophet Jeremiah: "I remember thee the grace of thy youth, the love of thine espousals, how thou wentest after Me in the wilderness, in the land unsown."

Pondering these antecedents and the indelibly etched memories of the desert, one can better understand the ancient yearning of the desert nomad, metaphorically evoked in Psalm 23: "The Lord is my shepherd, I shall not want; he maketh me to lie down in green pastures, he leadeth me beside still waters, he restoreth my soul." The symbolic meaning of the Bedouin tent is conveyed, again by Jeremiah, as he laments: "My tent is spoiled and my cords are broken; my children have left me and are gone, and there is none to erect my tent any more and set up my curtains."

The Bedouin still pitch their tents of goat hair and camel hair in the shadowy, water-carved ravines beneath the awesome cliffs of Sinai and Edom and the Negev. Their nature and tradition are to care nought for political boundaries and to disregard temporal powers. Modern international realities, armies, and technology, alas, are compelling them to conform and to abandon their ancient ways. Yet the diehard Bedouin try to resist change, and cling stubbornly to their traditions that have been transmitted from generation to generation, from father to son and from mother to daughter, without ever having been written down. It is no less powerful for that. The rules and customs composing this tradition evolved over the many centuries, in response and adaptation to the requirements of life in the desert. So important are these rules and customs that one cannot begin to understand traditional life in the desert without knowing something about them.

We ask ourselves at the outset what is the secret of the Bedouin. Do they possess an innate physiological adaptation to the dry climate? The answer is negative. Although persons living in the desert can become, to some limited degree, physiologically acclimatized, as an ethnic group or race the Bedouin seem to have no unique or superior aptitude for achieving this. For instance, they are no better able than we are to live and function without water. Their adaptation is primarily a matter of strategy, behavior, and lifestyle, involving dress, shelter, and work habits. Perhaps it is also a matter of attitude. Psychologically, they seem able to withstand heat, thirst, hunger, and other physical discomforts and privations without complaint. They are indeed superior in this respect to most of us Westerners, pampered and comfort-craving creatures that we have come to be.

Wandering has traditionally been imperative for the Bedouin. Given

Bedoui flocks drinking and resting during the shadeless midday at a well in the Northern Negev. The land around the well is completely denuded of vegetation by overgrazing.

their stage of technological development, they could subsist only by roaming the land in constant search of water and pasture for their flocks. Nomadism required that all possessions be portable. No nonessential article must be owned, for it could become a hindrance. Making do with the fewest material goods possible was not merely a virtuous precept but a practical necessity. Economy and simplicity were the guiding principles. All the traditional furniture of the Bedoui and most of his other belongings are made of wool, leather, or wood, all lightweight and easy to transport, yet sturdy and durable. The original Bedouin were pure nomads who never cultivated land and never engaged in any activity requiring permanent attachment to a specific location or plot of land. The Bedouin of the Negev, however, had long undergone a process of transformation and had become seminomadic. But though they had taken up the sporadic cultivation of patches of land here and there, they did not become villagers and house dwellers, choosing instead to remain tent dwellers.

To the Bedoui, the tent is house and home, and he calls it that quite literally (*beit she'ar* or "woolen house"). The picturesque tents of the Bedouin are practical. Ideally, housing in the desert should be cool by day and warm by night. Thick walls and small windows help to achieve this in stone or mud houses, but these are hardly suited to nomadic life. The great black tents of the Bedouin do very well, however. They provide dense shade by day, and store up heat for the night.

The Bedouin

A Bedoui family tent, with a section reserved for domestic animals.

Often the Bedouin use different tents for winter and summer. The winter tent is especially sturdy, made of numerous pieces of thick cloth firmly sewn together by the women of the household. Typically the roof is woven of pure goat hair, which is strong, durable, and naturally water-repellent, therefore providing excellent shelter in winter. The side walls and partitions of the tent are knit of sheep wool and designed to insulate the tent against cold winds. Each part of the tent is given a distinctive name, based on the imagined anatomical parts of a crouching mythical creature. The roof is called "back"; the opening, "mouth"; the front poles, "arms"; and the rear poles, "legs." The typical tent is supported by three rows of poles. Compared with the winter tent, the summer tent is a rather flimsy structure, often made of worn woolen cloth or even sackcloth. The locations of the winter and summer tents also differ.

The winter tents are placed in sheltered hollows or on the lee side of a hill, where they are protected from the direct blast of the chill winds. (However much they seek shelter from the winds, the Bedouin do not, under any circumstances, place their tents in the wadi bed, where they might suddenly be flooded and even swept away without warning.) In most cases the tents are oriented with their openings facing east, while the rear—slanted, firmly anchored, and sealed—faces the westerly winds. In the summer the Bedouin seek greater exposure to the cool breezes, so they erect their tents higher on the hillsides or on a plateau. In either case the encampment must not be too far from a source of water.

The family bonds and tribal solidarity of the Bedouin are outstanding examples of how circumstances dictate social organization and individual behavior. The desert is a hostile and dangerous environment. Agony and death constantly threaten anyone who ventures alone into its emptiness. Vital resources, especially water and pasture, are so scarce as to be the objects of fierce competition. An individual, or even a small family, could hardly expect to survive under these harsh circumstances; but cohesive families, associated into tribes sharing common ancestry, whose members can rely utterly on one another, can and do survive. Such groups depend on the unswerving loyalty of each individual.

Thus, the absolute foundations of Bedouin society are family and tribe. Father (and mother or mothers), sons (and wives), and grandchildren constitute a nuclear family, which moves together as an inseparable unit and sets up its tents in a cluster. Several such families having common recent (male) ancestry form an extended family, in which cousins intermarry. Wherever possible, extended families remain in close proximity. A related group of such extended families composes a clan, and several clans, a tribe. Finally, a number of tribes may be associated in a larger intertribal group, an alliance of common background and common interests.

In the absence of written records, incidentally, it is amazing how the Bedouin remember their genealogy and ancestral associations. However, tribal and intertribal groups may include families or even clans that are not necessarily related by blood, such units having joined the group under various circumstances (such as war or some other cause of dislocation). In any case no Bedoui can exist as an unattached individual. In the absence of any permanent place of abode, his tribe is in fact a Bedoui's only address and his primary frame of reference. In a larger sense a Bedoui belongs to the "peoplehood" of the Bedouin. Only incidentally, if he ever thinks of it, does a Bedoui consider himself a member of the nation or state within the political boundaries of which he happens to reside.

A most important aspect of the traditional life of the Bedouin is their unwritten code of law. Rigid rules to govern proper conduct were formulated in times long past, and have been hallowed by tradition. Nowadays we find that long after the original circumstances changed, the code, and the set of values from which it derived, persist even though they are at variance with the modern state's legal code. In view of the fact that the "law of the desert" was never recorded or institutionalized, but only transmitted orally from generation to generation, it is remarkable that this "law" is so uniform and widespread.

Disputes among Bedouin may involve damages to a person's body, property, or honor, the last being no less important than the others. Justifiable grievances demand redress. In any dispute a Bedoui does not stand alone; his family and tribe stand with him. Knowing that they are protected even from afar allows the Bedouin to disperse widely in search of their livelihood. The mutual responsibility of family members knows no bounds of time or location. If an individual culprit, having committed a crime or a shameful act, wanders off or hides in the desert, his family is held accountable. Redress can be sought of his father, brothers, sons, grandsons, great-grandsons, on to the fifth generation. This five-generation partnership of blood relatives is called *el khams*. Each male member of the family must be willing not only to suffer the consequences of the acts of each of his relatives, but also to avenge each relative's life if that life is taken by adversaries. Thus, a family must discipline and constrain its men, lest by an impetuous act any one of them implicates or endangers the group as a whole.

Likewise, it is the family's and the tribe's collective responsibility to protect each of its members. Family and tribe being his lifeline, a Bedoui can be called upon to kill or die for them. The ever-present, time-unlimited, and place-unlimited threat of vengeance against anyone who murders a member of the family or tribe, though it may seem terribly violent and even barbaric to Westerners, can be perceived as a powerful deterrent against crimes of violence in an environment that requires fierce competition and that makes it easy to commit violent acts unobserved and to escape personal accountability.

Sanctions of the utmost severity were needed to enforce unity and responsibility within each tribe. The most terrible of the sanctions was expulsion, which usually meant an agonizing death in the desert. Any family or clan could expel any of its sons who might prove to be incorrigible. This act is called *tashmis* (Bar-Tsvi 1979), from the word *shams*, meaning sun. The clear and terrifying implication is that the offending person is to be cast out from the protective shade of his family and exposed to the merciless sun of the desert: alone, frail, and defenseless. A terrifying fate, reminiscent of God's punishment of Cain: "A fugitive and a vagabond shalt thou be in the earth."

If murder is committed and the murderer and his family do not make appropriate amends, there begins a blood feud that may, in extreme cases, last for generations. One killing calls for another, and the reciprocating chain of violence can become interminable. Blood vengeance committed on behalf of the family is considered to be a most honorable and courageous deed. The vendetta ends only when a final *sulkha* is declared, generally after elaborate negotiations and payment of compensation by the family responsible for the original offense. Achieving such an accommodation is sometimes facilitated by the intervention of a particularly venerable sheikh, whose prestige, once laid on the line, neither side wishes to defy.

The more positive side of the coin is the Bedouin tradition of hospitality. The common experience of perilous life in the desert generates a sympathy that at times transcends rivalry. The desert nomad who has himself undergone the agony of thirst, and perhaps even the lonely terror of vengeful pursuit, will generally not deny succor to a wanderer though he be a total stranger and possibly a fugitive. Perchance the wanderer or fugitive is merely a guiltless victim of misfortune, accident, or misunderstanding. If so, granting him temporary refuge may allow his difficulty or his quarrel to be resolved. This perception gave rise to the unique generosity and hospitality of the Bedouin, and their custom of protecting those who ask for help.

Reception of guests is in fact one of the highlights of Bedouin life, a relief from the boredom and drudgery of their generally uneventful daily lives, and a chance to compare circumstances and to learn the news of other places. (Before the age of the transistor radio, the Bedouin had no other source of news.) The guest honors his host with his presence and his trust. Both must behave appropriately, for any infraction or disregard of the ancient rules of hospitality is seen as insulting and uncivilized.

The elaborate and ritualized practice of hospitality consists of much more than supplying the guest's physical needs of food, drink, and shelter. If the guest is in trouble, the proper host will protect him as long as the man remains his guest. A grace period of three days is traditionally observed, during which no questions are asked. A guest ought not to remain longer, lest he abuse his host's hospitality. (However, in extraordinary circumstances, the guest may request—and be granted—the privilege of joining the host's household permanently.) The act of hospitality is not entirely altruistic, for it enhances the host's prestige and connections. One who is not a gracious host stands to lose his reputation and to be regarded with contempt. Moreover, the recipient remains beholden to his benefactor, and he and his family will always be willing to reciprocate with a favor of at least equal value. It is a subtle line of credit.

A special honor bestowed upon a particularly deserving or high-ranked guest is the holding of a feast. The assembled guests and local notables sit barefoot on the carpeted ground, and are given soft cushions to lean upon. Coffee is prepared from its fundamental ingredients. The beans are roasted in a long-handled metal spoon, held in the ashes of the aromatic fire that smolders continually in the tent. The roasted coffee beans are then placed in a wooden mortar, and the men take turns pounding them rhythmically with a wooden or stone pestle, using a staccato that broadcasts the festive occasion over the still evening air and can be heard a mile or more from camp. It conveys an invitation to all who can hear it to come and partake. This is the epitome of desert hospitality, simple and strong. The ground coffee is then mixed with water in a copper vessel and slowly brought to a simmer, again and again. Spices are added, and soon a dense fragrance fills the tent. When ready, the brew is a full-bodied coffee-cardamom distillate, sharp and uncloying, to be savored in small, slow sips.

All the while, conversation flows. Bedouin conversation is a highly developed art form. It, too, is to be savored unhurriedly. Its subjects range from gossip and news of contemporary affairs to desert lore, camels, and wildlife. Humorous anecdotes are told with great relish, as are elaborately embellished ancient tales of prowess and courage. The conversation diminishes only slightly when food is brought in, item by item. The main offering is a large tray piled with rice or a wheat mush covered with juicy chunks of broiled mutton. No utensils are needed. The assembled men partake of the food by hand. The meat and mush are rolled into balls with the fingers. A loud belch is a sign of heartfelt appreciation. The good host, using his well-licked fingers, offers choice morsels to his appreciative guest of honor.

The guest must be appreciative, for otherwise he might insult his gracious host. It is equally uncouth and ungrateful for the guest to ask for anything other than what is offered, or to refuse any of the offered items of food and drink, or to eat too little or too much, or to cast eyes upon the women of the household, who may be revealed from time to time whenever the partition between the "parlor" section of the tent and the kitchen section is opened to bring in additional food. The women and children, incidentally, partake of the leftovers at meal's end, and the final remains are fed to the dogs. Nothing is wasted.

The feast is indeed a special occasion, for the normal fare of the Bedouin is very much more modest. Most eat only one meal a day, and it consists of little more than dry bread, a mush of wheat flour or soured leban from camel's or goat's milk, and perhaps some dried fruit, washed down with sweet tea.

The Bedouin women are strictly subservient to the men. The birth of a male child is greeted with joy, that of a female with resignation. A growing son mingles with the men of the clan and learns the ways of the world. He adds strength to his family, clan, and tribe. A growing daughter remains with her mother until she is able to work. Then she is sent out to herd the lambs. She is also expected to gather firewood and weave woolen cloth. All the while she is confined to her own family. Her childhood ends very quickly, for she is generally betrothed before age 15 and married (often without being consulted) to a much older man, able to pay her father the going price for a bride. Once married, she is subservient to her husband, and if she lives long enough to survive her husband, she becomes subservient to her sons. If divorced, she returns in shame to her father's household. Taking a more positive view, however, we should note that the Bedoui woman is cherished and protected. Any harm done her is treated with the utmost severity, and violation of her honor can be cause for a family to mete out the death penalty to her violator.

Thus far we have described the traditional ways of the Bedouin. The fact is that, for better or for worse, their ways are changing. For even while the Bedouin are fond of recalling their glorious past, and wax nostalgic about it, their present circumstances are increasingly at variance with that past. They remember when they were autonomous and lived undisturbed, a law unto themselves, when they carried weapons and were a formidable force, respected and feared. Around the turn of the century, the Turks began to limit the freedoms of the Bedouin. Through a system of rewards (payments to compliant sheikhs) and punishments (military raids against defiant tribes and confiscation of their livestock), the Turks imposed their rule on the desert provinces. Resentment of this oppressive regime induced some of the Bedouin to rally to the rebellion instigated by Lawrence of Arabia during the First World War.

The British, who in turn ruled over Palestine, Trans-Jordan, and Sinai until after the Second World War, extended their power even more than the Turks and imposed many additional restrictions. Bedouin raids were no longer tolerated, and acquisition of arms was prohibited. Central courts were set up to adjudicate disputes, and police stations were established in key locations, with patrol units actively supervising regional affairs.

The establishment of Israel brought about the greatest change affecting the Bedouin of the Negev. Water, schools, roads, housing, agricultural development, machinery, jobs, and regional security were provided, and resulted inevitably (though not immediately) in a profound modification of Bedouin life in the Negev. Although changes in the customs and values of a society always lag behind the changes in circumstances, the Bedouin of the Negev are now much more sedentary than nomadic, and are in the process of substituting villages and permanent housing for portable tents.

Prior to 1948 there were more than 50,000 Bedouin living in the Negev. The war and upheaval associated with the establishment of Israel caused many of them to escape to the regions of Hebron, Sinai, and Gaza. When the situation was partially stabilized in 1953, there were only 11,000 or so Bedouin in the Negev, organized in 19 tribal units (Marx 1979). By 1960 their numbers had grown to 16,000, by 1970 to 22,000, and by 1980 to nearly 30,000. Because of the serious security problem that prevailed in the Negev in the early 1950s, the authorities concentrated nearly all the Negev's Bedouin in the northeastern corner of the region. Confined to a subregion of 1,000 square kilometers—less than 10 percent of the Negev—the Bedouin necessarily gave up wandering and took up farming, and their young men sought remunerative employment as laborers on construction projects, on Israeli farms, and in industry. At the same time they continued to be pastoralists and to raise livestock, though in a smaller area and increasingly for market rather than for pure subsistence. They still herd small family flocks of 10-100 sheep and goats, but the total number of their animals probably approaches 100,000 (including perhaps as many as 10,000 camels).

I lived among the Bedouin in the early and mid-1950s, and knew them before they became "modernized." Their status was still uncertain then, and some of them were living in dire circumstances. The most hopeless among them were those who remained "unofficially" in the Negev highlands, where they were caught in the crossfire, as it were, between the warring Israelis and Egyptians. A few of the Bedouin remaining in the Negev highlands col-

A Bedoui girl wearing her dowry.

laborated with saboteurs who repeatedly disrupted traffic by mining roads and ambushing passing vehicles.

It was in these tense circumstances that I attached myself one day to a contingent of Druze soldiers patrolling the area. I was curious to see what was then still unknown territory, and I did not expect any trouble. But as the convoy of jeeps and command cars rode up the tortuous dry stream bed and emerged on the Matred Plateau, we caught sight of numerous Bedouin. These were obviously some of the "lawless" Bedouin living outside the control of Israeli authorities, which at that time was still very tenuous in the mountainous parts of the Negev. The Bedouin had evidently heard our convoy coming, and were scurrying to escape. Some had already folded their tents, and were hastily retreating with all their belongings on camelback. Most, however, had left their tents and belongings behind, and were scattering on foot in every direction. Surrounding the plateau were low hills separated by winding wadis, and it was toward these wadis that the Bedouin were heading. Several stragglers were just leaving their tents as our convey approached.

Sporadic shots greeted us from the hills, and the Druze soldiers became visibly excited as they sensed action. The officer in command had no orders to destroy the Bedouin, only to warn them not to collaborate with the saboteurs. "Don't kill, just catch a few alive!" he shouted to his men as his driver sped toward the first cluster of tents. The other vehicles raced toward the hills to head off some of the stragglers, and caught a few old men, women, and children. Then they proceeded to knock down the tents, one by one. The military vehicles rolled over sagging black curtains, popping ropes and uprooting pegs. In the melee frightened goats, sheep, and asses stampeded every which way in total confusion.

When the captives were brought together, they turned out to be a wretched lot, shriveled old men and women in tatters, and skinny children with frightened eyes. One by one they claimed to know nothing about saboteurs from across the border, and were innocent even of the name of their sheikh. It soon became evident that the interrogation was useless. But the warning had been made: avoid helping the infiltrators, or be driven out of the territory, back to totally barren Sinai. The captives kept their stoic silence. They neither begged nor cowered, and as they were released and began to walk away without a word, I felt a sudden admiration for their dignity and a compassion for their sorry state. I wondered later about Jeremiah's exhortation: "Arise ye, go up against Kedar and spoil the children of the east; their tents and flocks shall they take; they shall carry away their curtains and all their vessels and their camels; and they shall proclaim against them a terror on every side; and their camels shall be a booty, and the multitude of their flocks a spoil." Was there never any mercy in the age-old struggle between settled and nomadic?

The Bedouin

A Bedoui plowing a plot of rain- and runoff-wetted ground at slope bottom, after seeding it to barley early in the rainy season.

After this incident I began to take a personal interest in the Bedouin. I befriended a small tribe living south of Beersheba, and spent days at a time, during each of the seasons, living among them and listening to their discourse about the desert they knew so well. They had such a keen eye for detail: they could discern the tracks of passing men and animals where I could see practically no signs at all, save for a stone here or there that had been moved slightly, or a piece of crusted soil pried loose. Their ability to describe what had passed over the land, and when, was uncanny. Furthermore, I was repeatedly astonished at how much they knew about the hydrology or water regime of the territory, and how little they did about it. They knew the history of the floods, and could accurately predict whether a culvert or dike built by the hasty Israelis would likely withstand the coming winter's flash flood or — as happened all too often — would fail to do so. It later occurred to me that their reluctance to translate observational knowledge into practice by actually building runoff control systems was due less to sloth than to a deeply ingrained uncertainty over land ownership. No individual could ever be sure that any particular wadi or catchment belonged to him and that his rights to the land would be respected. Neither could the tribe as a whole be sure that it would not be moved arbitrarily at any time.

In the ensuing years the lot of the Negev's Bedouin has greatly improved.

The lively Bedouin's market at Beersheba.

As former nomads living in a modern state, their standard of living and of health has risen enormously. Many of their young people now reside in homes and wear Western clothes. Their lives, which for so many centuries had been a long and arduous saga of wanderings, dispossessions, droughts, famines, floods, sandstorms, diseases, poverty, and insecurity, at last seem stable and secure. And yet I must confess a feeling of regret that their ancient way of life is apparently doomed. Some readers may dismiss this as an excess of sentimental romanticism that shows little understanding of the needs of our times, and even less regard for the ultimate welfare of the Bedouin themselves. There is, however, a case to be made for at least seminomadic pastoralism as a way of using land in the Negev highlands. Cannot the Bedouin's previous condition of dire poverty be alleviated without so radical a change in their way of life? Must their remarkable and ancient culture, so finely tuned to their unique environment, necessarily be destroyed so that the Bedouin, like so many other reluctant peoples, are pushed into the last decades of the twentieth century "for their own good" as perceived by others? Are we not being conceited to assume that every group wants, needs, and must have the stamp of modernity and conformity impressed upon it, whether voluntarily or otherwise?

We ought not to acquiesce in the fact that whole segments of the world's population suffer deprivation and poverty — but must they be deprived of their culture and distinctiveness as the price of their economic betterment? Bedouin

A prosperous modern Bedoui.

are not slum dwellers, underprivileged, oppressed, or exploited. They are, in their own way, aristocrats, imbued with pride of tradition and identity, living in essential harmony with nature. Their environment is clean and beautiful, each individual's place in society is secure, and their qualities of self-reliance and self-respect are admirable. How many contemporary societies can claim as much?

The traditional Bedouin are, to be sure, often difficult to govern and mindless of regulations, but these are insufficient reasons for extinguishing their culture. Of course, some regulation is necessary to prevent overgrazing and erosion, and to ensure against droughts and other misfortunes. Land and water rights must be allocated equitably. Yet, with all competing demands and requirements, there is still room, one hopes, for the Bedouin who wish to continue their traditional pastoral life in the Negev and elsewhere. If the Bedouin must be contained in the interest of overall development, let development, too, be contained. Let us beware of the sort of unbridled development that can become destructive. We lose so much of value when ancient cultures are abruptly terminated for being anachronistic, and gain so little when all people are homogenized into a conforming mass of traditionless modernity.

In the meanwhile the Bedouin still exist, despite political and economic changes, throughout the Near East, and many still cling stubbornly to their old ways even in the rapidly developing Negev. One takes some comfort from knowing that the fires fed with the dry, aromatic twigs of desert shrubs still smolder in countless black tents pitched in the desert hollows; that the bittersweet spiced coffee is still being sipped as ancient stories are retold, camels are sold, and marriage contracts are sealed; that keen-eyed men still ride their soft-treading camels across the shimmering expanse of the sun-drenched wilderness; and that the lilting, plaintive tunes of a reed flute are still being played for naught but the ears of sheep lazily grazing in nameless boulder-strewn wadis. One feels a strange spiritual yearning to be there again and to find it all as ageless and unspoiled as in the days of yore.

22

Irrigated Agriculture

> Be like a tree
>   planted by streams of water,
> That provideth its fruit
>   in its season,
> And whose leaf shall not wither.
>
> Psalms 1:3

Historically, the Negev's principal agricultural activities were rainfed farming in the semiarid northern plains, runoff farming in the arid northern highlands and their foothills, and grazing throughout the region. Regular irrigation, developed in ancient times in the Near East's river valleys, was practiced in the Negev only on a very limited scale in a few oases of the extremely arid Arava Valley, where the groundwater of alluvial fans could be tapped by means of chain-well systems. Nowadays, in contrast, irrigation has become the Negev's major method of agriculture. In 1950 the extent of irrigation in the Negev was minuscule: only 880 hectares out of a total cultivable land area then estimated to be 44,200 hectares. By 1975, however, the cultivable land area in the Negev had been increased to over 120,000 hectares, of which 30,000 were under irrigation. In short, the irrigated area in the Negev had been increased 34 times.

This rapid development illustrates the important role of irrigation in the modern agricultural development of the Negev. The principal site of this development has been the northern plains subregion, where over half the land area is arable and potentially irrigable. This subregion is also, fortuitously, nearest to the sources of irrigation water, which are in northern Israel. The other subregions of the Negev have a much smaller agricultural potential: less than 10 percent of the land area in the Negev highlands subregion, and less than 1 percent of the Arava Valley, is cultivable.

The development of intensive agriculture based on irrigation in the Negev resulted directly from the construction of Israel's National Water Carrier, which diverted large quantities of water from northern Israel to the Negev. Within the 20-year period from 1955 to 1975, the amount of water piped to the Negev increased more than fourfold, from 30 million cubic meters to about 125 million cubic meters, or 11.5 percent of the total amount of water allocated to agriculture in Israel. Production ranges from field crops (such as wheat, barley, corn, sorghum, cotton, forage crops) to vegetable crops (potatoes, tomatoes, onions) and fruit trees (citrus, peaches, apples), as well as various specialty crops (such as ornamental flowers and medicinal plants). About 90,000 hectares, incidentally, are cultivated in the northern Negev in a system of rainfed farming without irrigation, mostly for grain production (such as barley and grain sorghum). However, although the area of unirrigated land under cultivation in the Negev is three times greater than the area of irrigated land, the former represents only 18 percent of the total value of the region's agricultural production.

The geography of Israel is such that by far most of its water resources are in the north, whereas its major land reserve is in the south. At the outset of Israel's agricultural development, there was some deliberation and disagreement over the desirability of interregional transfer of water. Some hardheaded advisers pointed out that there is enough irrigable land in the northern regions of the country, and that it would be much more efficient to utilize the limited water supply close to its source rather than transport the water over great distances and expend the energy to lift it to considerable heights above its point of origin. Indeed, the construction of the National Water Carrier required a tremendous investment, not only in initial construction but in annual operation as well. It involves the collection of water from three principal sources: the Jordan River (over 200 meters below sea level at the Sea of Galilee); the shallow, unconfined groundwater aquifer of the coastal plain; and the underlying deep, confined limestone aquifer that outcrops in the Galilean, Samaritan, and Judean highlands. Furthermore, the scheme involved the mixing the these waters for salinity control and their conveyance under pressure in closed conduits to nearly every region of the country—including the northern Negev.

Those who advised against the large-scale conveyance of water to the arid Negev spoke in the name of prudent economics. Their arguments have since been corroborated by recent findings that irrigation water-use efficiency (the yield of a crop per unit of irrigation water used) is lower in an arid than in a relatively humid region, not only because of the greater supply of natural precipitation in the latter but also because of its smaller evaporational demand. However, such arguments miss the important point that the settlement

Irrigated Agriculture

of the Negev was a national imperative for Israel, a task to be achieved regardless of strictly economic considerations.

With water so expensive and so scarce, it was obvious from the outset that every effort must be made to conserve and utilize it as efficiently as possible, particularly in the Negev. In the 1960s and early 1970s, I served for some time as head of the departments of soil and water sciences of Israel's Agricultural Research Institute and at the Hebrew University, directing and coordinating research on the efficiency of water utilization by irrigated crops. We began by taking what was then the conventional approach to irrigation, an approach developed three decades earlier in California. It was based on the hypothesis that soil moisture remains practically equally available to crops until evaporation and extraction by roots deplete it to some residual moisture (different for each soil) called the wilting point. In practice, this hypothesis resulted in an irrigation regimen of low frequency, designed to periodically wet the soil to its maximal "field capacity," then to await depletion almost to the wilting point before replenishing soil moisture by making up the "deficit" to field capacity.

The conventional irrigation cycle thus consisted of a brief episode of irrigation followed by an extended period of extraction of soil moisture by the crop. Correspondingly, the soil surface was periodically saturated (with a resulting disruption of soil aeration) and then allowed to desiccate excessively, to the detriment of the roots in the surface layer. Practical limitations on the frequency of irrigation by the conventional methods (such as water impoundment over the field or in furrows, or high-intensity sprinkling) have made it difficult to test alternative methods of irrigation designed to continuously maintain an optimal level of soil moisture in a well-aerated and well-fertilized root zone.

The traditional mode of irrigation seemed to make good economic sense because most of the conventional irrigation systems are more expensive to run at a higher frequency than at a lower one. Therefore, with these systems it is desirable to minimize the number of irrigations per season by increasing the interval of time between successive irrigations. For example, if the cost of portable tubing is a dominant consideration, it obviously pays to make maximal use of such tubes by minimizing the amount of tubing required per unit area, shifting the available tubing from site to site so as to cover the greatest overall area possible before having to return to a particular site for the next irrigation. Reducing irrigation frequency in practice involved applying heavy irrigations to store the greatest possible amount of water in the soil, and then waiting as long as possible before replenishing the "soil reservoir." The question was, thus, how dry the soil can become before the crop experiences a "significant" reduction in yield. The hypothesis that availability of soil moisture to crops remains undiminished even though the soil is being depleted, until it suddenly falls at a particular value of soil moisture, and the supposition that this value is independent of plant and climate, were interesting examples of how we humans—in this case scientists (who can be altogether *too* human)—can lead ourselves to believe what is convenient to believe. Or what some unquestioned authority once told us to believe.

Gradually the contradictions became too apparent to ignore. Evidence was accumulating that soil moisture is not "equally available," but in fact becomes gradually less readily available as it is depleted. Therefore, it finally dawned on some of us that we ought to try the opposite approach and irrigate as frequently as possible. For others, however, this represented too radical a departure from conventional wisdom. In an arid environment, irrigate more frequently rather than less frequently? No, they said, that would increase water use per unit of land area. But smaller water use per unit area never was an end in itself. A better criterion is water use per unit of production. And this is where the new approach eventually proved itself. Instead of asking the crop (as we once asked humans) to go thirsty without showing any signs of diminished peformance, we began to ask the plant how much better it can perform if it is never made thirsty.

Irrigation researchers had focused for so long on plant behavior in the dry range of soil moisture that they seemed to be oblivious to what might happen in the wet range. A fact that now seems obvious, but that somehow remained unnoticed for many years, is that crops may show a pronounced increase in yield when irrigation is provided in sufficient quantity and frequency that water never becomes a limiting factor. I first noticed this fact in the early 1960s in the data obtained by a graduate student who was preparing his doctoral dissertation under my supervision, and I encouraged him to publish his findings (Rawitz 1969) even though they seemed to be at variance with the then prevailing view of crop-soil-water relations. Corroborating evidence was not long in coming (Acevedo et al. 1971; Hillel and Guron 1973; Rawlins and Raats 1975).

But how to maintain soil moisture in the root zone at a high enough level to keep suction low while avoiding wetting the soil excessively, so as not to impede aeration, or leach out nutrients, or waste water? Such conditions could not easily be achieved by the traditional surface and sprinkler irrigation methods. Fortunately, newer irrigation methods had been developed in recent years that could be adapted to deliver water in small quantities as often as desirable, without additional cost for the extra number of irrigations. These include permanent installations of low-intensity sprinklers, subirrigation by means of porous tubes, and—especially—the technique of drip or trickle irrigation.

Since a high-frequency irrigation system can be adjusted to supply water at very nearly the exact rate required by the crop, we no longer depend on the soil's capacity to store water. The consequences of this fact are far-reaching: now, new lands, until recently considered unsuited for irrigation, can be brought into production. One outstanding example is sands and gravels, where natural moisture storage is minimal, and surface conveyance and application of water would involve inordinate losses by rapid seepage of the water beyond the depth of rooting. Such soils can now be irrigated quite readily, even on sloping ground without leveling, by means of a drip system, for instance.

With high-frequency irrigation the farmer need no longer worry about when available soil moisture is depleted or when plants begin to suffer stress. Such situations are avoided entirely. To the old question "when to irrigate?" the best answer might be "as frequently as practicable; daily, if possible." To the question "how much water to apply?" the answer is "enough to meet the evaporational demand and to prevent salinization of the root zone."

Raising crops by the old method of infrequent heavy irrigations seems analogous to the raising of babies by force-feeding them on Sunday, then waiting the full week, until they are practically famished, before stuffing them once again. By the same analogy, modern high-frequency irrigation is like spoon-feeding a baby with frequent, small portions so that it is not overfed or underfed at any time.

In the technique of drip irrigation (also called trickle irrigation), water is provided to plants (even large trees) drop by drop, at a slow rate that can be regulated precisely to meet the water requirements of the crop. This method was developed in Israel and was first tried on a field scale in the Negev in the mid-1960s. It has gained widespread recognition, and is now being introduced into many countries. Although the idea itself is not new, what has made it practical at last is the recent development of low-cost plastic tubing and variously designed emitter fittings capable of maintaining a uniform discharge of water throughout the field, as well as a controlled rate of drop discharge through the narrow-orifice emitters with a minimum of clogging. The application system has been supplemented by ancillary equipment such as filters, timing or metering valves, and fertilizer injectors. Field trials in different locations have resulted in increased yields of both orchard and field crops, perennial as well as annual, particularly in adverse conditions of soil, water, and climate. Drip irrigation has also been found to be suitable for greenhouses and gardens, and lends itself readily to labor-saving automation.

With drip irrigation it is possible to obtain favorable moisture conditions even in problematic soils such as coarse sands and clays, which are ill-suited to conventional ways of irrigation. It is also possible to deliver water uniformly over a field of variable elevation, slope, wind velocity and direction, soil texture, and infiltrability. Still another potential advantage is the ability to maintain the soil at a highly moist yet unsaturated condition, so that soil air is continuously capable of exchanging gases with the atmosphere. High moisture reduces the soil's mechanical impedance to root penetration and proliferation. As only part of the surface is wetted, evaporation is reduced.

Where salinity is a hazard, as where the irrigation water is somewhat brackish, the continuous supply of water ensures that the osmotic pressure of the soil solution will remain low near the water source. Furthermore, drip irrigation, applied as it is to the soil underneath the plant canopy, avoids the hazard of leaf scorch and reduces the incidence of fungal diseases. Since drip irrigation wets the soil only in the immediate vicinity of each emitter, the greater part of the surface (particularly the inter-row areas) remains dry, and hence less prone to weed infestation and soil compaction under traffic. In summation, properly managed drip irrigation offers an opportunity to optimize the water, nutrient, and air regimes in the root zone.

The justifiable enthusiasm for the new method, however, carries certain dangers. Drip irrigation in and of itself is no panacea. It is just as easy to be inefficient in the operation of a drip system as it is in the operation of conventional systems. The fact that drip irrigation wets only a small fraction of the soil volume can also become a problem. While it is a proven fact that even large trees can grow on less than 20 percent of what is generally considered to be the normal root zone of a field (provided enough water and nutrients are supplied within this restricted volume), the crop becomes extremely sensitive and vulnerable to even a slight disruption in the operation of the irrigation system. If the system does not perform perfectly and continuously, crop failure may result, since the soil moisture reservoir available to the plants is so small.

Apart from the technical problem of maintaining the water delivery system in perfect operation without interruption, there is the initial problem of tailoring the emitter spacing specifically for each crop and stage of development, the optimization of per-emitter discharge rate in relation to soil infiltrability and lateral spread of the water, the optimization of irrigation pulse duration and frequency, and determination of irrigation quantity variation during the season.

Other possible problems associated with drip irrigation are the accumulation of salts at the periphery of the wetted circle surrounding each emitter (an occurrence that can hinder the growth of a subsequent crop), and the excessive throughflow and leaching that can take place directly under the drip emitters. In most cases such problems can be overcome by good management. Clogging of emitters is a frequently encountered problem, due to the presence of suspended particles or algae or salts that tend to precipitate. Mechanical clogging can be prevented by proper filtration, while chemical and biological clogging can often be reduced by acidification and algacide treatment of water.

The technique of drip irrigation is only one example of a larger conception, based on recognition that water is a precious and scarce resource, to be managed with meticulous care and painstaking attention to detail. This conception, born of absolute necessity, is one of Israeli agriculture's greatest contributions. Irrigation farmers everywhere tend to overirrigate. "If giving a little water is good for the crop, giving more must be better" seems to be the

Irrigated Agriculture

guiding principle. But "more" is not necessarily better. If it exceeds the optimal requirement of the crop, more water is worse rather than better, and may result in reduction of crop yield.

The correct amount of water to satisfy crop requirements can be determined only if all processes involved are known quantitatively. The problem is that such important processes as transpiration, soil moisture evaporation, and deep percolation are invisible, and cannot be assessed by a farmer's intuition. In many places water is subsidized or assigned a low and unrealistic price. This encourages waste. Some irrigation projects are based on the supply to the farmer of a fixed quantity of water according to a fixed schedule, regardless of whether the full amount is needed. This also encourages waste. Such is not the case in Israel, where water carries a high price and is made progressively more expensive as more of it is used per unit area. This pricing policy, coupled with a strong educational program to develop awareness and expertise, accounts for the high levels of irrigation efficiency and water-use efficiency that are the hallmarks of agriculture in that country. Overall, agricultural production in Israel has been increased 1000 percent within a single generation, and much of that increase is due to the reclamation and judicious management of land and water in the Negev. The legacy of the ancient Israelites and of the Nabateans has not been forgotten; it is being applied.

23

Sdeh-Boker and Ben-Gurion

> Son of man, set thy face toward Yemen,
> And preach to the south,
> And prophesy to the forest of the field in the Negev.*
> Ezekiel 21:2

Sdeh-Boker, founded in early 1952, was the first agricultural settlement in the Negev highlands subregion. It was preceded, however, by the establishment in 1943 of the experimental outpost of Revivim in the plains just northwest of the Negev highlands. Revivim, too, is in a zone of 100 millimeters of average annual rainfall. At the outset the main concerns of the settlers at Revivim were the loessial soil's erodibility and crusting tendency, and the extreme dryness of the air. They searched for drought-resistant and salt-resistant plants capable of serving as windbreaks without requiring irrigation, and put much faith in the ability of dew to sustain plants and even to restore soil moisture (De Angelis 1979).

Their initial approach to each of these problems was unrealistic. Disregarding the rule that unirrigated (rainfed) farming is generally impossible where annual rainfall is below about 250 millimeters, they tried to grow grain on the wide loessial plain, believing that deep plowing would somehow make up for the lack of water. The Negev played a trick on them. The 1944/45 season was an extraordinarily wet one, with 146 millimeters, and the crop actually grew, though it gave practically no yield. However, this deception ended the following year, when the rainfall total was considerably below average. Still stubbornly optimistic, the Revivim settlers attempted to plant trees on

---

*The place names Yemen and Negev also connote "south".

the dry plains, watering them at first from barrels carried on mule-drawn wagons, in the expectation that once the roots penetrated deeply enough, these trees would somehow continue to thrive without irrigation. This experiment, too, was doomed from the outset.

Finally realizing that there was not enough rain to grow crops over the entire land area, the settlers of Revivim began to search for ways to crop part of the land while using the remaining area as a source of runoff water for irrigation. Attempting to dam and store the floodwaters of the large nearby wadi, they encountered problems with the surface storage of the water over the permeable soil, and tried to coat the soil with watertight asphalt, which cracked badly after a few months. Better results were achieved with levels basins of land where floodwater from the wadi could be impounded so as to wet the soil for subsequent planting of crops.

Revivim's efforts in these directions were interrupted by the 1948–49 war. When it was over, the long-suffering members of this settlement were understandably tired of experimentation, and demanded that irrigation water be piped from the north. They also cultivated lands in the more humid northern Negev subregion, where rainfall was found to be sufficient to obtain adequate crops in most years.

In 1949, after Israel's establishment, a village named Mashabei-Sadeh was established in the same area. One of its settlers' earliest attempts was to find water by drilling. In this they initially failed. Attempts to obtain irrigation water by diversion from a nearby subregional wadi met with only partial success, the operation being of doubtful economic feasibility. Cultivation of distant lands in the northern Negev did not provide local employment. Finally, Masahbei-Sadeh joined Revivim in demanding the installation of a pipeline, which was done in 1956. Another pipeline was laid in 1961. Both villages now irrigate sizable tracts of land, and have become veritable oases in the bleak desert of the plains and foothills subregion.

Sdeh-Boker was initially something of a reaction to the easy solution of the pipeline. The very name, meaning "Herdsman's Field," announced our intention to raise both livestock and crops, to utilize the desert range as well as to engage in runoff farming, and thus to resolve the age-old conflict between pastoralists and cultivators, much as the Nabateans had done long ago. We were determined to rely entirely on the development and utilization of local water resources, particularly runoff. In principle, Sdeh-Boker was more favorably situated for this enterprise than its predecessor settlements, Revivim and Mashabei-Sadeh, since it was located in the highlands proper, close to the headwaters of the wadis, where the floods are gentler and easier to manage. In time, however, it did not adhere to its original intent. It is now very much like the other two villages, depending on imported water for its agriculture, which is mostly pipeline-irrigated.

All three villages are kibbutzim — self-governing, democratic, collective

Scenes from the first two years of Sdeh-Boker
1. A wadi flood breaching laboriously built dikes.
2,3. Harvesting hay in the wadi.
4. A heavy tractor mired in the mud behind a water-spreading dike.
5,6. Camping in the Boker Valley, 5 kilometers west of the main settlement.

communities in which property is shared and social and economic equality prevails. Membership is entirely voluntary. The villages are self-employing enterprises, with some light industry as well as agriculture, and enjoy a rising standard of living. The members reside in comfortable, architect-designed, modern houses, in villages green with ornamental shrubbery, shade trees, and well-tended lawns. They have a rich cultural life and many amenities, including swimming pools and modern recreational facilities. All members are fully insured economically and medically, and are encouraged to pursue higher educational goals at all age levels. Life in a tightly knit communal society helps the members to avoid the loneliness and sense of isolation that might otherwise become oppressive in the desert.

Sdeh-Boker's transformation from a fiercely independent pioneering maverick to an "ordinary" Kibbutz can be traced to a chance and seemingly innocuous event that took place on May 21, 1953. We were working inside the compound that afternoon, constructing a storage shed, when we noticed in the distance an army convoy traveling south on the unpaved road skirting the plain on which our little settlement stood. The convoy did not consist of trucks, as was usual, but of jeeps, command cars, and, in their midst, an improbable black limousine. It bypassed our settlement, apparently heading for the newly opened spectacular descent into the Ramon Crater, some 50 kilometers to the south. Then, strangely, the convoy halted abruptly, turned around, and drove onto the spur road leading to our encampment. Soon the vehicles reached us and stopped. The great cloud of dust had scarcely dissipated when the door of the limousine was flung open, and out stepped a stocky, white-haired man whom we all recognized instantly as Israel's first, and as yet only, prime minister, David Ben-Gurion.

We were more than a little startled by this sudden visitation, and scarcely had time to recover composure before he began asking us questions.

"What are you doing here?" he demanded to know.

"Trying to build an agricultural settlement," we replied.

"An *agricultural* settlement in the middle of the desert? Whose idea is this?"

"Our idea."

"But who assigned you here? The army? The National Settlement Agency? The Ministry of Agriculture?"

"None of these. They all tried to discourage us. We came on our own."

The old man looked incredulous. With a hint of suspicion, he asked, "To what political party do you belong?"

"To none. We are unaffiliated, nonpolitical."

"Unaffiliated?" (In the Israel of those days, it seemed almost nothing was, or could be, nonpolitical.) Ben-Gurion was obviously intrigued.

"Who has been advising you? Who are the experts?"

"We have our own scientist here [the men pointed to me, and I didn't know quite where to hide], and we're all becoming experts."

"And what about security?" Ben-Gurion knew that Israel's hold on the Negev was still very tenuous, and it was contested by the neighboring Arab states. To them Israel's control was an affront, a dagger thrust into their territory, severing the land link (and the ancient pilgrim route) between North Africa and Arabia. The borders of the Negev were open to incursions from both Egypt on the west and Jordan on the east.

"Well," we hesitated, "we lost two of our original members during our first year here. The army has been patrolling the trafficable roadways, while the marauders blend into the hills and hide in the ravines."

"Who is in charge of security here?"

"I am," said Judith, who had earlier come out of the makeshift kitchen and—improbable as this may seem—was still wearing an apron.

"You? What is your training?"

"I was an artillery officer in the Israeli Army, and before that I fought with the partisans in eastern Europe," she said.

"And the others?"

"All had been trained in the army."

"Hm. Hm. How many are you?"

"We started with twelve. Two were killed, one left, and six others joined. So now we are fifteen."

"But surely you need more members!"

"Of course, but they must be the right sort."

"What's the right sort?"

"Dependable, compatible, willing to work hard."

"Any age limits?" he inquired. "Would you accept an elderly couple if they were willing to work?" Here the Old Man glanced at his wife, Paula, and so did we. I shall never forget the expression of astonishment on her face.

"Well, yes," we said, "if they can prove that they are hard workers." We all laughed. The high-ranking army officers escorting the Old Man also laughed. Obviously he was referring to himself and Paula, and he was being facetious.

But Ben-Gurion was not facetious. Humor was not his forte. Earnestly and insistently, he wanted to know more, and kept asking questions. Nervously his escorting officers fingered their watches and reminded him of the schedule they must meet, but he paid them no heed. He asked to see our agricultural experiments. So we walked together down into the wadi, and we showed him the terraces and dikes; our fruit trees, vegetables, and reseeded pasture. When he was through inquiring about the land and the availability of water, we took him to the edge of the Chasm. And there he stood silently for a long while, as if transfixed, as if entranced. As he gazed at the mountains looming above the deep valley, he mumured: "Oh that I could find a wayfarers' lodge in the wilderness. . . . " The words were probably not meant to be heard, but I happened to be standing next to him. Whimsically, I asked the impertinent question: "Do you mean the rest of the passage, too?" He looked at me intently for a moment, then shook his head. "No, of course not." There was a hint of a smile in his eyes as he added, "I see you know the Bible." It was the beginning of a long private friendship between a very wise old man and a very brash young one. Ben-Gurion then bade us farewell and ordered his escorts to cut the trip short and return to Tel-Aviv.

That evening I reread the ninth chapter of Jeremiah. After the first sentence spoken by Ben-Gurion, the passage continues: ". . . that I might leave my people and depart from them, for they are . . . an assembly of treacherous men who speak not the truth. . . . For the mountains I will take up a weeping and wailing, and for the pastures of the wilderness a lamentation, for they are so scorched. . . . "

A week later we received the following letter, dated May 28, 1953, and written on the prime minister's official stationery:

> To the comrades in Sdeh-Boker—
> Dear Comrades—
>
> I have just read in the newspapers that your settlement is now one year old. Characteristically, you did not mention this jubilee when I was with you last week, and I therefore send you this note without connection to the anniversary. In the forty-seven years of my life in this country I have seen a number of pioneering ventures, and I know that only thanks to them and to the pioneering ventures that preceded my arrival were we able to attain the measure of success we have: the beginning of independence in our renewed homeland. Nevertheless forgive me if I say that I have never in all my days seen a pioneering venture quite like that of Sdeh-Boker, which would indeed have been impossible prior to the establishment of the State.
>
> I have never envied a person or a group of persons for their wealth or appearance or other qualities, even though I willingly bow my head to many of my colleagues for their qualities. But when I visited with you I found it difficult to suppress a sort of feeling of envy in my heart: Why haven't I been privileged to participate in such a deed?
>
> Since I am certain that you do not need praises and encouragements, I shall not tell you all that I think about your venture, that is to say, about you. But I could not restrain myself from writing you just a few words.
>
> Be blessed and successful.
> Yours,
> D. Ben-Gurion.

Within a month Ben-Gurion announced his resignation from the government and his decision to join the struggling little village of Sdeh-Boker in the Negev highlands. The press was incredulous: How could the Father of the State, as he was called, then at the peak of his influence, abandon the seat of power and go to the remote desert? It made no sense.

But that is just what came to pass. A wooden hut was hastily built for

The Ben-Gurions at Sdeh-Boker
1. His first visit.
2. The Ben-Gurions with their sometime housekeeper in front of their hut.
3. Paula Ben-Gurion in the settlement's kitchen.
4,5. David Ben-Gurion working in the field, preparing plants for reseeding.

Paula and David Ben-Gurion, and for his collection of books and papers. Within a few weeks, the resignation a fait accompli, the elderly couple moved to their new home in the Negev.

When Ben-Gurion arrived, we had a problem: what to do with him, and how to carry on our own lives and work? His was a presence that could not be ignored. I was appointed to put him to work, and I tried to assign him some interesting task that would not overly tax him. First, it was helping prepare nursery-grown seedlings and saplings for transplanting in the field. Then it was feeding and caring for the lambs and kids of our flock. Supervising his work brought me into daily contact with him. Particularly meaningful were the evening visits to his hut, ostensibly to discuss the morrow's assignment but actually to converse with him. "Converse" is not exactly the right word. The exchange was asymmetrical: he spoke, I listened. He was in a contemplative mood, in the process of collecting his notes and recollecting his experiences, sifting and winnowing through the records of his stormy life and eager to discourse on past events. And I was an avid listener. Occasionally these engaging conversations lasted beyond midnight. Then Paula would charge into the small study and shoo me away, feigning outrage at my *chutzpah* in keeping the great man awake. I was fortunate that Paula liked me, if only because I was "the American." She, too, considered herself a bit American, for, although born in Poland, she had spent her youth in New York. The 35 years or so that

Laying the pipeline to Sdeh-Boker.

she had since lived in Palestine (later to become Israel) did not erase her sentiment for America.

Ben-Gurion was, as the expression goes, a legend in his own time. Although the purported greatness of famous men often tends to fade under close observation, his unique quality remained intact even after prolonged daily contact under circumstances that must have been very difficult for him. And he remained an enigma. I could never decipher just what Ben-Gurion had sought in coming to the Negev: sanctuary or challenge, retirement or renewed activity, symbolism or reality. At one and the same time, the man was inextricably engaged and involved in contemporary affairs, yet curiously detached from immediate circumstances, as if living in two realms—the contemporary and the historical. He was deeply rooted in history, and particularly in the Bible. To Ben-Gurion the Bible was not of the past but of the present. His allusions to biblical characters and events sounded almost like personal reminiscences. On occasion his pronouncements on current issues reverberated with a unique sense of history, and his words echoed those of the ancient Hebrew prophets. Anyone else speaking thus would sound incongruous and anachronistic, but coming from him the words sounded entirely natural. To be sure, Ben-Gurion was a very fallible man. With familiarity his foibles became increasingly apparent. But as my awe of him abated, I grew to be fond of him, not despite his human failings but more likely because of them.

One of his more amusing foibles was his irrepressible showmanship. Though essentially an aloof man, Ben-Gurion cultivated the image of a man of the people. To impress his important visitors at Sdeh-Boker, he sometimes put on his best *kibbutznik* act. Instead of eating his habitual lunch (made by Paula of fruits or vegetables blended with yogurt) at his own hut, he would escort his guests to the common dining room, which was then a rather hot and noisy and unesthetic place. There he would preside over a strategically located table and carry on a loud conversation with any member who happened to catch his eye. I recall walking unsuspectingly into the dining room on a number of such occasions and falling right into his act. "Danny!" he would shout familiarly as I entered, "what's new in the fields?" So I had to come over and play the straight man, keeping a serious expression under the barrage of B. G.'s semirhetorical questions: "How are the fruit trees? And the vegetables? The squash? The corn? And have you checked the soil moisture?" Etcetera. . . .

Even after his return to the government in 1955, Ben-Gurion would often rush back to Sdeh-Boker and put on his khaki working clothes just in time to greet (and impress) such special dignitaries as U Nu of Burma, Dag Hammarskjold of the United Nations, or Edward R. Murrow of CBS News.

Though Ben-Gurion was quite innocent of the details of science, he had a great vision of how science was destined to "conquer" the desert. In his view,

David and Paula Ben-Gurion with the author (between them) on a grain drill, planting barley in flood-irrigated land.

good science and good scientists were those who served the cause of development, and in his faith in development he was quite unencumbered by economic or environmental limitations. Scientific constraints to development were dismissed out of hand (as were economic feasibilities). Scientists who argued against various development schemes on grounds that they might cause environmental damage and do more harm than good were labeled with the uncomplimentary epithet "British experts." I tried on occasion to argue with him, but was singularly unsuccessful at convincing him that the Negev is destined to remain a desert and that developers should not try to subdue it, but to harmonize with it.

Ben-Gurion's was a literal understanding of the first chapter of Genesis, in which God blesses man to have dominion over all the earth, and to subdue it and all that grows and lives on it. Once I tried to interest him in the Bedouin of the region, and argued in favor of granting them possession over some tribal territories, on condition that they adopt soil and water conservation practices. "Sheyitgairu," was his one-word nationalistic reply, meaning "let them become Hebrews." Ben-Gurion seemed to have no halftones in his register of vision. Rather, he saw the world in primary colors, often in black and white. He admired certitude and decisive action, and despised doubt. He knew truth and untruth, belief and unbelief; outwardly, at least, he recognized no hesitating retinue of intermediate shades.

In the context of Israel and the Negev, incidentally, the term "British expert" derived from an interesting historic fact. In 1946 a U.N. commission was appointed to deliberate over the fate of the country, then ruled by Britain under a mandate of the League of Nations. In the course of its inquiries, the U.N. commission received the "expert" testimony of the British administrators, who had been in charge of the country for some 30 years, "proving" that the country's productive potential had already been reached and that there was no more arable land nor water to permit any substantial increase in agricultural production (and hence in population). When Israel was established two years later, its population was about three-quarters of a million, and it was barely able to produce half its food requirements. Now, one generation later, the population is five times as great, and the country's agriculture is producing (either directly, or indirectly by exporting and earning) the entire food requirements of this vastly increased population. In other words, agricultural production has been multiplied tenfold within about 30 years. In view of this remarkable achievement, Ben-Gurion's original and intuitive contempt for pessimistic experts seems to have been well justified.

Ben-Gurion's influence on Sdeh-Boker, and ultimately on the region as a whole, was overwhelming. Prior to his arrival our small settlement was dedicated to developing a modern version of the ancient desert agriculture, based entirely on the region's indigenous water resources. As such, it was a unique experiment in which scientific findings were meant to be put to immediate practical use. The very remoteness and isolation of the place protected the experiment from succumbing to such easy "solutions" as receiving water from the north or living off tourism. The immediate real benefit of Ben-Gurion's arrival was to eliminate the security problem. The settlement was surrounded by protective barbed-wire fences and a Regular Army unit was stationed there to patrol the area constantly. Wanting to control our own grazing territory independently, however, we set up a small camel-riding patrol to keep surveillance of the wadis and cisterns within a radius of about 15 kilometers around the settlement. Ben-Gurion himself, just prior to joining us, contributed his own money (1,200 Israeli pounds, then worth about U.S. $1,000) for the purchase of the first two camels. We bought a total of six from a friendly tribe of Bedouin.

For several months, on and off, I rode with this patrol, and it was a great adventure. Perched precariously on the teetering saddle of a swaying camel, high above the desert floor, sailing along narrow paths on the edge of a precipice, simultaneously experiencing both vertigo and—incredibly, in the middle of the desert—acute seasickness, or being lulled into delirium by the plodding beat and the merciless and shadeless heat, all the while suffering silently the pain of an underside rubbed raw by the relentless friction, I was nevertheless intoxicated with it all. In my fantasy I was transported back into the age of the Ishmaelites and Midianites, and I expected to meet an Abraham, a Moses, or an Elijah around every turn. Within a few months, however, the territory had become so pacified by the increasing activity of both military and civilian groups that we decided to disband the camel patrol and to sell the camels back to the same Bedouin.

A few of the secondary blessings that accrued from Ben-Gurion's presence were of somewhat dubious benefit. Sdeh-Boker attained instant fame, and suddenly became a major tourist attraction. Soon there was money to widen and pave the road linking the region to the north, and to lay a pipeline. Schemes that had formerly been inconceivable now became feasible. State funds were allocated for construction of an access road to the springs in the canyon and for restoration of the ancient Nabatean city of Ovdat, which quickly became a major center of tourism, with the food and fuel concessions given to Sdeh-Boker. The settlement itself was besieged by scores of applicants suddenly eager to join. Sadly, we had to reject nearly all of them after realizing that they were drawn only by the delusion of fame. The entire development of the region, which had been proceeding slowly, was greatly accelerated by the presence of Ben-Gurion. That was a positive effect, on the whole, except for the danger that accelerated development might be hastily conceived or even ill-conceived.

The idea motivating Sdeh-Boker's experiment, in any case, fell prey to the temptations of "easy" state financing. With subsidized irrigation water so readily available, raising and selling fruit to tourists at roadside kiosks became much more lucrative than the back-breaking, and at times heart-rending, task of building dikes to trap and spread the desert's own runoff waters. In this way Ben-Gurion may have, quite inadvertently, impeded the pioneering venture that he had so admired and had aspired to join. The free spirit of adventure and self-driven inquiry does not often lend itself to being institutionalized. As the settlement became fashionable, it was joined by groups that would not have joined it otherwise. Concurrently, some of the original founders, having lost the special sense of challenge and fascination that had drawn them initially, departed. Research into the region's potentialities became the exclusive activity of professional academics. One well-endowed group descended from the University of Jerusalem and set up comfortable quarters at the foot of newly reconstructed Ovdat. Self-promotion and somewhat inflated claims of originality notwithstanding, they did indeed carry out very valuable work in deciphering, reconstructing, and reactivating ancient runoff farming systems and in developing new ones (Evenari et al., 1971). L. Shanan and the late N. Tadmor were particularly important in this effort.

Regional research was further institutionalized with the establishment of the Ben-Gurion University of the Negev at Beersheba, and its annex, the Desert Research Institute, at the Sdeh-Boker campus. The latter is located just

The Valley of Zin, as seen from David and Paula Ben-Gurion's final resting place at the Sdeh-Boker Desert Institute.

south of the village of Sdeh-Boker, at the southern end of the loessial plain. And there, at the very edge of the cliff overlooking the great chasm known as the Valley of Zin, stands the library that houses Ben-Gurion's records. At the base of that building, near the spot to which we took David and Paula Ben-Gurion on their first visit and where he recited the words of Jeremiah ("Oh that I could find a wayfarers' lodge in the wilderness . . . "), they are buried side by side. It is a singularly appropriate final resting place, and it has quite properly become a shrine and a place of pilgrimage. The inspired vision of a mortal man combines there with the eternal spirit of the desert.

Ben-Gurion believed that "the greatest test of the Israeli nation in our generation is not in its struggle with hostile forces from without, but in its ability, through science and pioneering, to conquer the desolation of the Negev." He pronounced his own vision in early 1958, when the first telephone cable was extended to Sdeh-Boker: "The trees are multiplying in our settlement, and I can see the expanse of the Negev highlands turning green and the hills covered with forests. For the time being it is my imagination, but in the future it will become reality."

Epilogue
Modern Implications

> "The energy contained in nature—in the earth and its waters, in the atom, in sunshine—will not avail us if we fail to activate the most precious vital energy: the moral-spiritual energy inherent in man; in the inner recesses of his being; in his mysterious, uncompromising, unfathomable and divinely inspired soul."
>
> David Ben-Gurion

We have come to the concluding chapter of our book on land and water development and utilization in the Negev, past and present. Yet our exploration has been only cursory. We have given only a few highlights. Far from being exhausted, the subject is of growing interest and relevance. Indeed, the quest for more exact and detailed knowledge of the desert's ecology, and of the consequences of its human management, is bound to intensify in the years to come. The interest is not merely academic, not merely archaeological or historical. It is as contemporary as the needs and requirements of our own civilization. The age-old challenge of the desert is more pressing today than ever, and knowledge of the way ancient civilizations met this challenge can guide our own activities.

The challenge of the desert today is worldwide. A significant portion of the earth's population is concentrated in arid lands along the fringes of deserts. And it is a disturbing fact that so many millions of this population—in some cases including entire nations—subsist today at a level below that achieved by the ancient desert civilization of the Negev two millennia ago. Progress is neither automatic nor inevitable. In some arid regions civilization has retrogressed so markedly that where magnificent and prosperous towns once stood, emaciated children now roam aimlessly and often die of disease or malnutrition before they become adults. If we are to answer the cry for a better and fuller life for all the world's children, then we must husband some of the arid lands and make them productive. The achievements of past civilizations in specific localities can be repeated and extended, and even surpassed, on a larger scale.

In Israel as elsewhere, the desert represents practically the last reserve of habitable land, of unemcumbered open space. Moreover, the desert is blessed with an abundance of a resource so long taken for granted but now recognized as being invaluable: sunshine, or solar energy. The possibility of harnessing this energy on a large scale is very probably one of the greatest challenges and opportunities of our age. As our earth's population increases inexorably, and its known resources seem to diminish, we are drawn more and more to explore the great empty deserts. Finding the climate to be surprisingly pleasant in many cases, our space-hungry civilization seems bound to colonize desert areas. As it does so, it must certainly contend with the desert's ecological fragility and, above all, with its shortages of water and arable soil.

The desert of this book, the Negev of Israel, is but a small spot on the world map, and its conditions are in some ways specific. Its history, most certainly, is unique. Yet, in a sense, it is a microcosm of deserts in general. Human history has made it a testing ground, a place where pioneers in times long past labored and learned, suffered and survived, experimented and prevailed. Many of the principles upon which they based their successful venture in desert land and water husbandry, and many of their inventions and techniques, are universal and should be applicable, as a matter of principle, in other arid areas no less than in the Negev.

Quite obviously the principal barrier to settlement of the desert is the paucity of water there. The expression "paucity of water" implies not the total absence, but the presence in strictly limited quantities, of water. Hence the crux of the problem — indeed, the challenge — is to discover what water is available, to devise ways and means to obtain and conserve it, and to utilize it efficiently. It is the contention of this book, using the Negev as a case study, that the development and utilization of local water resources, meager yet potentially significant, offers important possibilities for regional settlement in desert areas. These water resources are too often ignored or discounted.

In common parlance a desert is "a place without water," whereas in fact it is a place with little water. There is a world of difference between "no water" and "little water." Because water in the desert is scarce, and because it appears in isolated locations and at odd times (as in sporadic rains and flash floods), it is difficult to develop and utilize local water resources. It is difficult, but by no means impossible or impractical, as was amply demonstrated by the ancient Negevites. The secret lies in water collection and water conservation methods, often quite elaborate and complex but nearly always based upon simple and readily understandable principles that were discovered long ago by those

Negevites. That their ancient methods are as sound today as when they were first devised has been established beyond doubt in the same locations, where ancient cisterns and conduits and terraced fields have been restored.

The fact that ancient methods have proved to be workable today does not mean, however, that we must copy them without change. Even while employing the same principles, we have at our command greatly improved techniques of water management and very powerful machines that are the obedient slaves of our mechanized civilization. Nowadays, using tractors and bulldozers and concrete mixers, all undreamed of by the ancients, we can build in a few weeks works that would require many man-years of labor in the older days. Above all, we have the tools of scientific exploration. We know a great deal more than the ancients knew about where water can be found, and how much. And we can plan and implement engineering works on a far greater scale. We can discover aquifers and drill for groundwater. Where runoff constitutes the principal source of water, we have the means to study the probability and frequency of its occurrence, as well as its rate and amount. And we have an arsenal of chemicals and machines with which to seal and shape land surfaces so as to induce much greater runoff yields than are produced naturally.

Despite all this, modern techniques of runoff inducement and utilization in desert areas are still in their infancy. This is so not because we lack the basic tools required for the task, but because our engineers, hydrologists, and chemists have heretofore devoted too little attention to the problem. The need for fundamental and applied research cannot be overstressed. Among the problems to be studied are the selection, and methods of application, of low-cost and durable agents for surface sealing, methods of land preparation, methods of water storage and evaporation reduction, and choice of crop plants and cropping practices best adapted to desert runoff-farming. New forms of intensive agriculture being tested are the controlled-environment (greenhouse) production of vegetable crops and of algae by means of aquaculture.

Solutions for the problems related to the management of arid lands are being sought in a number of research centers in the United States, Australia, Mexico, India, Egypt, and several other arid-zone countries. And much is being done in Israel. In the Negev itself, right next to Sdeh-Boker, there is now the Desert Research Institute, affiliated with the Ben-Gurion University of the Negev.*

The State of Israel is determined to develop the Negev, and this development may take many forms, some of which will not at all resemble the ways of the past. Rather than build upon the achievements of ancient civilizations, the

---

*There could be a danger, however, in the tendency to institutionalize research excessively. The danger is that a comfortably tenured staff in a formally structured bureaucracy will lose or fail to generate enthusiasm, spontaneity, and originality. And those who disregard the work of their predecesssors may, unknowingly, condemn themselves to repeating rather than extending it.

present and future developers of the desert may regard those achievements as mere historical curiosities, interesting but irrelevant. Rather than accept the fundamental principles of land and water husbandry in the desert, discovered and applied so successfully in antiquity, modern developers may choose to deviate greatly from those principles. It is impossible to foretell just how future development schemes will modify the natural environment, but modify it they will.

Such projects as establishing a Mediterranean-Dead Sea canal, railroads, industrial parks, airfields and associated installations, supply depots and service facilities, military training grounds and maneuvering areas, fire zones and fortifications—all undeniably essential—are altogether too likely to change the face of the land irreparably. We can only hope that these new forms of land use will not shatter the fragile environment of the region altogether.

Perhaps the greatest danger is inherent in the very phrase we use to describe ourselves, that high-sounding but insidiously arrogant title "Masters of the Desert." It behooves us to think of ourselves more humbly as custodians. There are indeed vast resources in the desert, but they are not simply available to all for the taking. First, we must find them, then husband what we find prudently. The word "husband" implies a familial relationship.

Let us respect and love the desert, and seek to live with it, not rape or despoil it. Considering the special character of the Negev, and the profound meaning of its rich history, we must refrain from regarding it merely as a place for economic development. Man's spiritual needs are as great as his economic needs. The balance we seek between the two is always tentative and tenuous, and the environment within which we seek it is itself an ever-precarious one. Total appropriation of the desert for the one set of needs denies the other. In the Negev we can still find places where silence and solitude reign, where spiritual communion with primeval nature and with human history are possible, where the memory of God's revelation yet echoes in the still, small voice. May such places always remain, even as we proceed to develop the resources of this and other deserts, and to utilize them for the betterment of life upon earth.

Bibliography

Aase, J. K., and W. D. Kemper. 1968. Effect of ground color and microwatersheds on corn growth. *J. Soil Water Conserv.* 23: 60–62.

Acevedo, E., T. C. Hsiao, and D. W. Henderson. 1971. Immediate and subsequent growth response of maize leaves to changes in water status. *Plant Physiol.* 48: 631–36.

Adolph, E. F. 1947. *Physiology of Man in the Desert*. New York: Wiley Interscience.

Aharoni, Y. 1977. The settlement of the Negev during the Israelite period. In *The Desert*, E. Sohar, ed. Tel-Aviv: Reshafim.

Aharoni, Y., M. Evenari, L. Shanan, and N. H. Tadmor. 1960. The ancient desert agriculture of the Negev. V. An Israelite settlement at Ramat Matred. *Israel Exploration J.* 10: 23–36, 97–111.

Alijibury, F. K. 1973. Drip irrigation; practices and applications. *Calif. Farmer* 238(12): 28a–c.

Amerman, C. R., D. Hillel, and A. E. Peterson. 1970. A variable-intensity rain simulator with a rotating disc. *Soil Sci. Soc. Amer. Proc.* 34: 830–32.

Amiran, D. H. 1950. Geomorphology of the central Negev highlands. *Israel Exploration J.* 1: 107–20.

Amiran, D. H. K. 1963. Effects of climatic change in an arid environment of land-use patterns. *Arid Zone Res.* 20: 437–42.

———. 1965. Arid zone development; a reappraisal under modern technological conditions. *Econ. Geogr.* 41: 189–210.

Amiran, D. H. K., and M. Gilead. 1969. Early excessive rainfall and soil erosion in Israel. In *Arid Lands in Perspective*, 4: 286–95. Tucson: Univ. of Arizona Press.

Andrews, Roy Chapman. 1956. *Quest in the Desert*. New York: Viking.

Anon. 1965. *Soil Erosion by Water—Some Measures of Its Control on Cultivated Lands*. Agric. Develop. Paper 81. Rome: FAO.

———. 1967. *Water for Peace: Proceedings of the International Conference on Water for Peace.* Washington D.C.: Government Printing Office.

———. 1972. *Desert Encroachment on Arable Lands: Significance, Causes, and Control.* Washington, D.C.: Office of Science and Technology, U.S. Agency for International Development.

———. 1974. *More Water for Arid Lands: Promising Technologies and Research Opportunities.* Washington, D.C.: National Academy of Sciences.

Arnon, I. 1972. *Crop Production in Dry Regions, I, Background and Principles.* New York: Barnes and Noble; London: Leonard Hill.

Ashbel, D. 1967. *Climate of the Negev.* Jerusalem: Hebrew University.

Atlas of Israel. 1956. Jerusalem: Department of Surveys, Ministry of Labour, and Bialik Institute, Jewish Agency.

Aubert, G. 1962. Arid zone soils. *Arid Zone Res.* 18: 115-37.

Bagnold, Ralph A. 1935. *Libyan Sands.* London: Hodder.

Bagnold, R. A. 1954. The physical aspects of dry deserts. In *Proc. Symp. Biology of Deserts. Inst. Bio.*, pp. 7-12.

Bar-Tsvi, S. 1979. Characteristics of Bedouin life in the Negev prior to settlement. In *The Land of the Negev,* Israel Ministry of Defense, Tel-Aviv.

Benson, Lyman. 1950. *The Cacti of Arizona.* Tucson: University of Arizona Press.

Benson, Lyman, and Robert A. Darrow. 1954. *The Trees and Shrubs of the Southwestern Deserts.* Tucson: University of Arizona Press; Albuquerque: University of New Mexico Press.

Bentor, Y. K., and A. Vroman. 1954. A structural contour map of Israel (1:250,000) with remarks on its dynamics interpretation. *Bull. Res. Counc. Israel* 4: 15-25.

Bentor, Y. K., A. Vroman, and I. Zak. 1963. Geological Map, Southern Israel. D/2821. Tel-Aviv: Geological Survey of Israel.

Bentor, Y. K. 1979. Geology of the Negev. In *The Land of the Negev.* Israel Ministry of Defense, Tel-Aviv.

Bernstein, B. 1979. *Sinai, the Great and Terrible Wilderness.* New York: Viking Press.

Biology of the Deserts. 1954. London: Institute of Biology.

Bibliography

Bitoun, M., R. D. Burman, L. J. Erie, D. D. Fangmeier, D. F. Heerman, D. Hillel, R. B. Norgaard, R. T. Ramage, L. R. Swarner, and J. van Schilfgaarde. 1979. *Water Conservation in California.* Sacramento: Department of Water Resources, State of California.

Blaney, H. F. 1957. Monthly consumptive use of water by irrigated crops and natural vegetation. *J.A.I.H.S.* (Association Internationale d'Hydrologie Scientifique) 431–39.

Bodenheimer, F. S. 1935. *Animal Life in Palestine.* Tel-Aviv: Devir.

―――――. 1953. Problems of animal ecology and physiology in deserts. *Desert Res. Publ.* no. 2, pp. 205–09. Jerusalem: Research Council of Israel.

―――――. 1960. *Animal and Man in Bible Lands.* New York: Humanities Press.

Boers, Th. M., and J. Ben-Asher. 1979. Harvesting water in the desert. In *Annual Report, International Inst. Land Reclam. and Improve.* Wageningen, Netherlands: ILRI, pp. 6–23.

Bouma, J., D. Hillel, F. Hole, and C. R. Amerman. 1970. Field tests of unsaturated hydraulic conductivity by infiltration through artificial crusts. *Soil Sci. Soc. Amer. Proc.* 35: 362–64.

Bourlière, François. 1960. *The Natural History of Mammals.* New York: Alfred A. Knopf.

Bowden, Charles. 1977. *Killing the Hidden Waters.* Austin: University of Texas Press.

Boyko, H. 1947. On the climax vegetation of the Negev with special reference to arid pasture problems. *Pal. J. Bot.*, Rehovot ser. 7: 17–35.

Bremaud, O., and J. Pagot. 1962. Grazing lands, nomadism and transhumance in the Sahel. *Arid Zone Res.* 18: 311–24.

Briggs, Lloyd Cabot. 1960. *Tribes of the Sahara.* Cambridge, Mass.: Harvard University Press.

Brown, G. W. (editor). 1968. *Desert Biology I.* New York: Academic Press.

Burdass, W. J. 1975. Water harvesting for livestock in Western Australia. *Proc. Water Harvesting Symp. Phoenix, Ariz.* ARS W-22, USDA: 8–26.

Butler, M. A. 1933. Irrigation in Persia by kanats. *Civil Engineering* 3(2): 69–73.

Button, B. M., J. Ben-Asher, and M. Evenari. 1980. Modelling intensity duration relationships of precipitation at Avdat, Israel. In *Report of the Institute for Desert Research.* Sdeh-Boker, Israel: the Institute. pp. 1–39.

Butzer, K. W. 1961. Climatic change in arid regions since the Pliocene. *Arid Zone Res.* 17: 31-56.

Bybordi, M. 1974. Qanats of Iran. *J. Irrig. and Drain. Div. Proc. Amer. Soc. Civil Eng.*, 100: 245-53.

Capot-Rey, R., A. Cornet and B. Blaudin 1963. *Glossaire des principaux termes géographiques et hydrogéologiques sahariens.* Algiers: Institut de Recherches Sahariennes, Université d'Alger.

Carder, D. J., and G. W. Spencer. 1971. *Water Conservation Handbook.* South Perth, Western Australia: Soil Conservation Service, Department of Agriculture.

Chapman, V. J. 1960. *Salt Marshes and Salt Deserts of the World.* New York: Wiley Interscience.

Christiansen-Weniger, F. 1961. Alte Methoden der Wassergewinnung für Bewasserungszwecke in Nahen und Mittleren Osten unter besonderer Berucksichtigung der Kanate. *Wasser u. Nahrung* 2: 32-39.

Cloudsley Thompson, J. L. 1964. Terrestrial animals in dry heat. Arthropods. *Handbook of Physiology*, New York: Academic Press, pp. 451-66.

Cluff, C. B. 1979. The use of compartmental reservoir in water harvesting agrisystems. In *Arid Land Plant Resources*, J. R. Goodin and D. K. Northington, eds. Tucson: Univ. of Arizona Press, pp. 482-500.

Cluff, C. B., G. R. Dutt, P. R. Ogden, and J. K. Kuykendall. 1972. *Development of Economic Water Harvesting Systems for Increasing Water Supply, Phase II.* Office of Water Resources Research Project no. B-015-ARIZ. (Available as Report no. PB-214-128, National Technical Information Service, U.S. Department of Commerce, Springfield, VA 22151.)

Cooley, K. R. and L. E. Myers. 1973. Evaporation reduction with reflective covers. *J. Irrig. and Drain. Div. Am. Soc. Civ. Eng.* 99: 353.

Cooley, K. R., A. R. Dedrick, and G. W. Frasier. 1975. *Water Harvesting: State of the Art.* Phoenix, Ariz. USDA.

Cressey, B. 1958. Quanats, karez and foggaras. *Geogr. Rev.* 48: 27-44.

Cressey, George B. 1960. *Crossroads: Land and Life in Southwest Asia.* London: J. B. Lippincott.

Dale, Edward Everett. 1949. *The Indians of the Southwest.* Norman: University of Oklahoma Press.

Bibliography

Dan, J., and H. Koyumdjisky. 1963. The soils of Israel and their distribution. *J. Soil Sci.* 14: 12–20.

Davis, S. N., 1974. Hydrogeology of arid regions. In *Desert Biology II* (G. W. Brown, editor). New York: Academic Press, pp. 1–31.

Dawson, W. 1964. Terrestrial animals in dry heat: Desert birds. *Handbook of Physiology*, New York: Academic Press, pp. 481–92.

De Angelis, Y. 1979. The settlements of Ramat Hanegev: Revivim, Mashabei-Sadeh, and Sdeh-Boker. In *The Land of the Negev*. Israel Ministry of Defense, Tel-Aviv.

Debenham, F. 1953. *Kalahari Sand*. London: Bell.

Dedrick, A. R. 1974. Water harvesting. *Agric. Eng.* (36): 9–10.

―――. 1975. Storage systems for harvested water. *Proc. Water Harvesting Symp. Phoenix, Ariz.* pp. 171–191. ARS W-22 USDA.

DeJong, R. L. A., and T. J. Wallace. 1975. Chemical water harvesting. *Proc. Water Harvesting Symp. Phoenix, Ariz.* ARS, W-22. USDA.

Descroix, P. 1951. La récupération de l'humidite atmosphérique. *L'Eau* 8: 127–29.

Diole, Philippe. 1956. *Sahara Adventure*. Paris: Julian Messner.

Dixey, F. 1962. Geology and geomorphology, and groundwater hydrology. *Arid Zone Res.* 18: 23–52.

Doughty, Charles M. 1922. *Travels in Arabia Deserta*. New York: Random House.

Draz, O. 1954. Some desert plants and their uses in animal feeding. *Publications de l'Institut désert d'Egypte* no. 2: 1–95.

Dutt, G. R., and T. W. McCreary. 1975. Multipurpose salt-treated water harvesting system. *Proc. Water Harvesting Symp. Phoenix, Ariz.* pp. 310–20. ARS W-22 USDA.

Duvdevani, S. 1947. An optical method of dew estimation. *Quart. J. Royal Met. Soc.* 73: 282–96.

Edney, E. B. Animals of the desert. In *Arid lands*, E. S. Hills, ed., pp. 181–218. London: Methuen.

Ehrler, W. L., F. H. Fink, and S. T. Mitchell. 1978. Growth and yield of Jojoba plants in native stands using runoff-collecting micro-catchments. *Agron. J.* 70(Nov.–Dec.): 1005–09.

Engel, C. E., G. Engel, and R. P. Sharp. 1958. Chemical data on desert varnish. *Bull. Geol. Soc. Amer.* 69: 487-518.

Erickson, A. E. 1972. Improving the water properties of sand soil. In *Optimizing the Soil Physical Environment Toward Greater Crop Yields*, D. Hillel, ed. New York: Academic Press. pp. 35-42.

Erickson, A. E., C. M. Hansen, and A. J. M. Smucker. 1968. The influence of subsurface asphalt barriers on the water properties and the productivity of sand soils. In *Transactions Ninth International Congress of Soil Science, Adelaide, Australia*, 1: 331-37.

Etherton, P. T. 1948. *Across the Great Deserts*. New York: Whittlesey House McGraw-Hill.

Evans, D. D., and J. L. Thames. 1981. *Water in Desert Ecosystems*. Stroudsberg, Pennsylvania: Dowden, Hutchinson, and Ross.

Evenari, M., Y. Aharoni, L. Shanan, and N. H. Tadmor. 1958. The ancient desert agriculture of the Negev. III. Early beginnings. *Israel Exploration J.* 8: 231-68.

Evenari, M., L. Shanan, and N. H. Tadmor. 1959. The ancient desert agriculture of the Negev. IV. Chain well systems in the Wadi Arava. *Ktavim Records Agric. Res. Sta. Rehovot* 9: 223-40.

―――. 1968. Runoff farming in the desert. I. Experimental layout. *Agron. J.* 60 (Jan.-Feb.): 29-32.

―――. 1971. *The Negev: The Challenge of a Desert*. Cambridge, Mass.: Harvard University Press.

Evenari, M., L. Shanan, N. Tadmor, and Y. Aharoni. 1961. Ancient agriculture in the Negev. *Science* 133: 979-96.

Fahn, A. 1964. Some anatomical adaptations of desert plants. *Phytomorphology* 14: 93-102.

Fairbourn, M. L. 1975. Field evaluation of microcatchments and vertical mulch systems. *Proc. Water Harvesting Symp. Phoenix, Ariz.* ARS W-22 USDA.

Fairbourn, M. L., and W. D. Kemper. 1971. Microwatersheds and ground color for *Crops and Soils* (Apr.-May.)

Fairburn, M. L., and W. D. Kemper. 1971. Microwatesheds and ground color for sugarbeet production. *Agronom. J.* 63: 101-104.

Bibliography

Fink, D. H. 1970. Water repellency and infiltration resistance of organic-film-coated soils. *Soil Sci. Soc. Amer. Proc.* 34: 189–94.

Fink, D. H., and K. R. Cooley. 1973. Water harvesting for improved grazing efficiency. *Proc. Water-Animal Relations Symp.* USDA Twin Falls, Idaho, pp. 200–08.

Fink, D. H., K. R. Cooley, and G. W. Frasier. 1973. Wax-treated soils for harvesting water. *J. Range Management* 26: 396–98.

Fink, D. H., and G. W. Frasier. 1975. Water harvesting from watersheds treated for water repellency. In *Soil Conditioners. Proc. Symp. Experimental Methods and Uses of Soil Conditioners.* Soil Sci. Soc. Am. Spec. Publ. 7: 173–82.

———. 1977. Evaluating weathering characteristics of water harvesting catchments from rainfall-runoff analysis. *Soil Sci. Soc. Am. J.* 41: 618–22.

Fink, D. H., G. W. Frasier, and L. E. Myers. 1979. Water harvesting treatment evaluation at Granite Reef. *Water Res. Bull.* 153: 861–73.

Flavius, Josephus. 1956. *The Jewish Wars.* 2 vols. Loeb Classical Library. London: Heinemann; Cambridge, Mass.: Harvard University Press.

———. 1956. *Jewish Antiquities.* 6 vols. Loeb Classical Library. London: Heinemann; Cambridge, Mass.: Harvard University Press.

Frasier, G. W. 1975. Water harvesting for livestock, wildlife and domestic use. In *Proc. Water Harvesting Symp. Phoenix, Ariz.*, ARS W-22 USDA.

Frasier, G. W., L. E. Myers, and J. R. Griggs. 1970. Installation of asphalt-fiber glass linings for reservoirs and catchments. U.S. Water Conservation Laboratory, Report no. 8. Phoenix: Agricultural Research Service, USDA.

Frith, J. L. 1975. Design and construction of roaded catchments. *Proc. Water Harvesting Symp. Phoenix, Ariz.*, pp. 122–27. ARS W-22 USDA.

Frith, J. L., R. A. Nulsen, and H. I. Nicol. 1975. A computer model for optimizing design of improved catchment. *Proc. Water Harvesting Symp. Phoenix, Ariz.*, pp. 151–58. ARS W-22 USDA.

Fuller, W. H. 1974. Desert soils. In *Desert Biology II* (G. W. Brown, editor). New York: Academic Press, pp. 32–102.

Furon, R. 1967. *The Problem of Water: A World Study.* New York: American Elsevier.

Gardner, H. R. 1975. An analysis of the efficiency of microwatershed systems. *Proc. Water Harvesting Symp. Phoenix, Ariz.*, pp. 244–50. ARS W-22 USDA.

Gardner, W. R., and D. Hillel. 1962. The relation of external evaporative conditions to the drying of soils. *J. Geophys. Res.* 62: 4319-25.

Gardner, W. R., D. Hillel, and Y. Benyamini. 1970a. Post-irrigation movement of soil water: I. Redistribution. *J. Water Resources Res.* 6: 800-10.

———. 1970b. Post-irrigation movement of soil water: II. Simultaneous redistribution and evaporation. *J. Water Resources Res.* 6: 811-19.

Gautier, E.-F. 1935. *The Great Desert*. New York: Columbia University Press.

Gerster, George. 1961. *Sahara: Desert of Destiny*. London: Coward-McCann.

Ginzbourg, D., and D. H. Yaalon. 1963. Petrography and origin of the loess in the Beer Sheva basin. *Israel J. Earth Sci.* 12: 68-70.

Glueck, N. 1959. *Rivers in the Desert*. London: Weidenfeld and Nicholson.

———. 1965. *Deities and Dolphins*. New York: Farrar, Strauss, and Giroux.

Gourou, P. 1966. Civilisation et desert. *L'Homme* 6: 112-19.

Hadas, A., and D. Hillel. 1970. Steady-state evaporation through nonhomogeneous soils from a shallow water table. *Soil Sci.* 113: 65-73.

Hanson, C. L., E. L. Neff, and D. A. Woolhiser. 1975. Hydrologic aspects of water harvesting in the northern Great Plains. *Proc. Water Harvesting Symp. Phoenix, Ariz.* ARS W-22 USDA.

Heaton, K. G. 1979. Water harvesting by wax. *Soil Conservation* 45(5): 8-9.

Hillel, D. 1953. Summary of the 1952/53 growing season in the Negev highlands. *Hassadeh* 33: 112-20.

———. 1954. Summary of the 1953/54 growing season in the Negev highlands, *Hassadeh*, 34: 249-60.

———. 1955. Summary of the 1954/55 growing season in the Negev highlands. *Hassadeh*, 35: 749-51; 830-32.

———. 1959. *Studies of Loessial Crusts*. State of Israel, Agricultural Research Institute, Bulletin 63. Rehovot, Israel.

———. 1960. Crust formation in loessial soils. In *Trans. 7th Int. Soil Sci. Congr., Madison*, 1: 330-39. ISSS, Madison, Wisconsin.

———. 1964. Infiltration and rainfall-runoff as affected by surface crusts. In *Trans. 8th Int. Soil Sci. Congr., Bucharest*, 1: 34-39. ISSS, Bucharest, Rumania.

———. 1967. *Runoff Inducement in Arid Lands.* Hebrew University Faculty of Agriculture Research Report. Rehovot, Israel.

———. 1968. *Soil Water Evaporation and Means of Minimizing It.* Hebrew University Faculty of Agriculture Research Report. Rehovot, Israel.

———. 1969. *Soil-Crop-Tillage Interactions in Dryland and Irrigated Farming.* Hebrew University Faculty of Agriculture Research Report. Rehovot, Israel.

———. 1970a. Artificial inducement of runoff as a potential source of water in arid lands. In *Food, Fiber, and the Arid Lands,* W. G. McGinnies, B. J. Goldman, and P. Paylore, eds., pp. 323-30. Tucson: University of Arizona Press.

———. 1970b. Soil moisture control for maximum plant response. In *Biology and Utilization of Grasses,* V. B. Youngner and C. M. McKell, eds., pp. 259-70. New York: Academic Press.

———. 1971a. *Research in Soil and Water Use Efficiency.* International Atomic Energy Agency. Vienna, Austria.

———. 1971b. *Soil and Water: Physical Principles and Processes.* New York: Academic Press.

———. 1972a. The field water balance and water use efficiency. In *Optimizing the Soil Physical Environment,* D. Hillel, ed., pp. 79-100. New York: Academic Press.

———. 1972b. Soil physics and technology. In *Optimizing the Soil Physical Environment,* D. Hillel, ed., pp. 15-25. New York: Academic Press.

———. 1972c. Soil pollution. In *The Environment of Israel.* Jerusalem: National Council for Research and Development.

———. 1972d. Some aspects of the field water cycle affected by soil surface conditions. In *Proc. Int. Symp. on Soil Structure and Soil Conditioning,* 37: 1114-31, Ghent: State University of Belgium, Med. Fak. Landbouwweeten.

———. 1972e. *Studies on Water Balance and Trickle Irrigation in Sand Dune Areas.* Tottori, Japan: Tottori University.

———. 1974a. *Infiltration and Runoff as Affected by Soil Conditions.* Hebrew University Faculty of Agriculture Research Report. Rehovot, Israel.

———. 1974b. Methods of laboratory and field investigation of physical properties of soils. In *Trans. 10th Int. Soil Sci. Congr., Moscow,* 1: 301-08. ISSS, Moscow, USSR.

———. 1975. Evaporation from bare soil under constant and diurnally fluctuating evaporativity. *Soil Sci.* 120: 230-37.

―――. 1976a. Effect of root growth parameters on the pattern of soil moisture extraction by non-uniform root systems. *Soil Sci.* 124: 307-12.

―――. 1976b. On the role of soil moisture hysteresis in the suppression of evaporation from bare soil. *Soil Sci.* 122: 309-14.

―――. 1976c. Soil management in arid regions. In *Yearbook of Science and Technology*, New York. McGraw-Hill, pp. 372-74.

―――. 1977a. *Computer Simulation of Soil Water Dynamics*. Ottawa: International Development Research Centre (IDRC).

―――. 1977b. International agricultural development: A case for conditional optimism. *IDRC Reports* 6(4): 20-23.

―――. 1977c. A new method of water conservation in arid zone soils. In *Arid Zone Development*. Y. Mundlak and S. F. Singer, eds., Cambridge, Mass.: Ballinger, pp. 99-108.

―――. 1977d. Water supply for an arid-zone city. In *Urban Planning in Arid Regions*, G. Golany, ed. New York: Wiley, pp. 112-25.

―――. 1978. A method of promoting penetration of water into tight, sloping soil under drip irrigation. *Soil Sci.* 125: 329-30.

―――. 1979a. Irrigation and crop response. In *The Role of Soil Physics in Maintaining the Productivity of Tropical Soils*, D. Greenland and R. Lal, eds. pp. 54-72. New York: Wiley.

―――. 1980a. *Applications of Soil Physics*. New York: Academic Press.

―――. 1980b. *Fundamentals of Soil Physics*. New York: Academic Press.

―――. 1982. *Advances in Irrigation*. New York: Academic Press.

Hillel, D., and Y. Benyamini. 1974. Experimental comparison of infiltration and drainage methods for determining unsaturated hydraulic conductivity of a soil profile in situ. In *Proc. FAO/IAEA Symp. on Isotopes and Radiation Techniques in Studies of Soil Physics, Vienna*, pp. 271-75. Vienna, Austria: International Atomic Energy Agency.

Hillel, D., and P. Berliner. 1974. Water-proofing surface zone soil aggregates for water conservation. *Soil Sci.* 118: 131-35.

Hillel, D., and W. R. Gardner. 1970a. Steady infiltration into crust-topped soil profiles. *Soil Sci.* 108: 137-42.

Bibliography

———. 1970b. Transient infiltration into crust-topped profiles. *Soil Sci.* 109: 69-76.

Hillel, D., and Y. Guron. 1973. Evapotranspiration and the yield of maize. *Water Resources Res.* 9: 743-48.

Hillel, D., and A. Hadas. 1970. Isothermal drying of structurally layered soil profiles. *Soil Sci.* 113: 30-35.

Hillel, D., and A. M. Hornberger. 1979. Physical model of the hydrology of sloping heterogeneous fields. *Soil Sci. Soc. Am. J.* 43: 434-39.

Hillel, D., V. Krentos, and Y. Stylianou. 1972. Procedure and test of an internal drainage method for measuring soil hydraulic characteristics in situ. *Soil Sci.* 114: 395-400.

Hillel, D., and E. Rawitz. 1968. A field study of soil surface treatments for runoff inducement. In *Trans. 9th Int. Soil Sci. Cong., Adelaide,* 1: 302-12. ISSS, Adelaide, Australia.

———. 1972. Soil moisture conservation. In *Water Deficits and Plant Growth*, T. T. Kozlowski, ed., pp. 307-37. New York: Academic Press.

Hillel, D., A. Schwartz, R. Steinhardt, and E. Rawitz. 1969. Laboratory tests of sprayable materials for runoff inducement on a loessial soil. *Israel J. Agr. Res.* 19: 3-9.

Hillel, D., and N. Tadmor. 1962. Water regime and vegetation in Negev highlands of Israel. *Ecology* 43: 33-41.

Hillel, D., H. Talpaz, and H. van Keulen. 1975. A macroscopic-scale model of water uptake by a non-uniform root system of water and salt movement in the soil profile. *Soil Sci.* 121: 242-55.

Hillel, D., and C. H. M. van Bavel. 1976. Simulation of profile water storage as related to soil hydraulic properties. *Soil Sci. Soc. Am. J.* 40: 807-15.

Hillel, D., C. H. M. van Bavel, and H. Talpaz. 1975. Dynamic simulation of water storage in fallow soil as affected by mulch of hydrophobic aggregates. *Soil Sci. Soc. Am. J.* 39: 826-33.

Hillel, D., C. van Beek, and H. Talpaz. 1975. A microscopic-scale model of soil water uptake and salt movement to plant roots. *Soil Sci.* 120: 385-99.

Hills, E. S., ed. 1966. *Arid Lands*. London: Methuen/UNESCO.

Hodge, C., ed. 1963. *Aridity and Man*. Washington, D. C.: American Association for the Advancement of Science.

Hollick, M. 1975. The design of roaded catchments for maximum runoff. In *Proc. Water Harvesting Symp. Phoenix, Ariz.* pp. 201-20. ARS W-22 USDA.

Hornaday, W. T. 1908. *Camp-fires on Desert and Lava.* New York: Scribner's.

Hult, J. L., and N. C. Ostrander. 1973. *Antarctic Icebergs as a Global Fresh Water Resource.* Report no. R-1255-NSF. Washington, D.C.: National Science Foundation.

Ionides, M. G. 1967. Water in dry places. *Engineering* (London) 27(Oct.): 662-66.

Jackson, R. D., and C. H. M. van Bavel. 1965. Solar distillation of water from soil and plant materials: A simple desert survival technique. *Science* 149: 1377-79.

Jaeger, E. C. 1957. *The North-American Deserts.* Stanford, Calif.: Stanford University Press.

Jones, O. R., and V. L. Hauser. 1975. Runoff utilization for grain production. In *Proc. Water Harvesting Symp. Phoenix, Ariz.* ARS W-22 USDA.

Karmeli, D., and J. Keller. 1974. *Trickle Irrigation Design.* Glendora, Calif.: Rain Bird Sprinkler Corp.

Kassas, M. 1966. Plant life in deserts. In *Arid Lands*, E. S. Hills, ed., pp. 145-80. London: Methuen.

Katsnelson, J. 1964. The variability of annual precipitation in Palestine. *Arch. Meteorol. Geophys. Bioclimatol.* ser. B 13: 163-72.

Kaul, R. W., ed. 1970. *Afforestation in Arid Zones.* The Hague: W. Junk.

Kedar, Y. 1956. The problem of the mounds of Tuleilat el Anab and their relation to ancient agriculture in the central Negev. *Bull. Israel Explor. Soc.* 20: 31-43.

―――. 1957. Water and soil from the Negev: Some ancient achievements in the central Negev. *Geogr. J.* 123: 179-87.

―――. 1967. *Ancient Agriculture in the Negev.* Jerusalem: Bialik Institute. (Hebrew).

Kendrew, Wilfred George. 1953. *The Climates of the Continents.* 4th ed. Oxford, England: Oxford University Press.

Kochavi, M. 1963a. Har Yeruham. *Israel Exploration J.* 13: 141-42.

―――. 1963b. Settlements of the Middle Bronze period in the Negev. *Mada* 8: 8-15. (Hebrew).

Koller, D., and M. Negbi. 1966. *Germination of Seeds of Desert Plants.* Project A10-Fs6. Hebrew University of Jerusalem, Israel.

Bibliography

Koller, D., N. H. Tadmor, and D. Hillel, 1958. Experiments in the propagation of *Atriplex halimus* L. for desert pasture and soil conservation. *Ktavim* (Records of the Israel Agricultural Research Station) 9: 93-106.

Kraemer, C. J. 1958. *Excavations at Nessana*, III, *Non-literary papyri*. Princeton: Colt Archeological Institute Princeton University Press.

Kramer, P. J. 1969. *Plant and Soil Water Relationships: A Modern Synthesis*. New York: McGraw-Hill.

Krutch, Joseph Wood. 1954. *The Voice of the Desert*. William Sloane Associates.

Laing, I. A. F. 1975. Sealing leaking excavated tanks on farms in Western Australia. In *Proc. Water Harvesting Symp. Phoenix, Ariz.*, pp. 159-69. ARS W-22 USDA.

Laing, I. A. F., and A. L. Prout. 1975. Bitumen, oil and clay surfaces on a deep sand to increase runoff from catchments for excavated tanks in Western Australia. In *Proc. Water Harvesting Symp. Phoenix, Ariz.* ARS W-22 USDA.

Lange, O. L., and A. Bertsch. 1965. Photosynthese der Wustenflechte *Ramalina maciformis* nach Wasserdampfaufnahme aus dem Luftraum. *Naturwissenschaften* 52: 215-16.

Lawrence, T. E. 1947. *Seven Pillars of Wisdom*. New York: Doubleday.

Lee, H. K. D. 1962. Application of human and animal physiology and ecology to arid zone problem. *Arid Zone Res.* 18: 213-33.

Lee, D. H. K. 1968. Human adaptation to arid environments. In *Desert Biology I* (G. W. Brown, editor). New York: Academic Press, pp. 518-56.

———. 1969. Variability in human response to arid environments. In *Arid Lands in Perspective*, Tucson: University of Arizona Press, pp. 229-45.

Leopold, A. S. 1976. *The Desert*. New York: Time-Life.

Leopold, L. B. 1974. *Water: A Primer*. San Francisco: H. W. Freeman.

Leopold, L. B., M. G. Wolman, and J. P. Miller. 1964. *Fluvial Processes in Geomorphology*. San Francisco: Freeman.

Levitt, J. 1972. *Responses of Plants to Environmental Stresses*. New York: Academic Press.

Logan, R. F. 1968. Causes, climates, and distribution of deserts. In *Desert Biology I* (G. W. Brown, editor). New York: Academic Press, pp. 21-51.

Logan, R. F. 1969. Geography of central Namib Desert. In *Arid Lands in Perspective*, pp. 129-44. Tucson: Univ. of Arizona Press.

Lowdermilk, W. C. 1958. Floods in the desert. In *Proc. Symp. Des. Res.*, pp. 361-374. Research Council of Israel, Jerusalem.

Manges, H. L., and L. T. Mao. 1978. *Harvesting runoff from precipitation on Irrigated Lands.* ASAE Paper 78-2559. Am. Soc. Agr. Eng., St. Paul, Minn.

Marcus, J. H. 1962. The problem of fatigue in a hot climate. In *Symposium, Climate and Man in Israel*, pp. 121-27. National Council for Research and Development (Hebrew) Jerusalem, Israel.

Marx, E. 1979. The Negev Bedouin during the sixties. In *The Land of the Negev*. Israel Ministry of Defense, Tel-Aviv.

Mayerson, P. 1959. Ancient agricultural remains in the central Negev: The Teleilat el Anab. *Bull. Amer. School Oriental Res.* 153: 19-31.

McCleary, J. A. 1968. The biology of desert plants. In *Desert Biology I* (G. W. Brown, editor) New York: Academic Press.

McGinnies, W. G. 1969. Arid lands knowledge gaps and research needs. In *Arid Lands in Perspective*, Tucson: University of Arizona Press, pp. 279-87.

McGinnies, W. G., B. J. Goldman, and P. Paylore, ed. 1968. *Deserts of the World: An Appraisal of Research into Their Physical and Biological Environments.* Tucson: University of Arizona Press.

Meidner, H., and D. W. Sheriff. 1976. *Water and Plants.* New York: Halsted Press, Wiley.

Meigs, P. 1953. World distribution of arid and semi-arid homoclimates. *Arid Zone Res.* 1: 203-09.

———. 1966. Geography of coastal deserts. *Arid Zone Res.* 28: 140.

Michelson, R. H. 1966. Level pan system for spreading and storing watershed runoff. *Soil Sci. Soc. Amer. Proc.* 30: 388-92.

Michelson, R. H., M. B. Cox, and Jack Musick. 1965. Runoff water spreading on levelled cropland. *J. Soil and Water Cons.* 20(2): 57-60.

Milthorpe, F. L. 1960. The income and loss of water in arid and semi-arid zones. *Arid Zone Res.* 15: 9-36.

Monod, T. 1959. Parts respectives de l'homme et des phénomènes dans la dégradation du paysage et le déclin des civilisations à travers le monde méditerranéen "lato sensu," avec les derniers millénaires. In *Congrès U.I.C.N. (Union internationale pour la conservation de la nature), Athens,* 1: 31-69. Paris, France.

Bibliography

Morin, G. C. A., and W. G. Matlock. 1975. Desert strip farming computer simulation of an ancient water harvesting technique. In *Proc. Water Harvesting Symp. Phoenix, Ariz.*, pp. 141–50. ARS W-22 USDA.

Morin, J., and Y. Benyamini. 1977. Rainfall infiltration into bare soils. *J. Water Resources Res.* 13: 813–17.

Morris, Yaakov. 1961. *Masters of the Desert.* G. P. Putnam's Sons.

Murray, G. W. 1968. *Dare Me to the Desert.* Cranbury, N.J.: A. S. Barnes.

Myers, L. E. 1964. Harvesting precipitation. *I.A.S.H. Pub.* no. 65, pp. 343–51. U.S. Water Conservation Laboratory, Phoenix, Arizona.

———. 1967a. *New Water Supplies from Precipitation Harvesting.* International Conference on Water for Peace Proc., Wash. D.C., paper no. 391. U.S. Govt. Printing Office, Washington, D.C.

———. 1967b. Recent advances in water harvesting. *J. Soil and Water Cons.* (May–June): 95–97.

———. 1975. Water harvesting 2000 B.C. to 1974 A.D. In *Proc. Water Harvesting Symp. Phoenix, Ariz.*, pp. 1–7 ARS W-33 USDA.

Myers, L. E., and G. W. Frasier. 1969. Creating hydrophobic soil for water harvesting. *J. Irr. and Drain. Div., Proc. Am. Soc. Civ. Eng.* 95(IR1): 43–54.

Myers, L. E., G. W. Frasier, and J. R. Griggs. 1967. Sprayed asphalt pavements for water harvesting. *J. Irr. and Drain. Div., Proc. Amer. Soc. of Civ. Eng.* 93(IR3): 79–97.

Nabhan, G. P. 1979. The ecology of flood water farming in arid south-western America. *Agro-Ecosystems* 5: 245–55.

National Academy of Sciences. 1974. *More Water for Arid Lands.* Washington, D.C.: National Academy of Sciences.

National Water Commission. 1973. *Water Policies for the Future.* Washington, D.C.: U.S. Government Printing Office.

Negbi, M., and M. Evenari. 1962. The means of survival of some desert summer annuals. Plant-Water Relationships in Arid and Semi-arid Conditions. In *Proc., Madrid Symp.*, pp. 249–59, UNESCO, Paris.

Negev, A. 1961a. Avdath. A caravan halt in the Negev. *Archeology* 14: 122–30.

———. 1961b. Nabatean inscriptions from Avdat (Oboda). *Israel Exploration J.* 11: 127-38.

———. 1963. Nabatean inscriptions from Avdat (Oboda). *Israel Exploration J.* 13: 113-24.

Negev, A. 1979. The Nabateans in the Negev. In *The Land of the Negev.* Israel Ministry of Defense, Tel-Aviv.

Nir, D. 1970. *Geomorphology of Israel.* Jerusalem: Academon. (Hebrew).

———. 1974. *The Semi-Arid World.* London and New York: Longman.

Oppenheimer, H. R. 1960. Adaptation to drought; xerophytism. *Arid Zone Res.* 15: 105-38.

Otterman, J. 1974. Baring high albedo soils by overgrazing: A hypothesized desertification. *Science* 186: 531-33.

Overton, D. E., and M. E. Meadows. 1976. *Storm Water Modelling.* New York: Academic Press.

Palmer, E. H. 1871. *The Desert of the Exodus.* 2 vols. Cambridge University, England.

Penman, H. L. 1948. Natural evaporation from open water, bare soil, and grass. *Proc. Royal Soc.* (London) ser. A 193: 120-45.

Pereira, D., D. Hillel, A. Aboukhaled, A. Moursi, and A. Felleke. 1979. *Opportunities for Increasing World Food Production from Irrigated Lands.* Ottawa: International Development Research Centre.

Peterson, D. F. 1969. Philosophical considerations of water resource importation. In *Arid Lands in Perspective,* W. G. McGinnies and B. J. Goldman, eds. pp. 398-405. Washington, D.C.: AAAS; Tucson: University of Arizona Press.

Rauzi, F., M. L. Fairbourn, and L. Landers. 1973. Water harvesting efficiencies of four soil surface treatments. *J. Range Mgt.* 26(6): 399-403.

Pickard, L. 1951. Geomorphology of Israel. *Bull. Res. Council Israel* 1: 5-32.

Ravikovitch, S. 1953. The aeolian soils of the northern Negev. In *Proc. Symp. Des. Res., Jerusalem,* pp. 404-33. Research Council of Israel, Jerusalem.

Rawitz, E. 1969. The dependence of growth rate and transpiration on plant and soil physical parameters under controlled conditions. *Soil Sci.* 110: 172-82.

Rawitz, E., A. Hadas, and D. Hillel. 1964. The effect of irrigation methods and cropping system on structural properties of a loess sierozem. *Israel J. Agr. Res.* 14: 4–10.

Rawitz, E., and D. Hillel. 1971. A method of characterizing the runoff potential of rainfall in water harvesting schemes. *J. Water Resources Res.* 7: 401–05.

———. 1973. Runoff collection and utilization in the Negev of Israel. In *Physical Aspects of Soil Water and Salts in Ecosystems*, pp. 315–24. Berlin: Springer-Verlag.

———. 1975a. Progress and problems of drip irrigation in Israel. In *Proc. Int. Conf. on Drip Irr., San Diego.*

———. 1975b. Water harvesting by runoff inducement for irrigation of an almond orchard in a semi-arid climate. In *Proc. Water Harvesting Symp. Phoenix, Ariz.* ARS W-22 USDA.

Rawitz, E., M. Margolin, and D. Hillel. 1972. An improved variable intensity sprinkling infiltrometer. *Soil Sci. Soc. Amer. Proc.* 36: 533–35.

Rawlins, S. L., and P.A.C. Raats. 1975. Prospects for high frequency irrigation. *Science* 188: 604–10.

Reifenberg, A. 1947. *The Soils of Palestine.* London: Thomas Murby.

———. 1955. *The Struggle Between Sown Land and Desert.* Jerusalem: Bialik Institute.

Rim, M. 1949. Dune sand movement and the formation of red sand soils in Palestine. Ph.D. dissertation, Hebrew University, Jerusalem.

Rita, U. 1977. The desert ecosystem. In *The Desert*, E. Sohar, ed. Tel-Aviv: Reshafim, pp. 85–91.

Roberts, Austin. 1951. *Mammals of South Africa.* New York: Hafner.

Rodda, J. C. 1970. On the questions of rainfall measurements and their representativeness. In *Symp. on World Water Balance, IASH, Reading, England*, pp. 173–85.

Saint-Exupéry, Antoine de. 1949. *Wind, Sand and Stars.* New York: Harcourt, Brace.

Schmidt-Nielsen, K. 1964a. Desert animals. In *Physiological Problems of Heat and Water.* London and New York: Oxford University Press, pp. 159–73.

———. 1964b. Terrestrial animals in dry heat: Desert reptiles. In *Handbook of Physiology*; sec. 4: 467–81. New York: Academic Press.

———. 1964c. Terrestrial animals in dry heat: Desert rodents. *Handbook of Physiology*, sec. 4: 493-509. New York: Academic Press.

———. 1981. Countercurrent systems in animals. *Sci. Am.* 244: 118-29.

Schmidt-Nielsen, K., and B. Schmidt-Nielsen. 1952. Water metabolism of desert mammals. *Physiol. Rev.* 32: 135-66.

Sears, Paul B. 1959. *Deserts on the March.* 3rd rev. ed. Norman: University of Oklahoma Press.

Seginer, I., and J. Morin. 1970. A model of crusting and infiltration of bare soils. *Water Resources Res.* 62: 629-39.

———. 1971. A model for surface drainage of cultivated fields. *J. Hydrol.* 13: 139-52.

Seligmann, N., Z. Rosensaft, N. H. Tadmor, J. Katznelson, and Z. Naveh. 1959. *Natural Pasture of Israel. Vegetation, Carrying Capacity and Improvement.* Tel-Aviv: Sifriat Poalim, Merhavia. (Hebrew).

Shalem, N. 1952. *La stabilité du climat en Palestine.* In *Proc. Int. Symp. on Desert Res., Jerusalem*, pp. 152-75. Jerusalem: Israel Research Council.

Shanan, L. 1975. Rainfall and runoff relationships in the Avdat region of the Negev Desert. Ph.D. dissertation, Hebrew University, Jerusalem.

Shanan, L., M. Evenari, and N. H. Tadmor. 1967. Rainfall patterns in the central Negev desert. *Israel Exploration J.* 17: 163-84.

Shanan, L., and N. H. Tadmor. 1976. *Micro-Catchment Systems for Arid Zone Development* Rehovot: Hebrew University of Jerusalem and Center of International Agricultural Cooperation.

Shanan, L., N. H. Tadmor, and M. Evenari. 1958. The ancient desert agriculture of the Negev. II. Utilization of the runoff from small watersheds in the Abde (Avdat) region. *Ktavim Records Agric. Res. Sta. Rehovot* 9: 107-28.

———. 1961. The ancient desert agriculture of the Negev. VII. Exploitation of runoff from large watersheds. *Israel J. Agric. Res.* (Ktavim) 11: 9-31.

———. 1970. Runoff farming in the desert. III. Microcatchments for the improvements of desert range. *Ag. J.* 62: 695-99.

Sharon, D. 1959. Geographical aspects of the Teleilat el Anab. *Geography of Erets Israel* 1: 86-94. (Hebrew with English summary). Jerusalem, The Hebrew University.

———. 1972. The spottiness of rainfall in a desert area. *J. Hydrol.* 17: 161-75.

Bibliography

Shkolnik, A. 1977. Physiological adaptations of mammals to life in the desert. In *The Desert*, E. Sohar, ed. Tel-Aviv: Reshafim. pp. 100–12.

Shmueli, A. 1970. *The Settlement of the Bedouin of the Judaea Desert.* Tel-Aviv: Gomeh. (Hebrew).

Shreve, Forrest. 1951. *Vegetation of the Sonoran Desert.* Washington, D. C.: Carnegie Institution of Washington.

Simpson, G. M. 1981. *Water Stress on Plants.* New York: Praeger.

Sinai, G., and D. Zaslavsky. 1976. *Rainfall in the Soil and near Its Surface.* Haifa: Agricultural Engineering Faculty, Technion, Israel Institute of Technology. (Hebrew).

Slayter, R. O. 1967. *Plant-Water Relationships.* New York: Academic Press.

Smith, H. T. U. 1968. Geologic and geomorphic aspects of deserts. In *Desert Biology I* (G. W. Brown, editor). New York: Academic Press.

Sohar, E., ed. 1977. *The Desert.* Tel-Aviv: Reshafim.

Sohar, E. 1979. Human physiology in a hot climate. In *The Land of the Negev*, Israel Ministry of Defense, Tel-Aviv.

Stanhill, G. 1962. Solar radiation in Israel. *Bull. Res. Council Israel* 11G: 34–41.

Starcky, J. 1955. The Nabataeans: A historical sketch. *Biblical Archeol.* 18: 84–106.

Swartzendruber, D., and D. Hillel. 1973. The physics of infiltration. In *Physical Aspects of Soil Water and Salts in Ecosystems*, pp. 3–15. Berlin: Springer-Verlag.

———. 1975. Infiltration and runoff for small field plots under constant intensity rainfall. *J. Water Resources Res.* 11: 445–51.

Tabor, H. 1962. Solar energy. *Arid Zone Res.* 18: 259–70.

Tadmor, N., O. P. Cohen, L. Shanan, and M. Evenari. 1966. Moisture use of pasture plants in a desert environment. In *Proc. X Intl. Grassland Conf.*, pp. 897–906, Beit-Dagan, Israel: *Volcani Inst. Agr. Res.*

Tadmor, N., M. Evenari, L. Shanan, and D. Hillel. 1958. The ancient desert agriculture of the Negev. I. Gravel mounds and gravel strips near Shivta. *Ktavim Records Agric. Res. Sta. Rehovot* 8: 127–51.

Tadmor, N., and D. Hillel. 1956a. *Observations on Reseeding Practices in Water-spread Areas in the Negev Highlands.* State of Israel, Agric. Res. Inst. Spec. Publ. 144.

———. 1956b. *Survey of the Possibilities for the Agricultural Development of the Southern Negev.* State of Israel, Agric. Res. Inst. Bull. 61, Rehovot.

———. 1957a. *Experiments on the Propagation and Cultivation of Some Desert Pasture Plants.* State of Israel, Agric. Res. Inst. Spec. Pub. 157, Rehovot.

———. 1957b. Natural conditions and range development in the Negev. In *Proc. FAO Conf. on Mediterranean Pasture and Range Development,* pp. 2-16, Rome, FAO.

Tadmor, N., D. Hillel, and Y. Cohen. 1969. *Establishment and Maintenance of Seeded Dryland Range Under Semi-arid Conditions.* State of Israel, Agric. Res. Inst. Res. Rept, Beit-Dagan.

Tadmor, N., B. Jogev, N. Seligman, and D. Hillel. 1965. *Seeded Dryland Range in the Northern Negev.* Israel National University Institute of Agriculture Bull. 510. Rehovot.

Tadmor, N., G. Orshan, and E. Rawitz. 1962. Habitat analysis in the Negev Desert of Israel. *Bull. Res. Council of Israel* 11D: 148-73.

Tadmor, N., L. Shanan, and M. Evenari. 1960. The ancient desert agriculture of the Negev. IV. The ratio of catchment area to cultivated area. *Ktavim J. Agric. Res. Sta. Rehovot* 10: 193-221.

Tadmor, N. H. 1970. Runoff farming in the desert. IV. Survival and yields of perennial range plants. *Agron. J.* 62: 695-99.

———. 1971. Runoff farming in the desert. V. Persistence and yields of annual range species. *Agron. J.* 63: 91-95.

Tadmor, N. H., and L. Shanan. 1969. Runoff inducement in an arid region by removal of vegetation. *Proc. Soil Sci. Soc. Amer.* 33(5): 790-93.

Taylor, A., ed. 1971. *Focus on the Middle East.* New York: Praeger.

The Future of Arid Lands. 1956. American Association for the Advancement of Science. Washington, D.C.

Thomas, G. W., and T. W. Box. 1969. Social and ecological implications of water importation into arid lands. In *Arid Lands in Perspective,* pp. 363-74. Tucson: University of Arizona Press.

Thornthwaite, C. W. 1948. An approach toward a rational classification of climate. *Geogr. Rev.* 38: 55-94.

Troll, C. 1963. Qanat Bewasserung in der alten und neuen Welt. *Mitt. Oesterr. geograph. Ges.* 105: 313-30.

Underhill, Ruth M. 1956. *The Navajos*. Norman: University of Oklahoma Press.

UNESCO. 1960. *Plant-Water Relationships in Arid and Semi-Arid Conditions. Reviews of Research*. Arid Zone Research Series, 15. Paris: UNESCO.

United Nations Conference on Desertification. 1977. *Desertification: Its Causes and Consequences*. Oxford: Pergamon Press.

U.S.S.R. National Committee for International Hydrological Decade. 1977. *Atlas of World Water Balance*. Paris: UNESCO.

Uvarov, B. P. 1928. *Locusts and Grasshoppers*. London: Imperial Bureau of Entomology.

van Bavel, C. H. M., and D. Hillel. 1975. A simulation study of soil heat and moisture dynamics as affected by a dry mulch. In *Proc. 1975 Summer Computer Simulation Conf., San Francisco*. La Jolla, Calif.: Simulation Councils, Inc.

―――. 1976. Calculating potential and actual evaporation from a bare soil surface by simulation of concurrent flow of water and heat. *Agric. Meteorol.* 17: 453-76.

Van der Post, L. 1962. *The Lost World of the Kalahari*. Penguin Books.

Van Keulen, H., and D. Hillel. 1974. A simulation study of the "drying front" phenomenon. *Soil Sci.* 118: 270-75.

Velasco Molina, H. A., and O. Aguirre Luna. 1972. Una estimación del costo de captar y almacenar agua de lluvia en regiones deserticas y semi-deserticas del norte de Mexico. *Agronomía* (Mexico) 145: 74-79.

Verma, H. N., R. Singh, S. S. Prihar, and T. N. Chaudhary. 1979. Runoff as affected by rainfall characteristics and management practices on gently sloping sandy loam. *J. Indian Soc. Sci.* 27(1): 18-22.

Wadham, S. 1961. The problem of arid Australia. In *History of Land-use in the Arid Regions*. Paris: UNESCO; *Arid Zone Res.* 17: 339-62.

Wallen, C. C. 1967. Aridity definitions and their applicability. *Geogr. Ann.* 49: 367-85.

Walter, H., and E. Stadelman. 1974. A new approach to the water relations of desert plants. In *Desert Biology II* (G. W. Brown, editor). New York: Academic Press, pp. 214-311.

Weeks, W. F., and W. J. Campbell. 1973. Icebergs as a fresh water source: An appraisal. *J. Glaciology* 12: 65.

White, G. E., ed. 1956. *The Future of Arid Lands*. Washington, D.C.: American Association for the Advancement of Science.

White, Gilbert E. 1960. *Science and the Future of Arid Lands.* Paris: UNESCO.

Wipplinger, O. 1958. *The Storage of Water in Sand.* Windhock: South-West Africa Administration.

Woolley, C. L. and T. E. Lawrence. 1936. *The Wilderness of Zin.* New ed. London: Jonathan Cape; 1st ed., Palestine Exploration Fund, 1915.

Wulff, H. E. 1968. The qanats of Iran. *Sci. Am.* 218: 94–101.

Yisraeli, T. 1966. Mesolithic sites of the Ramat Matred. *Yediot bahaqirat Eretz-Israel. weatiqoteha* 30: 23–32. (Hebrew).

Zeuner, F. E. 1963. *A History of Domesticated Animals.* London: Hutchinson.

Zing, A. W., and V. I. Hauser. 1959. Terrace benching to save potential runoff for semi-arid land. *Agron. J.* 51: 289–92.

Zohary, D. 1954. Notes on ancient agriculture in the central Negev. *Israel Exploration J.* 4: 17–25.

Zohary, M. 1945. Outline of the vegetation of Wadi Araba. *J. Ecol.* 32: 201–13.

———. 1947. A geobotanical soil map of western Palestine. *Pal. J. Bot.* 4: 24–35.

———. 1952. Ecological studies in the vegetation of the Near Eastern deserts. I. Environment and vegetation classes. *Israel Exploration J.* 2: 201–15.

———. 1962. *Plant Life of Palestine.* New York: Ronald Press.

———. 1966. *Flora Palestina.* I. Jerusalem: Israel Academy of Sciences and Humanities.

Zohary, M., and N. Feinbrunn. 1951. Outline of the vegetation in the Dead Sea region of Palestine. *Pal. J. Bot.* 5: 96–114.

Zohary, M., and G. Orshansky. 1949. Structure and ecology of the vegetation in the Dead Sea region of Palestine. *Pal. J. Bot.* 4: 177–206.

———. 1954. Ecological studies on the vegetation of Near Eastern deserts. V. the *Zygophyletum dumosi* and its hydrology in the Negev of Israel. *Vegetatio* 5/6: 340.

Index

Abraham (Hebrew patriarch), 107, 112, 198
Acacia trees, 19, 50, 79, 90
Adaptation to drought, 43
Aerial wells, 136
Aggregates, soil, 35
Aharoni, Yochanan, 113, 118
Air mass circulation, global, 16
Akbar the Great, 33-34
Alluvial fans, 22, 25, 170, 175, 176, 217
Alluvial soils, 36, 79, 157
Alluvium, 22, 90, 176, 177
Amalekites, 113, 114, 185
Angle of repose, sand, 20
Animal life in the desert, 53-61
Anticlines, 21, 79
Aqaba, Gulf of, 7, 25, 73, 81, 83
Aquifers, 10, 169, 171, 218
Arabian Desert, 5, 7, 13, 103
Arable soil, 74, 76
Arad, 112, 113, 118
Arava Valley, 7, 71, 74, 79, 81, 82, 83, 84, 112, 113, 114, 119, 170, 177, 200, 217
Archeological evidence, 110, 118
Arid zones, defined, 9-12
Arroyo (wadi), 26
Arthropods, 55
Aswan High Dam, 26
Atacama Desert, 6, 15
Atriplex (saltbush), 192-95
Australian Desert, 6, 15
Autotrophs, 45

Badlands, 19, 26, 27, 83, 160
Barbara, 104-05
Barkhans, 20
Basalt, 21
Bats, 54, 56, 132
Bedouin, 32, 66, 70, 71, 76, 89, 105, 106, 127, 133, 134, 136, 171, 180, 181, 182, 186, 187, 198, 202-16; code of, 206; disputes among, 207; hospitality of, 208; women of, 209
Beersheba, 70, 80, 104, 112, 113, 125
Ben-Gurion, David, 132, 182, 227-36; Paula, 228, 230, 233
Birds (desert), 54, 55, 56, 57
Blood feuds, 207
Body temperature, 63
Boustans, 180
Bronze Age, 111-12, 114
Buttes, 21, 22, 79
Byzantines, Byzantine period, 110, 124, 125, 135, 146, 147, 148, 161, 164, 180

Caliche, 36
Calvin cycle (photosynthesis), 50, 51
Camels, 58-60, 71, 104
Canals (diversion), 157, 158, 159, 161
Capillary rise, 33
Carnivores, 53, 56, 57
Carrying capacity (grazing potential), 186, 187, 196
Catchments, 146, 147, 148, 152, 155, 156, 168
Chad, Lake, 23
Chain wells (qanat, karez, foggaras), 84, 174-78, 217
Chalcolithic Age, 111, 112
Chalk formations, 21, 22, 76, 84
Channels, 131, 133, 147, 165; *see also* canals, conduits
Chenopod family (plants), 49, 90
Chihuahua Desert, 6, 15
Cisterns, 61, 62, 110, 117, 118, 127, 129-34, 136, 147, 172, 185, 197; plastering of, 117, 129, 130, 131
Clay, 37, 39, 41, 84, 144

263

Clearing of stones, 135–39, 141
Climate of the Negev, 74
Climatic changes, 109–11
Colorado River, 26
Colt expedition, 147
Conduits, 110, 146, 148, 149, 151, 174; *see also* channels, canals
Compaction of soil, 141, 143, 144
Conservation, soil and water, 10, 109, 121, 146
Continental drift, 15
Contour-strip runoff farming, 143, 153
Copper mining and use, 112, 114
Crassulacean acid metabolism (plants), 50; C3, C4 plants, 50–51
Creeks, 6; *see also* gullies, wadis
Crops and cropping, 147, 152, 163, 168, 169, 179–84
Crust, soil (surface crusting), 38, 39, 41, 94, 135, 138, 143, 144, 191, 192, 224
Cultivation, 9, 161, 163, 186, 187, 213
Cuticle, 48, 49

Dams, detention, 163, 164, 165, 166, 167; diversion, 157; failure of, 167, 168; storage, 156–57, 172
Dasht e-Kavir Desert, 6
Dead Sea, 7, 23, 24, 72, 73, 74, 80, 81, 82, 83, 84, 110, 121
Death Valley, 15
Deflation by wind, 79, 86
Dehydration, 57, 62, 63, 66
Desalinization, 32, 141
Desert agriculture, 121, 147, 152, 163, 168, 169, 179–84
Desert pavement, 29, 79, 86, 137, 138
Desertification, 10, 11, 187
Desert Research Institute, 235–36, 239
Deserts, defined, 9–12; distribution of, 14, 16; features of, 13–30
Desert varnish (patina), 29, 111
Dew, 51, 102–03, 136, 224
Dikes, 91, 95, 110, 148, 149, 151, 152, 155, 162, 167, 174, 180, 184, 226
Diodorus, 118
Diversion of floodwaters, 157–64

Dolomite, 21, 79
Drainage, 26, 33, 38, 39, 46
Drip (trickle) irrigation, 220–22
Drought, 9, 33, 53, 92, 141, 171, 184; adaptation to, 43; hazard of, 141
Drought tolerance (evasion, resistance), 43, 48, 49, 57
Dryland farming, 76
Dunes, 13, 20, 104, 189
Dust and dust storms, 29, 92, 198
Dust devils, 28, 29

Eastern Desert (Egypt), 7, 13
Ecological regions of Israel, 78
Ecology, desert, 4, 10, 12, 13, 42, 237
Ecosystem, desert, 42–44
Edom, 84, 112, 113, 119, 170, 203
Effective rains, 91, 181, 183
Ein (Spring of) Ovdat, 95, 172
Eolian deposits, eolian soils, 36, 76
Erosion, erosive processes, 26, 33, 36, 38, 40, 41, 99, 136, 137, 139, 140, 142, 147, 149, 160, 161, 168, 184, 187
Essenes, 17, 119
Estivation, 43, 56
Euphrates River, 33, 169
Evaporation, 33, 38, 41, 46, 49, 57, 59, 64, 65, 91, 97, 101, 131, 134, 138, 140, 156, 157, 177
Evaporative cooling, 64, 65
Evaporative demand (power) of the atmosphere, 46, 53, 65, 77, 218, 221
Evaporativity, atmospheric, 17, 50, 77
Evaporimeter, 77
Evapotranspiration, 101
Evenari, Michael, 140, 177, 184
Eytan, 197, 200–01

Fans, alluvial, 22, 25, 170, 175, 176
Farm systems (ancient) restored, 150, 151, 152, 183, 184
Fata morgana, 29
Fatehpur Sikri, 33–34
Faults, geological, 17, 21
Fences, 149, 185, 195, 199
Fertile Crescent, 10

Index

Flint, 22, 72, 76, 79, 137
Floods (flash floods), 6, 8, 26, 37, 38, 51, 72, 90, 93, 94, 95, 116, 128, 148, 154, 155, 156, 160, 184, 226, 238; harnessing of, 154–168
Flood-water irrigation, 91, 131, 146, 149, 151, 155, 166, 167, 168, 179, 189, 195
Foggaras (qanat, karez, chain wells), 174–78
Fossils, 16, 19
Fossil water, 97, 169

Galilee, Sea of, 24, 218
Gazelles, 57, 60
Geological erosion, 79
Geological history of the Negev, 74
Geological periods, 19
Geophytes, 50
Germination and seedling emergence, 38, 41, 49, 138, 181, 191, 192, 196; inhibition of, 49, 192, 194
Gilat, 153
Goats, 60, 61, 76, 89, 90, 127, 149, 187, 188, 195
Gobi Desert, 6, 16
Gran Chaco Desert, 6, 15
Granite, 19, 21
Gravel, 86, 90, 102, 170, 172; mounds and strips of, 135–39
Grazing the desert range, 9, 10, 131, 149, 180, 185–201; potential of, 186, 196
Great Salt Lake, 23
Gullies and gullying, 6, 22, 37, 86, 93, 99, 127, 149, 151, 160, 161, 168, 186
Groundwater, 26, 33, 41, 49, 50, 51, 76, 101, 117, 176, 178; recharge of, 41, 97, 170; tapping of, 169–78

Habitats, 39, 47; water regime of, 87–107
Hagar and Ishmael, 106, 107
Halutzah, 121, 189
Hammada, 29, 74, 79, 86
Heat balance, 63, 64
Heat dissipation (animals), 56, 57

Hebrew patriarchs, 112
Heatstroke, 63, 64, 66
Herbivores, 53, 57
Hermon, Mount, 24
Herod, King, 123
Herodotus, 175
History of the Negev, 108–27
Horizons (soil), 36
Hydraulic conductivity, soil, 36
Hydrophobization of soil, 142, 144
Hydrophytes, 47
Hyksos, 113

Ibexes, 57, 60, 111
Idumean Range, 7, 83, 122
Igneous rocks, 19, 85
Imperial Valley, 26
Indus River, 33, 169
Infiltrability, 36, 37, 38, 41, 94, 97, 137, 222
Infiltration, 36, 94, 101, 102, 138, 139, 141
Insectivores, 55
Insects (desert), 54, 55
Iranian Desert, 15
Iron Age, 114
Irrigated farming, 76, 145, 217–23
Irrigated land, 26
Irrigation, 11, 33, 101, 110, 147, 156, 159, 172, 217–23; efficiency of, 223; new methods of, 220–22
Isaac (Hebrew patriarch), 105–06, 112, 182
Ishmael, 106, 107
Israelites, 113, 115, 203

Jacob (Hebrew patriarch), 112
Jerboas, 56
Jerusalem, 17, 129
Jordan River, 23, 31, 33, 81, 110, 113, 121, 133, 169, 218
Judean Desert, 17, 74
Judean kings, Judean period, 113, 114, 115, 116, 117, 161

Kadesh Barnea, 113, 117
Kalahari Desert, 6, 15

Kangaroo rats, 56
Kara-Kum Desert, 6, 15
Karez (chain wells), 174-78
Karroo Desert, 6
Kedar, Yehuda, 136
Kibbutzim, 225-26

Land tenure, 181
Latent heat transfer, 64
Lavan, Nahal (wadi), 157, 160
Lawrence, T. E. ("of Arabia"), xvii, 122, 171, 210
Leaching of salts, 102
Lichens, 51, 52, 103
Limestone, 19, 21, 76, 79, 149, 157, 172
Lizards, 54
Locust, 54-55
Loess, loessial soils, 28, 38, 72, 73, 74, 76, 79, 87, 94, 101, 112, 138, 159, 184, 224
Loessial plains, 90, 98, 101, 182, 224, 236
Loessial wadi beds, 90, 95, 99, 160, 197

Makhtesh craters, 26, 79, 80
Mampsis (Mamshit), 118, 121, 156, 157
Marl, 84, 157, 171
Mashabei-Sadeh, 225
Masters of the desert, 240
Mesas, 21, 79, 86
Mesophytes, 47
Mesopotamia, 33
Mesquite, 50
Microwatersheds, 153
Midianites, 113, 114, 185
Mirage, 29-30
Mishor Haruach, 118, 161
Moisture available to plants, 39, 47, 50, 95, 100, 148, 219, 220
Moisture regime, 79
Mojave Desert, 6, 15
Moses, 113, 185
Moslem conquest, 127, 180
Mounds of stone and gravel, 135-39

Nabateans and Nabatean period, 110, 118, 119, 120, 121-27, 135, 161, 180
Nafud Desert, 6, 13
Nahal (wadi), 26, 106
Namib Desert, 6, 15
Nasser, Lake, 26
Negev, Avraham (archeologist), 122
Negev, defined, 73; history of, 108-27; subregions of, 76
Neolithic Age, 111
Nessana (Nitzana), 80, 121, 135, 147; papyri, 147, 182-83, 185
Nile River, 26, 31, 33, 169
North American Desert, 14, 15
Nubian sandstone, 74, 200

Oases, 13, 20, 54, 84, 86, 177, 217
Ogallala Aquifer, 34
Organic matter in soil, 35, 38
Orographic effect, 17
Ovdat, 121, 124, 135, 140, 150, 152, 157, 171, 174, 183, 197, 235; well of, 171-74, 197
Overgrazing, 11, 103, 109, 127, 186, 187, 191, 204
Overirrigation, 222-23
Overland flow, 37, 137, 144; *see also* runoff

Pan evaporimeter, 77
Panting, heat dissipation by, 60
Papyrus documents, 147, 182-83, 185
Pasture (desert range), 131, 162; grasses, 91, 189, 192, 193; pasturable shrubs, 192-95; reseeding of, 191-95
Patagonia Desert, 6, 15, pathways of, 50-51
Perched water table, 86, 90, 101, 170, 177
Percolation (seepage), 97, 101, 103, 170
Perspiration, 56, 57, 60, 63, 65, 66
Petra, 80, 119, 120, 121, 122, 124, 125, 200-01
Philistines, 114, 115
Phoenicians, 116
Photosynthesis, 45, 47, 50, 51, 52
Phreatophytes, 47, 171
Physiology of man in the desert, 62-66

Index

Pillars of Solomon, 18
Pistacia trees, 90
Plant-water relations, 45–52
Playas, 19, 23, 26, 84, 170
Potential evaporation, 74, 84
Potsherds, 118, 161, 164
Precipitation, *see* rainfall
Predators, 54, 56

Qanat (chain wells), 174–78

Radiation (solar), 4, 64, 101
Raindrop action, 6, 21, 37, 38, 92, 137, 139
Rainfall (precipitation), 9, 41, 43, 74, 79, 91, 94, 102, 135, 145, 152, 155, 156; distribution in Israel, 75; effectiveness, 91, 181, 183
Rainfall-evaporation ratio, 10
Rainfall simulator, 142
Rainfed agriculture, 76, 145
Rain penetration, 89, 90
Rain shadow, 17, 75
Ramat Matred, 118, 161, 212
Ramon, Makhtesh (crater), 118, 226
Range improvement, 131, 191–95
Red Sea, 51, 71, 80, 81, 83, 114, 116, 178
Reg, 74, 86
Regeneration of natural vegetation, 90
Rehovot (Ruheibe), 121, 171
Reifenberg, Avraham (Adolph), xix
Reptiles, 54, 55, 57
Residual soils, 36
Respiration, 45, 59, 64
Respiratory cooling, 57
Restoration of ancient farm systems, 150, 151, 152, 183, 184
Revivim, 70, 71, 80, 224–25
Rift Valley, 23, 74, 81, 170, 177
Rocky slopes, habitat, 87–90, 98, 101
Rodents, 54, 56
Romans and Roman period, 121, 123, 124, 125, 161, 164
Roots and root systems, 39, 46, 47, 49, 98, 99, 103, 104
Root-shoot ratio, 47

Root zone, 41, 91, 97, 153, 219, 221
Roughness, surface, 94
Rub al-Khali Desert, 6, 13, 21
Runoff, surface, 6, 22, 37, 41, 91, 94, 97, 101, 103, 145, 152, 178, 181, 239; collection and storage of, 128–34, 149; harvesting of, 135–44; inducement of, 38, 140–44, 153, 239; threshold, 141; utilization of, 117, 118, 152
Runoff farms, runoff farming, 102, 145, 146, 147, 148, 150, 151, 160, 161, 172, 180, 183, 185
Runoff-runon area ratios, 97, 147, 148, 153

Sabkhas, 23, 24, 170, 177
Sagebrush, 88, 89
Sahara Desert, 5, 6, 13, 15, 16, 169
Saint Exupéry, Antoine de, 4
Saline marshes, 23, 24, 170, 177
Salinity and salinization (of soil), 33, 41, 79, 89, 104, 221
Salivation, heat dissipation by, 57
Saltation (of sand), 20
Saltbush (Atriplex), 90, 192–95
Salton Sea, 26
Sand, 17, 19, 20, 28, 37, 39, 86, 172
Sand dunes, 13, 20, 21, 103, 104
Sandstone, 19, 21, 169
Sandstorms, 19, 29
Scorpions, 55
Sdeh-Boker, 80, 105, 131, 132, 154, 164, 165, 166, 167, 168, 172, 182, 183, 190, 191, 193, 194, 195, 196–99, 224–36
Sedimentary rocks, 19, 21, 74, 81
Sediments, 36, 38, 39, 84, 129, 140, 149
Seepage, 38, 41, 155, 156, 157, 171, 172, 175
Seifs, 20
Semiarid regions, 9
Serir, 29
Shale, 21
Shanan, Leslie, 140, 157, 161, 235
Sheep, 60, 76
Shivta, 80, 121, 124, 135, 147, 152,

160, 183
Silt and silting, 129, 136, 149, 156, 157, 161, 197
Sinai, 7, 13, 24, 25, 51, 61, 73, 90, 103, 113, 114, 119, 121, 169, 191, 203
Sind Desert, 6
Snakes, 54, 55, 132
Sodom, Mount, 83
Soil, characteristics of, 10; conservation of, 10; definition of, 35; desert types, 26; erosion of, 33, 41; formation of, 35–36; insulation properties, 56; profile of, 36, 39, 95; treatment of (for runoff inducement), 141–44
Solar still, 66
Sonora Desert, 6, 15
Spillways, 91, 148, 149, 155, 159, 160, 163, 165, 166, 174, 184
Springs, 56, 58, 61, 62, 101, 117, 129, 172, 173, 235
Springtime in the desert, 52, 93, 96
Steppes, 13, 78, 79
Stomates, 47, 49, 50
Succulents, 50, 51
Suez, Gulf of, 7
Survival in the desert, 66
Synclines and synclinal valleys, 21, 79, 90, 154, 168

Tadmor, Naphtali, xix, 104, 139, 143, 189, 197, 235
Takla-Makan Desert, 6, 15
Takyr, 170
Talus, 101, 102, 189
Tamarix (tamarisk) trees, 50, 90, 171
Tamilat, 171
Tectonic processes, 21, 81
Tent dwellers, tents, 204, 205
Terraced fields, terracing, 117, 118, 135, 136, 146, 148, 149, 151, 159, 160, 161, 165, 166, 174, 177, 179, 186
Thar Desert, 6, 15
Thermal inertia (body's), 59
Thunderstorm, 92
Tigris River, 33, 169
Trade routes, ancient, 119, 120

Transpiration, 45, 46, 47, 49, 97
Transpiration ratio, 51
Tributary wadis, 154, 186
Trickle (drip) irrigation, 220–22
Tuleilat el-einab, 136

Vapor condensation, 56
Volcanic rocks, 21

Wadis, 26, 38, 51, 72, 87, 94, 95, 133, 146, 149, 151, 155, 157, 158, 159, 161, 172, 180, 226; types of, 154
Wadi beds, 19, 87, 90, 91, 95, 98, 99, 101, 112, 135, 149, 160, 165, 170, 171, 186, 196, 197
Water balance, 63, 97, 101, 103, 104
Water conservation, 11, 51, 57, 110, 238; *see also* conservation of soil and water
Water harvesting, 141; *see also* runoff harvesting, runoff inducement
Water holes, 56, 129
Water proofing, 141, 142, 144
Water regime of desert habitats, 17, 87–107, 139
Water relations (physiological), of animals, 53–61; of humans, 62–66; of plants, 45–52
Water repellency, 49, 143
Water requirements, plants, 47, 148, 169
Water rights, 105, 147, 151, 181, 187
Watersheds, 146, 151, 153, 155, 156, 168
Water spreading, 90, 91, 146, 149, 155, 158, 160, 161, 162, 163, 196, 226
Water storage in soil, 95, 97
Water table, 33, 34, 39, 175, 176, 177; perched, 86, 90, 101, 170, 177
Water, universal dilemma of, 31–34
Water use efficiency, 223
Weathering processes, 35
Wells, 62, 90, 101, 106, 107, 112, 117, 129, 136, 171, 172, 174–78, 204; of Ovdat, 171–74
Western Desert (Egypt), 13

Index

Wind action, 19, 26, 28, 29, 36, 76, 79, 104
Windbreaks, 20, 28, 224

Xero-halophytes, 48
Xeromorphic features, plants, 48
Xerophytes, 47, 49, 101

Yamin Valley, 104, 189
Yerokham, 157, 171
Yotvata, 177

Zin, Nahal (wadi), xviii, 80, 95, 171; valley of, xix, 80, 173, 236; wilderness of, xvii, xviii, xix

About the Author

Dr. Daniel Hillel is an internationally renowned hydrologist and environmental scientist whose contributions in the areas of arid-zone ecology, the field water cycle and its management, irrigation, drainage, and the mathematical modeling of water dynamics in various regions are embodied in over 150 scientific papers and reports. He has authored or edited 8 definitive and widely used textbooks in fundamental and applied soil physics. Dr. Hillel has served recently as consultant on land and water development to various international agencies (including the U.N., the International Atomic Energy Agency, and the World Bank) and to various states (including the State of California, as well as the countries of Burma, Thailand, Japan, India, Pakistan, Iran, and Cyprus).

A native of California, Dr. Hillel has served as Professor and Head of Soil and Water Sciences at the Hebrew University of Israel, and as Professor of soil physics, environmental sciences, and hydrology in several leading universities in the United States. He has lectured and toured widely in Europe, Asia, and the Americas, and has been elected Vice-President for soil physics of the International Society of Soil Sciences.

Among Dr. Hillel's most interesting experiences was his active participation in the exploration and pioneering development of the Negev desert, a region which he has come to love and which he describes in intimate and graphic detail.